CHARLTON ATHLETIC

A HISTORY

DAVID C. RAMZAN

AMBERLEY

First published 2014

Amberley Publishing
The Hill, Stroud
Gloucestershire, GL5 4EP

www.amberley-books.com

British Library Cataloguing in Publication Data.
A catalogue record for this book is available from the British Library.

ISBN 978-1-4456-1657-5 (print)
ISBN 978-1-4456-1676-6 (ebook)

Typesetting by Amberley Publishing.
Printed in the UK.

CONTENTS

INTRODUCTION

Definition of a club: an organisation of people with a common purpose or interest who meet regularly and take part in a shared activity, a building, or facilities in which a club meets, a team, a cooperative unit, open to membership from the community.

As a lifelong Charlton supporter, one-time Charlton Community coach, and occasional cartoonist and illustrator for the club, when asked to produce a publication charting the history of the club, I wanted to record, as best as possible within these pages, not a concise club history (as there have been several such publications written by authors more eminent than I) but an account of the groups that have, over many years, been influential in the development of the club.

The organisations formed in support of the club included, The Charlton Athletic Former Players' Association, The Community Trust, The Disability Supporters Association, The Reminiscence Group, the Supporters' Club and the Valley Party, to name but a few, all played significant roles in the history and heritage of Charlton Athletic Football Club.

I should like to take this opportunity to express my appreciation and thanks to Charlton Athletic Club statistician Colin Cameron, who passed away in December 2012.

Colin had always been of great help over the years, offering much welcome support, help and advice. While I had been working on two previous Charlton Athletic historical publications, Colin supplied information, records and of course statistics for inclusion within those books, and in this latest publication.

1

IN SUPPORT OF A CLUB

When a group of teenage boys living in the Victorian terraced houses of lower Charlton formed a football club during the early 1900s, little did anyone realise that those football loving youngsters would be laying down the foundations of a club that would go on to record a long and illustrious history.

At the start of the summer of 1905, those boys from East Street and West Street, situated close to the bank of the River Thames in South East London, had been kicking a ball about for fun before deciding to take their only means of leisure more seriously by forming themselves into a football team. They named it Charlton Athletic and began playing organised friendly matches against other neighbouring football teams. Along with the newly formed Charlton Athletic, there were several other teams playing under the title of Charlton, which included Charlton Reds, once thought to have been the origins of the Athletic team, Charlton Albion, Charlton Villa, Charlton Invicta and Charlton United. It would be the Athletic team, however, which would become a professional League club within just fifteen years, leaving the rest of those other Charlton teams behind.

The club's first recorded match against Silvertown Wesley United took place on a piece of wasteland known as Siemens Meadow, located to the rear of a local public house the Derby Arms in Lower Charlton. The match was reported in *The Kentish Independent* on 22 December 1905, the Charlton Athletic team listed as Ellis, Silcox, Thomas, Burns, Marshall, Sudds, Bonner, Crawford, Jarvis, Lines and Mills. Charlton beat their opponents Silvertown 6-1. After Charlton's first recorded match, details on the club's football activities began to appear regularly in the local press sports pages. Following their entry into the Lewisham League Third Division, Charlton played in a series of friendly matches before the start of the 1906/07 season. They then went on to beat Nunhead Swift Reserves in an emphatic 6-1 victory over their opponents in the club's very first football fixture. Free-scoring Charlton Athletic were on their way to a record seventeen wins and one draw in eighteen League matches, after a loss in the final fixture was later overturned when their opponents were found to have fielded ineligible players in the team. Charlton Athletic were crowned division champions, winning promotion to the Second Division of the Lewisham League.

By the time Charlton had won promotion, several members of the local community had been recruited into the clubs ranks, including the club's first secretary, Jack

Mackenzie, who resided at York Street. The list also included president Harry Wells, licensee of the Crown public house, and committee members Harry Hughes, W. Higgs, J. Probert and a young Joe Merryweather, who was associated with the Merryweather steam-powered fire engine and tram production company of Greenwich. As the football club progressed, other local residents and businessmen began to invest their time, services, goods and, on occasion, funds into helping support the club. One local entrepreneur Arthur Bryan, who was later elected as the clubs vice president, owned a fish and chip shop at No. 77 East Street and it was through the club's association with the fishmonger that Charlton earned the nickname of the 'Addicks'. After home matches, Arthur Bryan would supply the players with haddock and chips (pronounced Addock in South East London).

The club's acquired nickname was used to great effect in the local press. A series of black-and-white line-drawn cartoons were published depicting Bryan's shop and the team's exploits on the pitch, accompanied by satirical captions commenting on the Addicks' triumphs over their opponents. Arthur Bryan used the fish connection to publicise his local business by parading around a haddock nailed to a pole at home matches. Shop owners, storekeepers and licensees of local public houses in the area of Lower Charlton, some of whose descendents continue to support the club to the present day, were ready to offer support for the boys' team. This ranged from transporting them to away matches on the back of a horse-drawn carriage, to storing kit, boots and goalposts in backyards and garden sheds.

During the early 1900s, sports participation generally conformed to class divisions. The wealthiest of society played tennis, or competed in rowing and yachting, while those educated within the public school system favoured athletics or rugby. The game of football was considered the sport of the working-class masses.

Football clubs such as Charlton Athletic had an important role to play in the community. They offered youngsters the prospect of playing a sport when there were not many other activities accessible to occupy them, outside of school, or at around the age of fourteen years after their working day was over. When Siemens Meadow was used by the land owners as a dumping ground (towards the end of the club's first season in the Lewisham League), Charlton relocated to Woolwich Common the following season. The football club then moved to Pound Park at the start of the 1908/09 season, close to the club's present site of The Valley, moving headquarters from the Crown public house to the Royal Oak on Charlton Lane.

To raise extra funds to finance Charlton's ongoing development, collections were taken during home matches. With the growth in player membership, the extra revenue gave the club the opportunity to run a second team for the very first time. Charlton Athletic were no different from hundreds of other small football clubs playing in the local Leagues, however, within ten years, the club from South East London had won promotion through all divisions of the Lewisham League, the Woolwich League and the Southern Suburban League. Both junior and senior divisions had also won the Woolwich Challenge Cup on four occasions and the club's success attracted an ever increasing number of supporters. By the outbreak of the First World War in 1914, Charlton had adopted senior amateur status, the first steps towards becoming a professional football club. After moving from Pound Park to the Angerstein Lane

Ground on Greenwich Marsh, they entered the FA Cup and FA Amateur Cup for the first time in the club's history.

With many of the team members off to fight for their country, the club was forced to close in March 1915 for the duration of the war and although Charlton recruited a few players to take part in some friendly matches to raise funds for local hospitals and wounded servicemen, the team would not take to the field again until 13 September 1919 for a competitive match in the Southern Suburban League. Charlton beat Summerstown 2-0 at a new purpose-built ground, later to become known as The Valley.

CHANGING PLACES

Since the only professional South East London football club, Woolwich Arsenal, had relocated from Plumstead to North London in 1913, a large number of their disassociated fans began attending Charlton matches. The team's outstanding performances on the pitch and remarkable progression up through the local Leagues, following their election to the Kent League in 1919, had been an attractive alternative to travelling across London to watch football at the new Highbury Stadium. Although officially known by the title of Woolwich Arsenal, the Royal Arsenal munitions' works' team originally went by the title of Dial Square, the name of a workshop located within the armaments site where players from the team were employed. Later changing the name to Woolwich Arsenal, although never actually playing any home matches in the area of Woolwich, the club played at grounds located in Plumstead.

Before moving to North London, Woolwich Arsenal had been attracting crowds in excess of 20,000 at the Plumstead Manor Ground. With Charlton moving into a new purpose built ground, there was potential to bring in a similar number of football-loving fans to support a new professional football club in the local area. After election to the Kent League in 1919, a proposal was put forward by several of the club's members for Charlton Athletic to turn professional, which caused a dispute among the members as to whether the club should retain its amateur status, or go down the route of professionalism. After Charlton played a friendly match against Tottenham Hotspur, it was reported in an edition of *The Kentish Independent* that Charlton Athletic would turn professional the following season. This would be supported financially by the Tottenham directors, who would have a representative to give advice on the Charlton Athletic playing staff.

THE PROFESSIONAL WAY FORWARD

Although any supposed takeover by Tottenham was fanciful at best, the ambitions of a majority of the Charlton members prevailed. At a meeting held on 1 July 1920 in the Antigallican public house situated on Church Lane, Charlton, it was decided, much against the wishes of several founder members of the club, for Charlton Athletic to apply to join the Southern League (one division below the Football League) to compete as a professional football club.

Once Charlton's application had been accepted, Walter Rayner, an experienced former non-League player and coach with Arsenal and Tottenham, was appointed the club's first professional football manager. After the club finished the first season in the Southern League just below mid-table, the directors took a further step forward by forming Charlton Athletic into a limited company with a share capital of £10,000, and applying for election to the Football League. In May 1921 at a Football League meeting held in the Connaught Rooms, Holborn, Charlton Athletic was elected to the Third Division (later Third Division South) of the Football League.

After Charlton's election, the directors set out to purchase the freehold of The Valley and appointed engineering and building firm Humphries Ltd to construct a main grandstand on the west side of the ground and areas of terracing to the north, east and south for standing and fencing around the ground, with gated entrances and turnstiles to admit the paying public. The completed works had been estimated to cost £14,000, however the final bill came to just over £20,000. Although the grandstand was not completed for the start of the 1921/22 season, an official gate of 13,000 was recorded at The Valley on 27 August 1921 for the club's first ever match in the Football League. Midfielder Tommy Dowling scored Charlton's first ever League goal in a 1-0 win over opponents Exeter City.

Supporters were now offered the opportunity to purchase season tickets to watch all Charlton's League matches. Prices ranged from £3 3s 0d for a reserved seat in the main stand, £2 12s 6d for admittance to the ground (and stand) and £2 2s 0d for entrance to the ground and enclosure. If you could not afford to purchase a season ticket, admittance to all first-team games would cost 1s for an adult and 6d for children. The first season competing in the Football League went as well as supporters could have expected: Charlton won ten games, drew six and lost five at home, with the average Valley attendance of 8,011 higher than the overall divisional average. Charlton's biggest gate of 16,000 came against neighbours Millwall, with Charlton beating the local rivals 2-1. Charlton's form away was not so good, resulting in a sixteenth place finish. The club made an overall financial loss of just over £7,000, which the directors had not expected, proving that playing in the Football League would not be as straightforward as they had thought.

CUP RUN MAKES HEADLINES

Although the progress of Charlton Athletic had been reported in the local newspapers, to a majority of the football nation, the club was just one of many competing in lower divisions and hardly worth a mention in the nationals. This would all change during the 1922/23 season, when Charlton went on an exceptional FA Cup run to make headlines on the sports pages of the day. Before the fifth round of the FA Cup, which would be the club's first appearance in the competition that season, Charlton had already won their first piece of silverware since turning professional by beating Second Division Crystal Palace 2-1 in the final of the London Challenge Cup. Although the club's League form had been average at best leading up to the home FA Cup tie against Third Division South opponents Northampton Town, Charlton won the tie 2-0.

In the sixth round, Charlton drew Third Division North side Darlington and beat them at The Valley 2-1 to go through to the FA Cup first round proper. The Charlton players now found themselves facing First Division Manchester City away, a club that had only lost one League match at home all season. With Manchester City limited to just one shot on target during the whole of the first half, Charlton took the lead 3 minutes before the half-time whistle blew. Although City drew level soon after the start of the second period, Charlton scored a second with just 7 minutes of the match remaining and won the game 2-1. Little Charlton Athletic, from a small suburban village on the outskirts of London, had captured the notice of the national football population, where their Cup exploits were written up in the daily nationals and their Cup tie highlights were shown on cinema newsreel sports reports throughout the country.

After beating one of the season's Cup favourites Manchester City, Charlton were drawn at home to play the losers of the previous year's FA Cup, Preston North End. For the second round tie, 22,490 football fans packed into The Valley on 3 February 1923, which at the time was a record home attendance. The Charlton Athletic players found themselves up against some tough opposition and, for the watching home supporters, First Division Preston seemed as if they would overwhelm the Third Division South team. As the match went on, the Charlton players began to grow in confidence and were soon taking control of the game, missing several good scoring opportunities before the break. Two minutes into the second half, Charlton's Abraham Goodman scored from a twenty-yard volley. With Preston going all out for an equaliser, teammate Stephen Smith hit a second to put Charlton into a 2-0 lead with just under 30 minutes of the tie remaining. Preston continued with their onslaught on the Charlton goal and were awarded a penalty for their efforts, which was then put wide. Charlton successfully held out until the final whistle to go through to the third round.

In the third round, Charlton were drawn to play at home and once again faced a strong First Division team. West Bromwich Albion arrived at The Valley with seven internationals, and were by far the best side Charlton had come up against in the Cup so far. The First Division team went into all-out attack from the outset. However, just as in the previous round, Charlton soaked up all the pressure and then began to turn the match around in the second half. Once more, Abraham Goodman opened the scoring for his team soon after the second half kicked off, with Charlton going on to win the match by the single goal. The 31,489 football fans, who packed out The Valley for Charlton's third-round FA Cup triumph, set another record attendance, which would then be surpassed when Charlton played Bolton Wanderers in the fourth round of the FA Cup two weeks later.

The official attendance of 41,023 on the day of the Cup tie was far too big a crowd to be accommodated safely in such a basic ground as The Valley. As a consequence of such high attendance, a section of railing surrounding the pitch collapsed prior to kick-off from the pressure of the crowd. Going 1-0 down after 35 minutes, Charlton were then awarded a free-kick close to the edge of the Bolton area. As Abraham Goodman lined up to take a shot on goal, a whole length of railing fell away and the match was held up while temporary repairs were made. The same happened again just before half-time, on this occasion spilling men, women and children out onto the pitch. The referee had to stop play while the injured were taken away and more repairs were made to the railing. After the restart, Charlton were unable to equalise, and the Cup run came to an end with Charlton losing 1-0 to the eventual FA Cup winners Bolton Wanderers. The money Charlton made from the gate receipts was reportedly paid as compensation for the collapsed railing incident.

Even though crowds at The Valley had broken records for figures of attendance at Cup ties, League gates had been poor, dropping below those of the previous season. Charlton eventually finished the season in a credible twelfth position. Before the season's end, rumours had begun to circulate among the fans that the directors were intending to move the club away from The Valley to share a ground with Catford Southend. Unsurprisingly, when these rumours turned out to be true, the news infuriated the club's supporters and the group which represented their views, the Charlton Athletic Supporters' Association. The Charlton Athletic Supporters' Association was independent from the football club. It first came to prominence when publishing the first supporters' newsletter, *The Charlton Athletic Supporters' Association Gazette*, made available for the match against Portsmouth on 18 February 1922. The gazette stated that The Charlton Athletic Supporters' Association was formed 'to bring together all those ladies and gentlemen who have an interest on the welfare of Charlton Athletic Football Club and to encourage and promote sport in general'. All Charlton supporters were invited to join the association for a membership fee of 1s.

2

A JOURNEY TO CATFORD MOUNT
AND BACK

At the Charlton Athletic AGM, which took place on 6 April 1923, representatives of the club's shareholders and Supporters' Association confronted the board of directors over their proposed decision to move the club from The Valley to Catford Mount, Catford Southend's ground. The board were reluctant to explain the full circumstances behind the decision to relocate, except to inform those present that it was the cause of 'outside influences'. In their opinion, they did not believe The Valley would bring in enough regular support to make the club financially viable. This explanation ignored the potential possibility for an increase in attendances, which had been proved by the record gates in Charlton's FA Cup run. After the club made a financial loss at the end of the season, and with money still owed to Humphries Ltd for the previous groundwork carried out at The Valley, the board assumed that a move to Catford would be financially beneficial to the club.

Members of the club's original committee, several of whom had opposed the move into professionalism and entry into the Football League, protested against any such move. Those who had joined the Charlton Athletic Supporters' Association now faced the prospect of supporting a club situated in Catford, at a ground located closer to the home of Second Division Crystal Palace than it was to the area of Charlton. This made the directors' decision to share a ground with Catford Southend, in the expectation of attracting bigger attendances, debatable. Arguably, local football fans were more likely to turn out to watch a football club playing in a higher division rather than attend matches of a club they had no affinity with, and competed in a lower division.

At a hastily arranged emergency board meeting on 23 April 1923, a resolution was unanimously carried forward in support of the move to Catford Mount. There was, however, more behind the move than the board of directors' hopes of an increase in gate money. At the AGM, Charlton manager Walter Rayner made it known that he had been approached by representatives from the district of Catford who were prepared to finance the move. Included in this proposal was an agreement to pay off club debts owed to Humphrey's Ltd. An agreement had also been made between Charlton Athletic and Catford Southend to merge into one. Clauses allowed the amateur side to resign from the London League with the two combined clubs continuing to compete in the Third Division South under the name of Catford

Southend, and wearing the Catford club's colours of dark-blue and light-blue stripes. Charlton directors later attempted to amend this agreement by requesting a change of colours to red and white stripes, and club name change to Catford FC. The attempt to merge clubs was soon put to an end by the Football League, who refused to permit a change of name if the club was to continue to play in the Third Division South. The move from The Valley to Catford Mount, however, went ahead.

Proposals were submitted to redevelop the Catford Southend ground, which included dismantling the Valley's West Stand, and re-erecting the structure at The Mount. Members of Charlton's original committee, in protest against the move, formed a rival amateur club, which they named Old Charlton. Disillusioned with their own club's plans to merge, they applied to join the London League and take the place of Catford Southend. Old Charlton were duly elected to the London League and formed a team consisting of former Charlton Athletic players who had played before the club turned professional, and also players from Catford Southend.

It was planned that Old Charlton would initially play home games at Morley Road then relocate to The Valley once Charlton Athletic had moved out. As building works at The Mount had not been completed for the 1923/24 season, the planned move was in chaos and Charlton Athletic were forced to continue playing their home games at The Valley. Charlton's move to The Mount was delayed for almost four months while the building works continued, leaving no time for the West Stand to be taken down and rebuilt before the first match took place against Northampton Town on 22 December 1923, the game ending in a 0-0 draw. After Charlton beat Accrington Stanley in an FA Cup first-round replay at The Mount, they were drawn at home to play Wolverhampton Wanderers, winners of the FA Cup in 1921. Even though the mighty Wolves had dropped down into the Third Division North, approval was requested from the FA to move the Cup tie back to The Valley, as The Mount was still undergoing building works and a large attendance was expected. On the day of the match, which ended in a 0-0 draw, there were over 20,000 supporters in attendance at The Valley, a much larger crowd than could have been safely accommodated at The Mount.

Edwin Radford, chairman of the Charlton Athletic Supporters' Association and one of the original directors of the football club, was approached by the Charlton board with a proposal to sell him The Valley for £6,000, an offer that he refused. The Charlton Athletic Supporters' Association, who were perhaps not as pro-active as they should or could have been in opposing the move to Catford from the outset, were now fully behind an attempt to bring Charlton Athletic back home. The Valley had not been left derelict after the first team and reserve team had moved out, as the ground was still being used. Since Old Charlton had first proposed taking over The Valley, the Charlton third eleven continued to play fixtures at the ground and were attracting more support than the first team were getting at The Mount. When attendances at The Mount dropped away towards the end of the season, the Shareholders and Supporters' Association continued ongoing communication with the board. Despite the ill feeling the move had caused, the association realised that this was an ideal opportunity to persuade the directors to bring the club back home.

It was clear to all those concerned that the board's expectations of an increase in attendances had failed to materialise, and the relocation had been a misguided and expensive mistake. The financial implications of continuing to play League football at Catford were grim, and the promised financial investment in the club had failed to materialise. Even more alarmingly, the club had been losing more money than when playing at The Valley. The whole relocation had become an absolute catastrophe, leading to speculation that if Charlton were to return to The Valley, it may be as an amateur club playing non-League football. The Supporters' Association chairman, Edwin Radford, wrote a letter to the Charlton board setting out the financial implications the club faced by continuing to play football at The Mount, with assurances that every effort would be made to rally support if the club made a return.

During the 1923/24 season the club made a trading loss of £11,369 due to the venture, or misadventure, of relocating to Catford. They were also in further financial debt with Humphrey's Ltd, following the building works required to get The Mount ready for League football. The letter from Edwin Radford to the Charlton board seemed to have tipped the balance. In the reply to the Supporters' Association chairman, he was informed that a unanimous decision had been made by the directors for Charlton Athletic to return to The Valley.

Old Charlton, the club formed with the intention of moving to The Valley, continued in its own right after the return of Charlton Athletic, and played for one season in the London League. Catford Southend reformed as a professional club to compete in the Kent League. They were managed by former Charlton Athletic player George Dodd, and Albert Mills, who was the only player to have represented Charlton Athletic in their first recorded match, played for Catford in the Football League. During the 1926/27 season, the club failed to meet its financial obligations and Catford Southend, following their suspension from the League, closed down altogether. As for Charlton Athletic, the return to The Valley did not solve the clubs financial worries, even though a rise in attendances during the 1924/25 season brought an increase in revenue through gate receipts. Prior to the start of the first season back at The Valley, the Football League held an enquiry into whether Charlton would be able to fulfil their League fixtures. They were only given permission to continue after the board gave assurances that the club was financially sound. The first home League fixture back at The Valley took place on Monday 1 September. Attracting an attendance of 5,000, the opponents were Northampton Town, the club Charlton played in the first match at The Mount.

On the following Saturday, Charlton beat Newport County 1-0 at The Valley with an increased attendance of 8,000. Provided this support would continue, football at The Valley would be sustainable. This was providing that the board would be able to put the club's finances in order sooner rather than later. With the losses the club made through relocation to The Mount, and their return to The Valley less than a year later, along with the outstanding debt owed to Humphrey's Ltd rising to £30,000, this was going to be an extremely difficult task to achieve. Mysteriously, on New Year's Day in 1925, a fire broke out at The Valley, destroying many of the club's records and papers, including the football company's books of accounts. Shareholders of the club were of the opinion the fire had been started deliberately to cover up financial fraud. At the end of the season, with Charlton finishing down in fifteenth place, changes were needed at both managerial and boardroom level.

This led to Charlton manager Walter Rayner being sacked, along with club secretary and director Sydney Hartgrove. Rayner was later suspended from football altogether after the FA held an enquiry into the affairs of the club while he had been the manager. The Supporters' Association chairman Edwin Radford was appointed Charlton Athletic chairman. Humphrey's Ltd also agreed not to foreclose on the debt they were owed, and took up an issue of debentures instead. A member of their staff, David Clark, was appointed to the board to look after the building firm's financial interests.

The club shareholders and the Supporters' Association had played their part in bringing the club back home. They would continue to perform a major role throughout the coming years to ensure Charlton Athletic FC remained a part of the local community, where the club had evolved and belonged. It should have been inconceivable for the Charlton board to believe that the decision to relocate the club from its place of origin would ever have received backing from the club's fan base, where the lack of support after the move was a major factor in the decision to bring the club back home.

In that very first newsletter, published by the Charlton Athletic Supporters' Association in February 1922, it was written that 'progress should be our "watchword and motto" through life', a phrase which the Charlton Athletic board of directors should have take more notice of before moving from the area where the club belonged. It seems, however, that lessons were not learnt from the past, as just over sixty years later a similar decision was made by a board of directors to relocate the club without any consultation with the fans. Following on from the administrative changes at board level at the end of the 1925/26 season, income exceeded the running costs for the first time since the club turned professional, a huge improvement over the previous year's financial turnover. During his first season in charge, the new Charlton manager Alex Macfarlane had been less successful on the field than the club had been financially successful off it. At the season's end, the club had to apply for re-election to the Third Division South, after finishing second from bottom. The poor finish was more due to lack of investment in the team than Macfarlane's lack of managerial skills, and he continued as manager for another eighteen months before leaving to take up the managerial position at Dundee United, a club he had once played for.

3

THE ARRIVAL OF THE TIMBER MERCHANTS

After only six months away, Alex Macfarlane returned to Charlton to take over from player-manager Albert Lindon in June 1928, and won promotion to the Second Division in his first season back. Although Charlton's financial situation continued to be an ongoing cause for concern, the promotion brought in bigger crowds to The Valley, with over 26,000 in attendance for the match against Crystal Palace. In Charlton's first season as a Second Division club, average attendances at The Valley had risen to 13,666. Although this brought an increase in gate receipts, the club continued to find it difficult to break even.

In October 1930, the board of directors held an AGM where discussions centred on Charlton's financial sustainability in the Second Division. The club had continued to make substantial loses each season, mainly due to offsetting the club's ongoing debts. The following year, director David Clark, representing the interests of Humphrey's Ltd, arranged to meet with two wealthy timber merchants, brothers Albert and Stanley Gliksten, who had shown an interest in investing in the club.

After the timber merchants made several visits to The Valley, a meeting was arranged at the Savoy Hotel in London between the Gliksten brothers; their accountant and club representative David Clark; chief accountant Arthur Arnott and managing director of Humphrey's Ltd, George Freeman. After going through the club's finances and accounts, thoroughly scrutinised by the Gliukstens' accountant, the brothers made an offer to buy the club whose finances were in an extremely poor state of affairs. The Charlton board of directors readily accepted the offer and Charlton Athletic FC passed into the hands of Albert and Stanley Gliksten.

The Charlton board members resigned. In February 1932, Albert Gliksten was appointed club chairman, with brother Albert taking on the role of deputy chairman. Their accountant, Arthur Arnott became a director, as did David Clark, who remained to oversee the interests of Humphrey's Ltd. Alex Macfarlane, who was acting as secretary-manager, was kept on to take care of team affairs for the foreseeable future. Money was not only invested in the club, but also in the playing staff, and Macfarlane used the funds to bring five new players into the squad. These signings undoubtedly helped Charlton to finish in the top half of the Second Division table at the end of the season.

The following campaign, however, did not go as well as planned. With the investments made to bring players into the club, expectations were high that

Charlton would finish at least in the top half of the table, if not higher. By Christmas 1932, with Charlton in the lower half of the table and struggling to get results, the board requested Alex Macfarlane's resignation. Assistant manager Albert Lindon took charge of the team and, even with this change of leadership, results failed to improve. Losing 3-0, away to Southampton in the penultimate game of the season, Charlton were relegated back into the Third Division South. Surprisingly, throughout this extremely disappointing season, attendances at The Valley had risen from those of the previous year.

Following the team's relegation, the Charlton board could not rely on maintaining the same level of support for the forthcoming season. The Gliksten brothers were immediately on the search for a new manager with the potential to take the club straight back up. On 17 May 1932, Charlton Athletic confirmed the appointment of Jimmy Seed as the club's new secretary-manager. The appointment had been made following a chance meeting between Charlton chairman Albert Gliksten and Jimmy Seed, who was manager at Clapton Orient at the time. Both had been attending a dinner to celebrate Arsenal winning the First Division title. Albert had met Jimmy Seed when the Gliksten brothers had been acting as advisors for Clapton Orient, and Arsenal proposed to take them over as their nursery team. At Arsenal's dinner, Gliksten and Seed began discussing their clubs' current fortunes, Charlton Athletic without a manager, and Clapton Orient without any money. Jimmy Seed suggested to Gliksten that he would be interested in taking on the role of manager at Charlton. After a meeting with the timber merchants at their office in Stratford, Seed was offered the position of secretary-manager, which he accepted without hesitation.

Jimmy Seed immediately set up a nationwide network of football scouts (including his brother Anthony, operating in the North East) to search out any potential signings for the club. Seed brought in four new players, moved several other players to different positions and let players go who were surplus to his needs. At the end of the season, Charlton finished fifth in the Third Division South and were only ten points off winning promotion.

The following season, two new players were recruited, centre-half Don Welsh from Torquay United and 'keeper Sam Bartram, who came down from the North East. Welsh had been serving in the navy and stationed in the West Country, before turning to football as his career. Bartram had been working at the pit and played football during his spare time for local team Boldon Villa before he was spotted by Seed's brother. Don Welsh, a centre-half whom Jimmy Seed moved to play in the centre-forward position, would become one of the club's greatest ever players, while Sam Bartram, although not Seed's immediate first-choice 'keeper, would become a Charlton legend.

Although Valley attendances had dropped to an average of 10,574 from the previous season, the Charlton supporters began to turn up in force for Jimmy Seed's second year in charge, and Charlton went into the new year unbeaten, winning ten matches and drawing one. Another of Seed's signings, forward Ralph Allen, scored thirty-two goals in twenty-eight matches to set a Charlton record that still stands today. With three matches of the season remaining, Charlton were at the top of the table, and as only the division winners were promoted, they required one point from their home game against Aldershot to win the title and promotion.

Charlton won the match 4-0 and Jimmy Seed achieved what he had been appointed to do – take the club back up to the Second Division. Even better was to follow, when Charlton went through the 1936/37 campaign unbeaten at home and made League history by becoming the first football club to win promotion from the Third to First Division in two consecutive seasons. The potential of attracting huge crowds at The Valley had been proved on many previous occasions when supporters had turned out in force to fill out the ground for Cup matches and local London derbies. During the promotion season, gates at The Valley averaged 22,026, the highest attendance of 46,713 coming against Tottenham Hotspur, Charlton winning the match 2-1.

TRAVELLING SUPPORT

For the club's first home match in the top division, over 30,000 supporters filed in through The Valley turnstiles to watch Charlton Athletic take on Liverpool, the game ending in a 1-1 draw. Apart from local derbies, which for Charlton now included playing Arsenal, Brentford and Chelsea, match attendances came mostly from the home club's supporters. When Charlton entertained Arsenal in a local London derby, the combined home and visiting support totalled 68,160, a record for a League match at The Valley that has never been broken. It is believed that the actual attendance was more likely 80,000 or more, as when The Valley gates were locked, thousands of spectators found their way into the ground without paying. In the midweek return fixture at Highbury, with Charlton on top of the table and Arsenal one place below, it was another lockout with just over 60,000 in attendance and thousands more supporters left outside, unable to gain entry.

Long distance travel for away supporters was not so easy. When eventual title winners Manchester City visited The Valley in February, the fixture attracted a gate of just over 35,000 and the majority in attendance would have been home supporters. On match days, a large proportion of football supporters in attendance at The Valley would have been workers from the local industries located on the Thames riverside, from Greenwich along to Woolwich. When Charlton were playing at home on a Saturday, after the local industries closed down for the weekend at midday, the workers would file out through their firms' main entrance, and make their way towards a local public house for a pint or two before heading to The Valley.

These industries employed thousands of workers who lived within the borough, industries that included Woolwich Arsenal, a huge firm that made armaments for Britain's fighting forces; Siemens, electrical and telegraph cable makers; Greenwich Power Station; Stone's, a ship propeller foundry; Johnson & Phillips, submarine cable manufacturers; Redpath Brown, a steelworks; British Ropes and Harvey's, a metal fabrication factory. These were all companies that collectively employed more than 50,000 workers, with around 30,000 coming from the Royal Arsenal alone.

Supporters following their team away were dependent on the availability of public transport, and during the 1920s and 1930s it would be highly unlikely that working class people, who made up a majority of football support, would have their own transport (aside from a pushbike). Journeying to home matches or to local derbies would have been relatively easy, as there were plenty of trams and, later, buses operating in towns and cities around Britain. Additionally, supporters of London clubs had the ever-reliable tube at their disposal. Charlton however, situated south of the Thames, was not serviced by the London underground system and relied on supporters getting to matches by using the tram, train and bus services. Those fans who peddled their way to the ground by bike would pay a couple of pence to park the bicycles in the front gardens of houses close to the ground. Albert North, one energetic young supporter, regularly cycled from his home in St Paul's Cray to matches at The Valley and back, a round trip of 16 miles. After coming out of the army in 1946, he had earned enough money to buy himself a small car for travelling to the games.

In Jimmy Seed's autobiography, published in 1958, the Charlton manager recalls the difficulties supporters had in attending matches at The Valley. He wrote

> One of Charlton's biggest crowd problems had always been transport ... Although London was glad to see the back of those old bone-shakers we called trams, it was a bad day for Charlton supporters when they were finally done away with. The trams held more customers, of course, and could be turned round quickly with an efficient shuttle service to pick up more supporters.

It was ironic therefore, that after the majority of London trams were taken out of service, they were then broken up at salvage yards in Charlton. Travelling supporters were eventually able to make good use of the ever-expanding local and national overground railway networks. Travelling from one end of the country to the other by train, to follow your club away, continued to be a difficult task, especially in the years after a report was published written by Kent born Dr Richard Beeching on how to make railways more cost effective. The report resulted in the closure of many of Britain's branch lines during the 1960s, an act which inadvertently generated more business for coach operators transporting supporters to away matches. Acknowledged as the man who changed the face of the national train network system, Beeching spent his early career working at a fuel research centre in Greenwich during the 1930s, at a time when Charlton's support was at its highest.

During an away fixture at Middlesbrough, after Charlton's promotion into the First Division, the Charlton players were surprised to hear a lone voice call out from the terraces 'come on Charlton', as it was unlikely they were expecting a Charlton fan to be in the crowd so far away from home. The lone Charlton supporters turned out to be 'keeper Sam Bartram's brother, who travelled from his home close by to cheer on the team. Although fans travelling to away matches were few in number during the 1930s, coach companies were organising limited group travel for home and away games. As early as 1921, the Royal Arsenal Co-operative Society placed an advert in the club's first League home programme, recommending supporters to 'Follow your favourite team in a McCleod Motor Coach – The most comfortable coaches in the district'.

With motorways yet to be built, the railway network system was still the most efficient, cost-effective and fastest method of travel when journeying long distances to watch your team play away. This was especially the case after restrictions were imposed on coach operating services in the Road Traffic Act 1930, which introduced a national system of regulation for passenger road transport and imposed a top speed limit of 30 mph for all coaches.

These speed restrictions were gradually lifted for buses and coaches on open roads, but it would not be until 1961 that a speed limit of 40 mph was increased to 50 mph. Journeying from Charlton to faraway football cities such as Manchester would have taken up to ten hours or more, travelling by coach (or charabanc as they were more commonly known) on Britain's old A and B road network system, supporters not returning from away matches until the early hours of the next morning. The players and management team had the luxury of travelling long distances outside of the capital by train, staying overnight at a hotel before being transported by bus to the opposition's ground on the day of the match. One of the club's first transport suppliers were Greenwich-based C. G. Lewis Safety Coaches, founded by Charles George Lewis in 1919. Lewis coaches, originally known as Greenwich Belle before a change of name in 1923, had been transporting the Charlton team to local away matches before they began running a service for the Robins Club, a group of travelling Charlton supporters, who were taken to watch the team play away matches throughout London. As travel to away games became more commonplace, supporters travelled to grounds all around the county for Cup and League matches. The Charlton Athletic Supporters' Club, which had their headquarters at The Warren in Charlton Church Lane, also began hiring double-decker buses, often twelve at a time, to transport supporters to local derbies and away matches within the suburbs of London.

During the early twentieth century, especially during the interwar years of the 1920s and 1930s, London's urban areas expanded faster than at any previous period of time. In the South East, suburban development expanded out into the neighbouring county of Kent. Although the greater part of Charlton's support had originally come from the South East London boroughs, supporters were now travelling in from the suburbs of Bexley, Bromley, Dartford and north-west Kent.

At the end of the 1936/37 season Charlton finished second in the table and were the fifth best-supported club in the First Division, with an average attendance at The Valley of 31,086. All receipts taken during that season totalled up to a record £40,393, give or take a few shillings and pence, which made club a very healthy profit indeed. The supporters carried out their own fundraising activities at matches by walking around the pitch holding out a large bedsheet for fans to throw loose change into and selling raffle tickets at a penny each to win the match ball. Supporters also had the opportunity to help the club financially by purchasing Charlton Athletic shares.

By the latter part of the 1930s, Charlton Athletic was established as major force in British football. The club's financial situation, however, never matched its successes on the pitch. Before the outbreak of the Second World War, Charlton suffered a financial loss for the season of just over £2,000, and three matches into the 1939/40 season, with war now raging in Europe, all football competition was suspended on instruction from the League. The Charlton board then took the decision to release all the club playing staff from their contracts, but to keep their registrations, and retain the services of the secretary-manager, trainer, assistant trainer, groundsman and club secretary. This reduced the staff wage bill down to £28 a week.

WARTIME WEMBLEY AND WINNING SILVERWARE

A majority of the playing staff released by Charlton continued playing friendly football matches after entering into a reserve occupation, either with the police, warden services or working at the local Woolwich Arsenal. Some players would later join the armed forces, serving on the home front and overseas. After a series of friendly matches were played during the first few months of the war, Charlton joined an unsuccessful attempt to organise a London, and later regional, League.

With bombing raids becoming a regular occurrence, match attendances for friendly games and local League fixtures were unsurprisingly poor. Games were often suspended during an air-raid alert, and the majority of the spectators would go home before the all-clear was sounded and the match resumed, even if a raid had not taken place. By the end of 1940, the League authorities made the decision to close all professional football competitions down for the duration of the war. Charlton manager Jimmy Seed and trainer Jimmy Trotter began organising coaching sessions for boys from the local area and, after playing a series of friendly matches, entered a junior team, Charlton Rovers, into the South Eastern Combination League for the 1941/42 season.

Following the Royal Air Force's success over the Luftwaffe during the Battle of Britain, which brought an end to the sustained strategic bombing raids over the United Kingdom (known as the Blitz), German daytime air raids became less frequent. With the full backing of the government, regional war-League competitions resumed, with the expectation that competitive football would bring some form of normality back to a nation under siege. Although the danger of falling bombs became less frequent, The Valley received several direct hits that caused some minor damage to the terracing, the pitch, an ambulance hut and the North Stand covered-end roof.

Local neighbours Millwall, however, fared much worse. When part of their main stand burned down after an air raid towards end of the 1942/43 season, the docklands club began playing home games at The Valley while a temporary stand was constructed. With the majority of Charlton players now scattered throughout the country, if not serving overseas, many featured as guest players for football clubs close to where they were stationed, worked or lived. Charlton fielded guest players who found themselves many miles away from their own clubs, including Manchester United's Frank Swift and Everton's Tommy Lawton. Other wartime players who would later join Charlton's playing staff included forward Charlie Revell, who went on to score eighty-two goals for Charlton during the war seasons, and winger Chris Duffy, who joined the club after the war and found fame in the FA Cup.

Charlton Athletic made two consecutive Wembley appearances during the war years in the Football League (South) Cup (which had replaced the FA Challenge Cup during hostilities). There were two regional League divisions, north and south, with a cup competition played out between teams in the Northern League and Southern League. The cup final winners of each League then met in an overall final, playing for the Alexander Charity Cup. Charlton won their way to the 1943 final after despatching Fulham, Crystal Palace and Luton in a series of home and away legs, winning all but one of the ties, and then beat semi-final opponents Reading 2-1 at White Hart Lane. In the final played in May at Wembley, Charlton played

Arsenal with 75,000 fans in attendance, a record for a War Cup final up to that date. Arsenal outplayed Charlton on the day to win the match 7-1, but then later lost to the northern winners Blackpool in the regional final at Stamford Bridge.

The following season Charlton were back at Wembley, this time making it through to the final without losing a match, knocking out Brighton, Crystal Palace and Brentford, before beating Tottenham 3-0 in the semi-final. In the Wembley final played on 15 April 1944, Charlton's opponents Chelsea were making their first appearance at the national stadium. A maximum capacity crowd of 85,000 supporters from both clubs packed into Wembley and broke the previous War Cup final record attendance figures. Although conceding a goal after 12 minutes from a Chelsea penalty, Charlton hit back before half-time with two goals from Charlie Revell, and one from club captain Don Welsh. The final finished 3-1 to Charlton and the Football League (South) Cup was presented to the winners by the future President of the United States, General Dwight D. Eisenhower.

After overcoming Chelsea, Charlton faced Aston Villa, the winners of the Football League (North) Cup, to compete for the Alexander Cup played at Stamford Bridge in aid of the King George charitable fund. The cup was named after First Lord of the Admiralty, Albert Victor Alexander, 1st Earl Alexander of Hillsborough and vice president of Chelsea FC. Aston Villa scored first, at just under the hour mark, through a goal from winger Eric Houghton. Charlton's Charlie Revell scored the equaliser with 13 minutes of the match remaining and the final finished in a 1-1 draw. With neither extra time nor a replay possible, due to transport restrictions and the threat of air raids, both teams shared the honours. Charlton and Villa received a cup each, which had never happened in a War Cup final previously and would never happened again. On 7 May 1945, two days after Charlton had played their last match of the 1944/45 season, the German High Command signed the instrument of surrender at Reims in France, which brought an end to the Second World War in Europe. Two weeks after the start of the 1945/46 Football League (South) season, total war was finally declared over after the Japanese command signed the documents of surrender aboard USS Missouri on 2 September 1945.

Although it would undoubtedly take some time for the nation to get back to any form of normality after six years of global warfare, the Football League resumed at the end of the 1945/46 war League season. Football clubs had already began competing in the FA Cup, which came back to replace the War Cup tournament at the beginning of that current season. For the first and only time in the history of the Cup, all ties from the first round proper up to the sixth round proper would be played home and away over two legs.

In the third round, first leg, Charlton were drawn to play Fulham at The Valley. For both teams, this was their first venture back into the FA Cup competition. Charlton went into a three-goal lead before Fulham scored to make it 3-1, which is how the first leg finished. In the return leg, played two days later, Charlton lost the match 2-1 but went through 4-3 on aggregate to meet Wolverhampton Wanderers in the next round. Charlton then beat Wolves 5-1 at The Valley and drew 1-1 at Molineux to make it into the fifth round. In the next leg, away to Preston North End, Charlton drew 1-1 and then beat their opponents 6-0 at home. After despatching Brentford in the next round 6-3 at The Valley, and 3-1 at Griffin Park, Charlton faced Bolton Wanderers in the semi-final (played at Villa Park). Just six months after hostilities had ceased, the semi-final attracted an attendance of over 70,000, raising receipts of £18,011 17s 6d, a record outside of London for an English League ground. Leading 1-0 through a goal from Chris Duffy 35 minutes in, Charlton were then under constant pressure going up to half-time. 5 minutes after the restart, Chris Duffy received the ball from a Don Welsh pass and then began dribbling his way up the pitch, taking on five players before shooting past the Bolton 'keeper Stan Hanson, to make it 2-1. Charlton made football history by becoming the only club to lose an FA Cup tie and still reach the final.

On Cup final day, which took place on 27 April 1946, four days before the domestic season had come to a close, Charlton's opponents Derby County had played in three previous FA Cup finals but had never been victorious. In an evenly matched final, Charlton's Bert Tuner scored for both sides with just 10 minutes of the final remaining, first deflecting a shot into his own goal, before his own shot at the Derby goal was deflected past the 'keeper a minute later to make it 1-1. The final went into extra time and Derby scored three more goals to win 4-1.

After the match it was reported that when one of the Charlton players told his teammates they would all be back again next season, Jimmy Seed, overhearing the remark, said to them all, 'That's right, boys, and next year we'll go one better and win the Cup,' a comment which he later said was simply made in an effort to cheer them all up. The Charlton players received two medals for playing in the club's first FA Cup final, one made of bronze was presented on the day, as gold had been in short supply after the war. The second, made of gold, was issued to the players some time later. Charlton finished third in the Football League (South) after their FA Cup final appearance, one point behind division winners Birmingham City and runners up Aston Villa, with both those clubs on sixty-two points. Charlton only lost one match at home all season and the faithful Charlton fans had come back to support the club in their thousands. Attendance figures at The Valley during the last season of the war averaged 6,165, however, once the global conflict was over and peace resumed, the average attendance increased to 28,991. From 1946 onwards, the Football League returned to the previous configuration of four divisions with Charlton now back in Division One. The initial two fixtures of the 1946/47 season were played away with Charlton only gaining one point from both matches. The third fixture of the season, played at The Valley against Manchester United, attracted an attendance of 44,088. Throughout the season, Charlton's League form was inconsistent, winning matches by three or four goals and then losing by a similar score line a week later. The supporters, however, continued to turn up at The Valley in huge numbers, with the largest home League attendance of 57,983 for a game against Arsenal, which ended in a 2-2 draw.

Although Charlton had not been playing well in the League, the team excelled once more in the FA Cup, winning all four Cup ties to go through to the semi-final. When Charlton entered the FA Cup in the third round on 11 January 1947, against Third Division (South) Rochdale, the team were then fifth from bottom of the First Division, with eighteen points from twenty-four matches. Charlton easily won the tie 3-1 and were then drawn to play Second Division West Bromwich Albion at The Hawthorns. Charlton captain Don Welsh was unavailable to play due to an injury and his place was taken by semi-retired thirty-nine-year-old George Robinson.

After going a goal down with less than 30 minutes of the match remaining, Charlton fought back and went on to win 2-1. This led to a fifth-round tie against Blackburn Rovers at The Valley on 8 February 1947, which became the first FA Cup tie, apart from the final, to be shown on television. The match, however, was hardly a television spectacle. The Valley pitch was in poor condition with the surface covered in mud, frost and ice. The football played was far from exiting, with neither side coming close to scoring a goal. Then, with just 3 minutes of the match remaining, and a replay the most likely outcome, Charlton almost lost the tie when 'keeper Sam Bartram came out to close down the onrushing Blackburn midfielder Jim Baldwin, only to slip over on an icy patch to leave his goal unguarded. Baldwin's shot somehow went wide of the target and from the following goal kick, Charlton's Gordon Hurst chased down the wing to force a corner. Taking the kick himself, Hurst hit the ball into the Blackburn area for teammate Tommy Dawson to rise up among a crowd of players, head the ball past the 'keeper, and score the winning goal for Charlton.

When the next round came along on 1 March 1947, Charlton were still languishing down towards the foot of the table in nineteenth place, while their opponents, Preston North End, were just five places off the top spot. With an attendance of over 56,000 at The Valley, and the majority of supporters cheering on the home team, Chris Duffy scored the first goal of the game to put Charlton 1-0 up, and although Preston levelled the tie before half-time, winger Gordon Hurst scored Charlton's second from a Charlie Revell headed-cross. The Preston players complained to the referee, claiming the ball had already gone out of play before Revell headed it on, and appealed for the goal to be disallowed. The referee refused to overturn the decision and Charlton won the tie 2-1 to go through to meet Second Division Newcastle United in the semi-final, played at Elland Road on 29 March 1947.

The evening before the match, with the Charlton team staying overnight in a Harrogate hotel, several of the players began suffering from food poisoning, believed to have been caused by the salmon sandwiches they had eaten while visiting a local factory during the afternoon. The suffering players were ill all through the night, and although prescribed some medicine by club physician Dr John Montgomery, Don Welsh, Gordon Hurst, Peter Croker, Bert Johnson and big Sam Bartram, five players who manager Jimmy Seed could hardly do without going into an FA Cup semi-final, were still feeling the effects the following morning. The newspapers had already backed Newcastle to go through to the final, even before half the Charlton team had gone down with food poisoning, and the Charlton management even considered flying up substitutes from London to replace the players still suffering.

The all-ticket semi-final was limited to an attendance of 48,000, with 12,000 tickets allocated to Charlton supporters, all of whom were relieved to see every one of Charlton's first-choice players running onto the pitch after news of the food poisoning incident had featured in the latest edition of the *London Evening Standard*.

The Charlton team line-up on the day was Sam Bartram, Peter Croker, Jack Shreeve, Harold Phipps, Bert Johnson, Charlie Revell, Gordon Hurst, Tommy Dawson, Bill

Robinson, Don Welsh and Chris Duffy. From the start of the match, Charlton went straight out on the attack, the Charlton supporters outcheering the Geordie fans at St James' Park. By half-time Charlton were beating Newcastle 3-0, with a goal from Tommy Dawson and two from skipper Don Welsh. The Newcastle United team, which included England internationals Roy Bentley, Jackie Milburn, Len Shackleton and Duggie Wright, plus Scottish capped Frank Brennan and Tommy Pearson, were no match for a rampant Charlton Athletic team. With the exception of Sam Bartram, who required a hot poultice applied to his stomach during the match, the players hardly showed any sign of suffering from food poisoning. On the back foot for most of the game, Newcastle United conceded a fourth goal in the second half, scored by forward Gordon Hurst, Charlton winning the tie 4-0. Carried from the pitch in triumph by the fans, Don Welsh then collapsed unconscious in the dressing room. After he recovered, Welsh told his teammates he had kept quiet about how poorly he had felt, hoping that it might console them if they believed that he at least was perfectly fit.

Back to Wembley for a second consecutive FA Cup final, the match was scheduled to be played on 26 April 1947, before the season had ended, and with Charlton still having six fixtures to fulfil. Although fourth from bottom and five points off a relegation position, manager Jimmy Seed remained confident that the team would not drop down into the Second Division. Leading up to the final there was an evident feeling of disharmony within the Charlton dressing room, as the players were unhappy about the share of the profits they would receive from the Wembley gate money. Starting up a financial pool themselves, the players charged the press a fee to take pictures of them, and Don Welsh produced an FA Cup final souvenir booklet, which was sold for 1s a copy. Manager Jimmy Seed agreed that the bonuses on offer to each player for appearing in the final and the early round matches were of small financial reward, however, he did not agree with the players refusing to let the press take their photographs unless they were paid, as their grievance was with the FA and not the press.

More funds were raised for the players' pool on the coach journey to Wembley from Brighton, where the team had been staying and training prior to the day of the final. After stopping off for luncheon at the Metropolitan Police Sports Club at Hayes, Dr Montgomery, unaware that the team coach would have a police escort waving them through any red traffic signals encountered when they set off on the final journey to the stadium, agreed to contribute a shilling to the pot if the coach went through any red lights, the players adding a shilling if the lights were green. On arrival at Wembley the club doctor had made a hefty contribution of £10 to the players' pool.

Although the team arrived with some extra funds to share out, they arrived at the game without any match socks. The team had used up all their allocated clothing coupons on a change of shirts and shorts, as Cup final opponents Burnley were playing in the club's home colours, which would have caused a colour clash. Charlton defender Peter Croker, who missed playing in the previous year's final after breaking a leg, managed to secure a full set of socks from the manufacturer through a sports shop owner he knew in Kingston. On the day of the final, Charlton's match socks arrived by special delivery, carried to Wembley in two parcels by Croker's parents, who picked up the socks en route.

The 1947 FA Cup final Charlton Athletic line-up included Sam Bartram, Peter Croker, Jack Shreeve, Harold Phipps and Bill Whittaker, who had been drafted in to replace injured Charlie Revell, Bert Johnson, Bill Robinson, Tommy Dawson, Chris Duffy, Gordon Hurst and club captain Don Welsh. The Cup final, played on a very hot day, was not as exciting as the 98,215 in attendance had expected. Burnley, a team heading for promotion from the Second Division, were considered favourites to win the Cup, due to both clubs' respective positions in their divisions, however, after 90 minutes with neither team creating very many clear-cut chances, the final went into extra time. With both defences dominating play, it seemed that the final would, most likely, be decided in a replay with just 6 minutes of extra time remaining. Charlton's Bert Johnson then passed the ball on to Bill Robinson, who dribbled the ball down the wing to put in a high cross to Don Welsh, who headed the ball back, and down towards Chris Duffy, who was waiting just inside the Burnley penalty area. Duffy then hit the ball with a powerful right-foot half-volley, past the motionless Burnley 'keeper Jim Strong and into the back of the net. For an instant, time almost seemed to stand still, then, raising his arms above his head, Duffy turned and ran back towards his own half with the rest of the Charlton players chasing after him in celebration. With only a few minutes of the final remaining and Charlton winning 1-0, Burnley had an opportunity to equalise when Charlton's Tommy Dawson lost possession of the ball, giving Burnley the chance to go on the attack. Sam Bartram was then called into action by diverting the ball onto the crossbar from a shot on goal. The rebound was cleared upfield and the referee finally blew his whistle to signal full time. Charlton Athletic had won the FA Cup for the first time in the club's history, becoming one of only three London clubs at that time to have lifted the world's most famous and prestigious domestic trophy. The Cup and medals were presented to the team by the Duke and Duchess of Gloucester, and, on this occasion, the medals were made of gold.

The team and members of the club then celebrated this fantastic achievement by holding a celebration dinner at London's Café Royal, and were later invited to attend a civic reception hosted by Mayor of Greenwich at the town hall. The players were driven around the borough in a Lewis coach to show off the trophy to the club's cheering supporters who had lined the streets of Charlton and Woolwich. What those happy fans were unaware of was that, shortly before the Cup went out on display with the team on the bus, Charlton manager Jimmy Seed had broken off the top of the trophy's lid. While getting into his car at The Valley, on the way to the civic reception, Seed dropped the lid and the top snapped off. A local garage provided a quick fix and welded it back on, and no one noticed the difference when the Cup arrived at Greenwich Town Hall. The next day Seed had the trophy professionally repaired by a silversmith. After the celebrations were over, it was then back to League football. With games in hand over the three teams below Charlton in the League, it was essential enough points were won in those final few matches to ensure the club kept clear of the bottom two relegation places.

Charlton's first of the six remaining fixtures ended 1-1 away at Sunderland. They then lost the next match 3-1 at home to Liverpool, leaving them third from bottom and needing three more points from the four remaining games to ensure they were safe from relegation. Returning from an away game against Blackpool at Bloomfield Road with a point, after drawing 0-0, Charlton had thirty-one points and the two teams below, Brentford (with twenty-five) and Leeds (with eighteen) could no longer catch Charlton with only two matches for each club remaining. At the season's end, Charlton finished fourth from bottom and even though this was the club's worse position since promoted into the First Division under manager Jimmy Seed, Charlton were the tenth-best-supported team in the division. During the three seasons following the club's FA Cup success, Charlton's League and Cup record was extremely disappointing. Finishing no higher than ninth position during that time, attendances at The Valley were far better than should have been expected. In the 1948/49 season, home gates at The Valley averaged 40,216, the best the club had ever had.

4

AT THE COST OF FINANCIAL INVESTMENT

With Charlton Athletic one of the best-supported clubs in the First Division, an investment in both the team and The Valley (the ground having had no major development carried out since the 1930s) may well have given the club an opportunity to become a major force in English football. At one time, The Valley had been considered a suitable venue for international matches and with European club football competition just over the horizon, the board of directors should have been planning for Charlton's future in the global game. Undoubtedly the name of Charlton Athletic was well known throughout the football world, in both Europe and South America, as the club had regularly been invited to travel overseas to play friendly matches. Charlton's first tour abroad came in 1924 when the club travelled to play two Belgium clubs, Liège and Ent Standard, Charlton winning both games. Then, once they had been promoted to the First Division, Charlton received offers to travel to all parts of the globe to compete against clubs which looked upon English football, and English teams, as the best in the world.

Charlton first competed against a full international side in 1937 when they played the French national team in Paris and beat Les Bleus 5-2. Other matches played against famous European teams overseas included Racing Club de Paris, Malmo and Benfica in 1946, Galatasaray and Besiktas in 1948 and Fenerbahçe in 1949, all clubs that would go on to play in European Cup competition. Two years after Manchester United became the first British club to compete in the European Champions' Cup, Charlton manager Jimmy Seed wrote in his autobiography, 'With the promise of new European Leagues and European Cup competitions, gates will boom and international soccer will become more and more important.' If the Charlton board of directors had made the necessary financial investments into the playing staff and ground development, as many other top clubs in the First Division had done prior to the formation of European Cup, supporters of Charlton Athletic may well have had the opportunity to watch the team compete in this highly prestigious and financially lucrative football tournament.

At the end of the 1949/50 season, receipts totalled just over £77,000, making the club a profit of £4,223 12s 8d, after paying off outstanding debts, running costs and staff wages. Manager Jimmy Seed was well aware that for Charlton Athletic to have any chance on making a serious challenge to win the First Division title, the directors would need to invest money back into the club. Where other clubs had been improving facilities for the comfort of supporters by covering all sides of their grounds and installing floodlights, not only to hold evening matches, but also to ensure that when it grew dark in the late afternoons during winter, supporters did not have to arrive for early afternoon kick-offs, there had been little significant improvements made to The Valley since the construction of a cover over the north terrace in 1932.

Charlton Athletic were a club that had always struggled financially, and after the Gliksten brothers had claimed back the assets initially invested, once the club became solvent and free from debt, there had been a reluctance to invest more money than the Glikstens believed was necessary back into the club. There was not much more manager Jimmy Seed could do than carry on as best as he could by improving the team through loan signings, free transfers, youth development and funds made available from players sold on, a familiar scenario that Charlton supporters would recognise in the modern game.

Jimmy Seed did not have to worry about negotiating players' wages, as during the late 1940s and early 1950s players were on a fixed maximum wage of £9 a week, plus a bonus of £2 for a win and £1 for a draw, which for married players with a family just about covered their outgoings. Single players without family commitments would, after paying the bills, have enough left over to spend on going out with teammates for a beer and attend local dances, with the expectation of meeting up with an attractive member of the opposite sex who was ready to walk out with famous football star. Other players would spend their free evenings betting at the new Charlton Greyhound Stadium located on Woolwich Road, not too far from The Valley. A few of the other Charlton players preferred a game of snooker.

Inside-forward Alex McCrae and midfielder Tommy Brown were the team's snooker hustlers, and would go around hotels and pubs that had snooker tables to take on all comers. Once at the table, both were unbeatable and they would play on all through the evening. However, they would never keep the winnings and always gave back the money to their beaten opponents, as staying at the snooker table was winning enough.

'Keeper Sam Bartram enjoyed meeting up with the locals for a pint and then serenading them with a few songs while a pianist played along. Bartram and his teammates also attended many of the Supporters' Club dances held throughout the season, and it was at one of these events where Sam met his future wife, and dedicated Charlton fan, Helen. A few players would also enjoy a night out at a private members club on Humber Road Greenwich, which was often raided by the local constabulary when drinking went on too long after hours.

THE ROBINS GO BOBBING ALONG

During the 1949/50 season, one supporter, Mr E. J. Baxter, took it upon himself to form a Charlton Athletic Supporters' Club, with the intention of organising group match travel for the club's fans. The Charlton board of directors, however, showed no enthusiasm for such an idea and refused to officially recognise the travel group as a supporters' club. The directors made the suggestion for a change of name, suggesting the 'Charlton Athletic Followers Club'. If the group agreed then they would be given permission to have their travel details printed in the matchday programme.

The travelling supporters group decided against this proposal for a new name and changed their title to 'The Robins Club', as Charlton had been using the nickname 'Robins' since the 1930s. At home matches the team would run out onto the pitch with a rendition of the popular song 'when the red, red robin comes bob, bob, bobbing along' played out over the grounds loud speaker system. Billy Cotton and his band recorded a version of the famous song especially for Charlton, after the team won promotion to the First Division in 1936. The big-band leader became a great friend of the Gliksten brothers through their association with theatrical agent Leslie Grade, a director of Leyton Orient football club. Many years later Leslie Grade's son, Michael, became a director of Charlton Athletic, the club he had supported ever since his father first took him to watch a match at The Valley in 1953.

Although Charlton fans now had more opportunities to follow their club to away games, it was at home where the support really needed to be maintained, as the club's lack of success may well have caused a sharp drop in attendances and, more importantly to the club, a drop in gate revenue. While attendances would never again reach those of the previous campaign, Charlton's average gate of 34,567 during the 1949/50 season was exceptional, especially as Charlton finished the season third from bottom and one place off relegation.

Team performances showed no improvement during the first part of the 1950/51 season and, by the new year, Charlton were positioned down towards the bottom of the division. Manager Jimmy Seed was in desperate need of a recognised goalscorer. The directors, however, were unwilling to release the amount of money Seed required to secure such a player.

Always on the lookout for alternative means to bring players in for very little financial outlay, when Seed was tipped off by a football acquaintance at IFK Norrköping that Swedish International forward Hans Jeppson was on his way over to London to attend business studies, the manager went out to sign him up. Jeppson was intending to look for a club to join during his short stay in the capital and was on his way to have talks with Arsenal. Seed met up with him before he had a chance to visit Highbury, immediately talking him into joining Charlton and playing under amateur terms. The Swedish striker scored nine goals in the eleven matches he played, goals which helped Charlton secure seventeen points and kept the club safe from any relegation worries. Jeppson scored a hat-trick in a 5-2 win over Arsenal at Highbury, the club he may well have joined if Seed had not got to him first. The defeat was the North London club's biggest at home in over twenty years.

Hans Jeppson departed the club a hero, and was presented with an inscribed cup from the Charlton supporters and a dinner set as a wedding gift from the club. Straight after his final match, Jeppson boarded a river launch down on the Thames which took him to Tilbury, so he could catch a boat back to Sweden in time for his wedding day.

Through his network of overseas football connections, Jimmy Seed had always been on the lookout for cut-price signings and prospective young talented players from abroad. He brought in a string of gifted players from South Africa, including inside-forward Syd O'Linn; 'keeper Albert Uytenbogaardt; forward Eddie Firmani and his defending brother Peter; midfielder Dudley Forbes; full-back John Hewie and forward Stuart Leary, who went on to become the club's record League goalscorer.

Three of those South African players came into the Charlton side during the 1951/52 season and although two of them (Leary and Firmani) only played a handful of League matches, the third, defender Hewie, made thirty-eight appearances during the season.

Charlton finished in a much more respectable position than the previous season, just above mid table. Attendance at The Valley however, had dropped to an average of 27,609. In 1951, just before Christmas, the club received news that chairman Albert Gliksten had died of a sudden heart attack while holidaying in British Honduras. This was not only very sad news for everyone associated with the club, it was devastating news for manager Jimmy Seed, who not only had a very good working relationship with his chairman, but had also become a very close friend. The relationship had built up between the two men since Seed had been appointed as Charlton's manager, and Albert had certainly helped him when all was not going too well out on the pitch. By the time of Albert Gliksten's death, the board of directors had become well aware of the signs of strain on the once good relationship between Seed and his number two, club trainer Jimmy Trotter.

One relationship which had grown and flourished however, while both men were working together as manager and player, was between Jimmy Seed and his 'keeper Sam Bartram, both men becoming friends for life. After Seed made Bartram Charlton's first-choice 'keeper, he was never dropped from the team. The manager made a promise that when he knew Bartram was no longer good enough to play in the first team, he would let him know. On 6 March 1954, in a 3-1 win over Portsmouth at The Valley, Sam Bartram made his official record-breaking five-hundredth appearance for the club. This milestone was later disputed, with some questioning whether this record came too soon, as the total number included three matches played prior to the outbreak of war in the 1939/40 season that were never recognised by the Football League. Nevertheless, Charlton Athletic statistician, Colin Cameron, made a good case for the record appearance against Portsmouth to stand, as the expunging of player appearances in the aborted 1939/40 season was never officially sanctioned by the football authorities at the time.

Valley attendances continued to fall during the mid-50s. Supporters were disappointed with team performances and the club's position in the division, and became disillusioned by the decision of the board to sell the best players to help balance the club's financial books. However, two young players Jimmy Seed brought in from South Africa, forwards Eddie Firmani and Stuart Leary (both goalscorers on Sam Bartram's big day), were soon bringing the crowds back to The Valley. At the end of the 1953/54 season the talented young forwards had scored thirty-six goals between them, Firmani with twelve and Leary with twenty-four. Charlton finished ninth in the division and were solvent for the first time in the club's history. One of the highlights of the season came in a home match at The Valley on 12 September 1953, when opponents Middlesbrough were beaten 8-1. Eddie Firmani's hat-trick, Sid O'Linn and Gordon Hurst's two goals each, and Stuart Leary's one made club history by recording Charlton's biggest ever League win.

Both Firmani and Leary became prolific goalscorers for the club and, along with another young forward, Bobby Ayre, who first joined the club in 1951 as an amateur player while serving in the RAF, they scored fifty-one of Charlton's seventy-six goals between them during the 1954/55 season. Although there were now some very good players in the Charlton line-up, Jimmy Seed lost the services of several of his most experienced squad members who were sold on for financial reasons. At the beginning of March, Charlton had been riding high, fourth in the First Division, just five points behind leaders Wolverhampton Wanderers. However, two months later, they had dropped down to fifteenth, which is where they stayed to the end of season, finishing six points off a relegation place. Although the club had become well run financially, the supporters were of the opinion there was an obvious lack of ambition shown by the board of directors for investing in the club's football future. This was soon to be proven correct when talented Eddie Firmani was sold at the end of the season to Italian giants Sampdoria, for a British record transfer fee at that time of £35,000.

The sale of Eddie Firmani brought the club a substantial financial boost going forward into the 1955/56 season, but the forward's goal scoring ability and football skills would be an obvious loss for the team. The Charlton supporters were, again, left extremely disappointed after losing such a prolific goalscorer. The young South African-born, Italian striker had attained heroic status while playing for just three seasons in Charlton's first team. Ireland-based Scottish forward Jimmy Gauld had been signed for a transfer fee of £4,000 and would take over Firmani's role up front. In his first season, Gauld scored eighteen League and Cup goals.

Playing alongside Stuart Leary, the pair struck up a prolific goalscoring partnership. The supporters were treated to some quality exhibitions of football at The Valley throughout that season, making Charlton the bookmakers' favourites to go on and win the FA Cup. After Charlton had beaten Burton Albion 7-0 in the third round and then knocked out Swindon Town 2-1 in the fourth round (both ties played at the Valley), Charlton were drawn to play Arsenal at home on 18 February 1956. The attendance on the day of 71,767 was just under double the figure of Charlton's biggest League gate of the season two months before, when eventual First Division champions Manchester United visited The Valley and were well beaten 3-0. Charlton had also recorded a 4-2 victory over their FA Cup opponents Arsenal at Highbury earlier in the season, but on the day of the Cup tie, the North London club went into a 2-0 lead within 30 minutes and Cup favourites Charlton, unable to reply, went out.

END OF A FOOTBALL ERA

A month later, Arsenal were back at The Valley for a League fixture on 10 March 1956. This would be Sam Bartram's last game as a professional player. After spending almost twenty-two years at Charlton, playing a record 623 League and Cup matches for his club, Bartram made the decision to retire from playing when an opportunity came along to take up the managerial position at York City, the club he had guested for while stationed at Harrogate during the early part of the war. The legendary 'keeper kept a clean sheet on the day and Charlton beat Arsenal 2-0, a fitting end to Sam Bartram's epic playing career. Charlton's second 'keeper Frank Reed took over in goal for the final eight matches of the season. Bartram's departure later proved to be a great loss.

After finishing fourteenth in the table, one place better than the previous year, supporters were in expectation of a further positional improvement by the end of the forthcoming season. They were soon to be disappointed when Charlton lost their first four matches of the 1956/57 season. After a humiliating record breaking 8-1 away defeat against Sunderland on 1 September 1956 (Jimmy Seed's first club as a professional player), the Charlton supporters were notified, through an article written for the following Saturday's home matchday programme, that Seed had resigned.

To a majority of Charlton supporters Seed's resignation was an astonishing decision for the manager to make, despite the team having lost the first five fixtures of the season. Within the programme notes, Seed's resignation was explained away by implying he was ill. It stated that 'the tremendous strain of office on a man in ill health could not have been endured much longer.' In reality, the reason behind his departure was that the board had relieved him of his duties. Sacked after more than twenty-three years of excellent service to the club, Seed had taken Third Division (South) mid-table Charlton Athletic up to the top division and to four Wembley finals, winning a War Cup and the most prestigious trophy of all, the FA Cup.

After the defeat by Sunderland, Jimmy Seed had been requested to attend a meeting at the business office of club chairman Stanley Gliksten. In the meeting, it was explained to the manager that due to the team's poor start to the season, the board believed it was time for a younger man to take over, suggesting that as Seed was unwell and getting old, it would be best for all concerned if he retired. Jimmy Seed was sixty-one years old at the time, his health no different from others of a similar age. Having already made plans to retire gracefully when reaching sixty-five, ever the gentleman and not wishing to cause the club grief, Seed, after some gentle persuasion by his chairman, succumbed to the request of the board and resigned to take early retirement. Following the loss of his job, Jimmy Seed did become extremely ill, the likely cause due to the stress and strain endured after being sacked from managing the club he loved so dearly.

Club chairman Stanley Gliksten then asked Seed who he believed would be a suitable replacement. The sacked manager suggested the board consider former Charlton inside-forward Benny Fenton, twenty-three years Seed's junior. Fenton, then player-manager at Colchester United, was a man Seed considered a very worthy and capable successor. However, a week after Jimmy Seed's forced retirement, the board, ignoring the former manager's recommendation, appointed first-team trainer Jimmy Trotter instead. Trotter was only three years younger than Seed so, in some respects, the club had chosen a younger man to take on the role of managing Charlton Athletic.

Charlton Athletic's supporters had, by then, lost all faith in the board of directors. Season after season since the club's triumphant FA Cup final win ten years earlier, they had failed to financially back the manager in building a team that would make Charlton a force in the Football League. At the end of the season, attendances at The Valley had dropped to an average of 20,370. This was not as low as perhaps it might have been, as Charlton were relegated after finishing at the foot of the table with just twenty-two points. Some could look upon the departure of the great Sam Bartram as a contributing factor to Charlton's poor run of form throughout the season, the team only winning 9 matches, drawing 4, losing 29 and conceding 120 goals. The consensus among fans for the cause of the club's ultimate downfall was the board's lack of financial investment during the preceding season, which had also cost Charlton's most successful manager Jimmy Seed his job.

After Jimmy Trotter's appointment, the Charlton supporters remained ignorant of the truth behind Jimmy Seed's departure from the club, especially as the local and national newspapers were publishing the club's carefully worded press statement that Seed had made the decision to leave the club due to poor health. Two years later, the truth came to light in Jimmy Seed's autobiography, published in 1958, where he wrote of the circumstances surrounding his departure and the day he was informed he had lost his job. He wrote

The date holds little significance for most people other than it was the seventeenth anniversary of Britain's second entry into a world war, but I shall never forget 3 September 1956 ... the day in which my own little world seemed to crash around me when, after twenty-three years as secretary-manager, I had been SACKED!

The Charlton Supporters' Club, grateful for the success the legendary manager had brought to the club, presented Jimmy Seed with an inscribed silver cigar case at a reception held to honour him in at the town hall in Woolwich. Attended by the Charlton players and former 'keeper Sam Bartram, the team presented their former boss with a handsome pen and pencil set. Before the Supporters' Club presentation, Jimmy Seed's services to Charlton Athletic, and football in general, had been recognised by the Football Writers' Association who presented him with a specially commissioned watch. This was the very first time football journalists had made such a presentation to a football manager. Jimmy Seed did not retire from football altogether. He later joined Bristol City as an adviser and then as acting manager, before moving to Charlton's local rivals Millwall, first as manager from January 1958 to July 1959, and then as advisor and director of the club, a position he held until his death in July 1966.

SUPPORT IN THE SECOND DIVISION
At the beginning of the 1957/58 season, Jimmy Trotter's first full season in charge, Charlton went on a seven-match unbeaten run and although it might have been expected that attendances at The Valley would have dropped for Second Division football, home gates were similar as those towards the end of the previous season. With the team at the top of the Second Division, there was an expectation among the club directors that Charlton would bounce straight back up to the First Division. Exactly halfway through the football season, with Charlton now down in sixth place but only three points behind leaders Liverpool, Huddersfield Town visited to The Valley on 21 December 1957 for a League match which would become unique in the history of football. There were only 12,353 supporters in attendance on the day, the majority followers of Charlton.

The low match attendance was due to the match being played on the last shopping day before Christmas, rather than down to the team's recent home performances, as Charlton had won each of the previous two home fixtures 4-1. With less than 30 minutes of the match remaining, hundreds of Charlton supporters decided they had had enough and headed for the exit gates. Charlton, now down to ten men, conceded a fifth goal to make it 5-1 to the visitors.

Manager Bill Shankly's mid-table Huddersfield Town had gone into a two-goal lead in the first half after Charlton defender Derek Ufton dislocated his shoulder and had to be taken off with only 17 minutes of the match played. After the half-time break, Charlton forward Johnny Summers pulled a goal back and, although a man short, the Charlton supporters were of the belief that there was plenty of time for their team to get an equaliser. Former Millwall forward Summers, a proven goalscorer who the previous Charlton manager had wanted to sign before the start of the 1956/57 season, moved to Charlton for £3,300, two months after the appointment of Jimmy Trotter.

Two minutes after Summers scored for Charlton, Huddersfield hit their third and then, within 12 minutes, scored two more to go into a 5-1 lead. With the attendance already one of the lowest for a League match at The Valley in over ten years, the huge expanses of terracing around the ground became even more sparsely populated as Charlton supporters gave up on the game as soon as Charlton conceded the fifth goal. As the fans that left early were walking down the roads leading away from the ground, a great roar came up from inside The Valley when John 'Buck' Ryan pulled a goal back for Charlton. Then, it was time for Johnny Summers to take centre stage, and he scored his second goal on 64 minutes, Summers then found the back of the Huddersfield net three more times to give Charlton a 6-5 lead with just 9 minutes of the match remaining. Although Summers was a natural left footer, the forward scored all five of his goals with his right foot. John Hewie, Charlton's Scottish International defender, then deflected the ball past his own 'keeper, Willie Duff, to make it 6-6 and the Charlton supporters who had decided to stay, were now cheering their team on to go for the winner.

From a Johnny Summers' cross, attacking midfielder Fred Lucas passed the ball onto 'Buck' Ryan who struck the ball home, past the Huddersfield 'keeper, to make it 7-6 to Charlton with only a minute of the match remaining. At the final whistle the supporters jumped the railings and onto the pitch, running up to surround the exhausted players as they attempted to make their way towards the West Stand tunnel and down into the changing rooms. The supporters, now unwilling to go home, gathered in front of the West Stand chanting for Johnny Summers to make an appearance. A huge cheer went up as the Charlton players came up into directors' box, acknowledging the well deserved round of applause they all received from the fans.

Along with the record 7-6 win over Huddersfield, Charlton were involved in two other high scoring games at The Valley during the season, beating Liverpool 5-1 and Middlesbrough 6-2, Summers scoring a hat-trick in the latter. The win over Middlesbrough on 15 February 1958 took Charlton back to the top of the table and two points ahead of second placed West Ham United. When West Ham then won a game in hand a week later, the East End club took top spot on goal average, staying there until the end of the season. With two teams promoted from the Second Division, Charlton were the most likely to take second place and secure promotion, even with both Liverpool and Blackburn Rovers close behind.

Prior to the last game of the season, Charlton and West Ham United were now both on fifty-five points, West Ham in top place only by goal average and Blackburn Rovers, now ahead of Liverpool, in third place, just one point behind. Charlton's last match of the season took place at The Valley on 26 April 1958 and their opponents on the day were promotion rivals Blackburn Rovers. The Charlton supporters turned out in force to cheer on their team and the attendance of 56,435 was a record for a Second Division match at The Valley. Charlton only needed a draw to ensure promotion and with only 4 minutes of the match gone, a header from Fred Lucas put Charlton into a 1-0 lead. Stuart Leary (second only to Johnny Summers that season for number of goals scored) then missed an easy opportunity to make it 2-0. After escaping conceding a second goal, Blackburn Rovers went on the offensive, scoring three goals without reply before half-time. In the second half, Charlton conceded a further goal from a penalty scored by England international Bryan Douglas.

Charlton's Peter Firmani pulled a goal back, and then with only 7 minutes of the match remaining, Charlton were awarded a penalty which was taken and scored by John Hewie. With Blackburn leading 4-3, Charlton supporters were cheering their team on, encouraging them to go forward in search of the equalising goal to take Charlton back into the First Division. Holding out with some resolute defending until the final whistle, Blackburn Rovers took second place and promotion from Charlton by a single point.

Although Charlton finished the season as top scorers, with 107 League goals, as well as winning more matches than any other team in the Second Division (one more than division winners West Ham United) they had failed to take enough points off their promotion rivals to ensure a return to the top division. Even though attendances at The Valley had increased during the promotion chasing season by 2,000 a match, thousands of once-loyal fans had now deserted the club.

At the beginning of the 1958/59 season, the board of directors, aware of the discontent growing among the Charlton support, made an appeal to the fans through the local media to band together and take more of an interest in the workings of the club and, in collaboration with the board, help Charlton Athletic continue as a first-class football club. The board of directors were now apparently also more willing to accept an official Charlton Athletic Supporters' Club, with its own headquarters, based at The Valley. The most sceptical of fans, however, were aware that the appeal may well have been an attempt to reduce the expected drop in match day attendances, which would severely hit the club financially through a fall in gate receipts, especially after the club made a loss of over £10,000 the previous season.

Although just over 21,000 supporters were in attendance at The Valley for Charlton's opening fixture of the season against Sheffield United (the match ending in a 1-1 draw), only four more matches during the season would reach such attendance figures. Performances throughout the season were inconsistent, giving supporters no confidence in the team or their chances of challenging for promotion. By Christmas, Charlton were in a mid-table position. Although third top scorers in the division with fifty goals, bettered only by leaders Sheffield Wednesday with sixty-five, and second place Fulham with fifty-five, Charlton conceded fifty-two, one goal more than both teams at the foot of the table, Lincoln City and Rotherham United.

It was a poor start to the new year. Charlton lost three matches in succession, which was not helped by horrendous weather conditions making The Valley pitch unplayable. The players, who would usually train on the pitch, had to make use of Harvey's sports ground off Woolwich Road to keep themselves match-fit. By this time, the Charlton supporters had become increasingly frustrated, not only with the lack of football played at The Valley, but more importantly, with the indifferent performances of the team, which the poor conditions of the pitch could not excuse. Supporters resorted to writing to the local newspapers to criticise the running of the club, player performances and training activities, in order to make the board of directors aware of their growing discontent. The board responded to the criticism in the next home match-day programme notes by stating that, in the opinion of the board, 'the players were training with absolute satisfaction'. However, performances and results throughout the remainder of the season showed no improvement. Even though the forwards scored plenty of goals (ninety-two in total), the defence let almost as many in, conceding ninety.

At the end of another disappointing season, Charlton finished in eighth position with forty-three points, and attendances at The Valley had dropped to a lowly average of 16,806. Not since the mid-1930s had the seasonal average home attendance been lower, and the Charlton board, attempting to direct the club's poor performances away from the lack of financial investment in playing staff, laid blame upon the Charlton supporters, claiming that a the lack of support had not helped in the club's objective of regaining their place back in the First Division. Charlton supporters, however, knew that the club's fall into what would eventually become football mediocrity, could be blamed on the failings of the Charlton board of directors.

Another high-scoring season was to follow with forwards Stuart Leary, Johnny Summers and Sam Lawrie each reaching double figures. Charlton suffered a humiliating defeat in an away fixture against top of the table Aston Villa on 14 November 1959, with the team conceding a record number of goals. Within an hour of the match Charlton were already 6-1 down when 'keeper Willie Duff then dislocated a finger. As no substitutions were allowed at the time, defender Don Townsend put on the 'keeper's jersey and took over in goal. After receiving some medical attention, Willie Duff then returned to take up the outside left position for the remainder of the game. Within 9 minutes of Townsend replacing Duff, Aston Villa scored three more goals, before Stuart Leary, who had been carrying an injury since the early part of the match, took over in goal. By the time the referee blew the whistle to signal the end of the game, which came as a welcome relief for all the Charlton players and a large contingent of travelling fans, Charlton had conceded two further goals and lost the match 11-1.

In the return fixture, which took place on 2 April 1960, Charlton recorded the biggest home gate of the season with 28,629 in attendance. With only seven matches of the season remaining, Aston Villa were still at the top of the table and Charlton were sixth. On this occasion, Charlton were the victors, although not winning by such a large margin as Villa had done, the match ending 2-0. Aston Villa went on to win promotion as champions and Charlton finished the campaign in seventh place, one place better than the previous year.

For the supporters however, this had been another unsatisfactory season, resulting in an overall drop in home attendances and more importantly for the football club, a further drop in gate revenue. It would be much the same for supporters the following season with Charlton scoring plenty of goals but letting almost as many in. The final position in the division was even more disappointing as the team could finish no higher than tenth. Attendances at The Valley were now the lowest since Charlton had been playing in the Third Division (South) during the 1933/34 season.

5

TRENDY DAYS OF FOOTBALL

The decade that became known as the swinging sixties, an age of fashion, cultural and musical revolution, was not much of a swinging era for the ever-suffering supporters of Charlton Athletic, where any hope of ever seeing their club playing in the top division of the Football League became less likely as the sixties rocked and rolled on. In August 1961, a year before the formation of one of the sixties most iconic rock bands of the age, the Rolling Stones, future lead singer and Charlton fan Mick Jagger had just left Dartford Grammar School, situated a few miles downriver from The Valley, to pursue a career in the music industry. Charlton kicked the season off with a 1-0 away loss to Leeds United. While young Jagger's fame and success in the world of rock and pop would rise, Charlton's success in the world of football went into decline.

After losing the opening fixture of the season, Charlton only managed a single win and two draws in the following eleven matches, leaving Charlton at the foot of the table with just four points. After five years as Charlton manager, Jimmy Trotter was unceremoniously sacked by the board and, as with the club's previous manager, the supporters were lead to believe that Trotter had handed in his resignation. Charlton carried on for six weeks without a permanent manager before former Scotland international Frank Hill was appointed by the board to take over a team entrenched at the foot of the table, Charlton only gaining nine points from seventeen of the forty-two matches already played.

The supporters knew that for Charlton to escape the drop into the Third Division the team would need to perform like promotion contenders, rather than relegation candidates, and going by previous performances, relegation seemed the most likely outcome, especially when they lost the first two matches under Frank Hill's management. Over the following six League matches, Charlton secured ten points from four wins and two draws. Despite this excellent run of form, the team were unable to climb up from the foot of the table. As Hill began to impose his playing style on the team, forward Stuart Leary found his goalscoring form again and two young talented players, midfielder Mike Bailey and defender Marvin Hinton, now regulars in the side, Charlton moved up to fifteenth place by the end of the season.

Before Charlton were safe from relegation, club chairman Stanley Gliksten died at his home in Buckinghamshire and was succeeded by his son Michael. On his appointment, the twenty-three-year-old Gliksten became the youngest ever chairman in the Football League. There was no doubt that, under Frank Hill, the team had performed miraculously to stay safe from what most supporters believed would be a certain drop into the Third Division. Although forward Dennis Edwards had finished the season as top goalscorer with sixteen League goals, Stuart Leary's inspirational performances during the latter part of the season had been instrumental in turning the season around. The club's change in fortunes had brought with it an increase in home attendances and gate revenue. The overwhelming relief which the supporters felt by the end of the season then turned into a feeling of despair when Stuart Leary was sold to Third Division Queens Park Rangers for a transfer fee of £17,000.

During the time Stuart Leary played football for Charlton, he also played first-class cricket in the football close season, not uncommon at the time among players talented in both sports. Before the start of the new season, Leary made a request to take some extra holiday time, which meant he would miss the first few Charlton fixtures. Not only was Leary feeling the wear and tear of playing football and cricket alternately throughout the year, he was also grieving over the recent loss of his friend and former Charlton partner up front, Johnny Summers, who had died from cancer at the young age of just thirty-four. Leary was informed by the club that his wages would be deducted for any extra time he took off and, if he did not like it, he could move on. This was an ultimatum which resulted in the Charlton record goalscorer leaving the club. Although Leary's association with the football club had come to an end on his retirement from playing football, he became an active member of the Charlton Athletic Supporters' Club. Stuart Leary then returned to South Africa in 1971 to pursue a career in football and cricket coaching, working in the townships with disadvantaged children. In August 1988, after having gone missing for several days, Leary's body was found at the bottom of a cliff on Table Mountain in Cape Town, a tragic end for a terrific sportsman.

After the fine end to the previous campaign, the beginning of the 1962/63 season did not live up to supporters' expectations. Short of one proven goalscorer, Dennis Edwards would not produce the form he showed during the previous relegation battling campaign and, by Christmas, Charlton were third from bottom with fourteen points from twenty-three games. Attendances at The Valley gradually fell away as results on the field showed little sign of improving.

In the penultimate match of the season, with Charlton rooted to the bottom of the table on twenty-seven points, a 2-1 win over Southampton at The Valley failed to move the club up the table. The result did draw Charlton level on points with Luton Town, one place higher on goal average, but were already relegated with all their matches played. Charlton's final match of the season and the last chance to avoid relegation was away to third from bottom Walsall, where a win would take Charlton above their opponents on goal average, sending Walsall down with Luton.

In the midweek match at Fellows Park on 21 May 1963, Charlton arrived during a downpour. After playing the first 45 minutes with neither side scoring, the referee abandoned the match at half-time because of a waterlogged pitch. In the rearranged fixture, played on the Friday evening of the same week, the tense encounter between two relegation-threatened teams failed to produce a goal for either side going into the half-time break, despite Walsall playing with ten men after their 'keeper fractured his cheekbone and was taken off. In the second half, 5 minutes before the hour, Charlton took the lead through a goal scored by young midfielder Keith Peacock, a player who joined Charlton in 1961 as an amateur at the age of sixteen and was now playing in the first team. Nine minutes later, winger Mike Kenning scored Charlton's second and it seemed as if the club's Second Division status was secured.

Even though Walsall were down to ten men and their forward Graham Newton was carrying an injury, the home team pulled a goal back with just under 20 minutes of the game remaining. An equalising goal from Walsall would have kept them up by one point to send Charlton down in their place. When the referee finally blew the whistle to end of the match, Charlton stayed up and Walsall were relegated on goal average, an extremely fortunate escape for the South East London side. Unsurprisingly, attendances at The Valley had dropped even more during the relegation threatened season, to an average attendance of 13,420.

In the 1963/64 season, the board decided to make some changes at the club, not in management or playing staff, but in change of kit colour and club nickname. What the supporters really wanted to see was some new quality signings, and an improvement in team performances. Charlton's new kit was changed from the traditional red shirts, white shorts and red and white socks, to an all white kit with bright red shoulder flashes.

The new nickname had been chosen through a competition run by the Charlton Athletic Development Association where the supporters had been invited to send in their suggestions. Once chosen, the new nickname Valiant's was adopted at a board meeting in October 1963. The new style kit and club nickname failed to have any effect over results on the pitch and Charlton lost the first three fixtures of the season. What the team really required was a goalscorer. In October, Charlton re-signed Eddie Firmani from Genoa for £12,500, after the supporters' former favourite forward turned down a move to Lazio. Scoring two goals in his first match back in a 3-1 win over Manchester City at Maine Road, Firmani then scored on his homecoming debut at The Valley a week later, in a 3-0 win against Bury.

With several young talented players now having established themselves in the team, including Mike Bailey (who would win international honours at the end of the season) and forward Roy Mathews, who along with winger Mike Kenning and forward Eddie Firmani, began scoring plenty of goals between them, attendances at The Valley started to improve. By the new year, Charlton had moved up into fourth place, just six points behind leaders Leeds United, and five points behind second place Sunderland and third place Preston North End. Although Charlton were unable to overtake the three teams at the top of the table, they remained in fourth position up to the season's end. The fine performances on the pitch had also seen an increase in match day attendances at The Valley, which had risen to an average of 18,283.

The Charlton supporters continued to turn out in force at the beginning of the 1964/65 season, with the hope that Charlton may be pushing for a promotion place. Although starting well, the team failed to produce the results the supporters were expecting and were soon dropping down towards mid-table. Although Eddie Firmani finished top scorer with sixteen goals, Charlton had dropped to fifth from bottom by the end of the season, escaping relegation by just three points. Supporters frustrated by the team's indifferent performances and the continuing lack of ambition shown by the board not signing the quality experienced players required, deserted The Valley once more. By the end of an unsuccessful campaign, the average home attendance was down by more than 5,000, supporters believing the club's days of playing First Division football had long gone.

The board, in their wisdom, then decided to sell top goalscorer Eddie Firmani to Third Division Southend United, giving supporters more reason to believe their club was going nowhere but downwards. The board decided not to renew Frank Hill's contract and he was replaced by former Bury player-manager Bob Stokoe. Under Stokoe's managerial care, which lasted only two seasons, Charlton finished in nineteenth and sixteenth place respectively. The only two football events Charlton supporters had that was worth remembering during those two unexceptional seasons, came through the club making history by fielding the first ever League substitute in 1965, and the national football team winning the World Cup in 1966.

Before the start of the 1965/66 season, a new League ruling allowed teams to make one substitution during a match, principally to be used to replace an injured player. In Charlton's first fixture of the season on 21 August 1965, away to Bolton Wanderers at Burnden Park, 'keeper Mike Rose sustained an injury 11 minutes into the game and was taken off for treatment. Defender John Hewie, who was no stranger to putting on the 'keeper's jersey for Charlton, took over in goal and Keith Peacock came on as the spare man, forever remembered throughout his career as the first ever Football League substitute.

As for England winning the FIFA World Cup, which took place at The Empire Stadium in Wembley on 30 July 1966, the only connection between Charlton Athletic and England winning was through the attacking midfield number ten. Bobby Charlton not only shared the same surname as the South East London club, he also made his debut for Manchester United against Charlton at Old Trafford on 6 October 1956, where he scored two goals in a 4-2 win. In the return fixture at The Valley on 18 February 1957, Charlton scored his first ever hat-trick for Manchester United in a convincing 5-1 win, Charlton Athletic helping England towards winning the World Cup by starting Bobby Charlton off on his legendary goalscoring career to become one of only eleven English players ever to have lifted the trophy.

While the Charlton-supporting schoolchildren of South East London now had eleven England World Cup winning stars to idolise, one player who would join Charlton during the close season soon became every young Charlton fan's very own football superstar. When the shaggy-haired midfielder-come-forward Harry Gregory first joined Charlton from Leyton Orient, it was in exchange for two of Charlton's talented players, midfielder John Snedden and forward Cliff Holton. Although the fans were sad to see the players go, the versatile Harry Gregory soon became a favourite of the fans through the passion and commitment he showed when playing in the red shirt of Charlton Athletic. This was a shirt that he regularly wore loose outside of his shorts in the style of George Best, and was copied by Charlton-supporting schoolboys who began wearing their shirts in the same style as Gregory.

Considered as one of the more flamboyant type of modern-day footballers, Harry Gregory not only became a popular figure among the supporters, but also a well-liked member of the team. After joining Charlton, Gregory moved into one of the club-owned houses situated at the end of Harvey Gardens, next door to Charlton 'keeper Charlie Wright. Gregory paid the club £4 weekly rent, out of his £25 a week wages, during a time when a footballer's income was slightly higher than the average UK wage. Gregory became good friends with teammates Billy Bonds and Peter Reeves, both greyhound racing enthusiasts who owned a greyhound bitch named Thick Legs that raced at Charlton Greyhound Stadium. When Peter Reeves decided to sell his half share in the dog, Gregory decided to make an investment and bought out his teammate's share. After winning just one race in twelve, the greyhound then went into heat and Gregory decided to take Thick Legs home, rather than pay kennel fees while the dog was unable to race, which cost Harry and his wife their Sunday lunch. When Gregory left the greyhound out in the garden one Sunday afternoon, the dog crept back in to the house and snatched a roast leg of lamb just taken out of the oven, off the table, and dashed back out into the garden at top greyhound speed, joint in mouth. Thick Legs devoured everything but the bone within 5 minutes, which not only put the greyhound in the dog house but Harry Gregory too, his wife not best pleased with his decision to bring the greyhound home from the kennel.

Not only had Harry Gregory become a local football celebrity, he was now a famous greyhound owner too, his fame bringing him the opportunity to present a winner's trophy for a big race meeting at Charlton Greyhound Stadium. Here, Gregory met up with Great Britain track and field athlete Lillian Board, who had also been invited along to present a winning trophy. Gregory remembered the occasion as one of the sporting highlights of his career, a memory that would stay with him forever, as not long afterwards, Lillian Board's life was cut short at the age of twenty-two after she was diagnosed with cancer.

MANAGERIAL MERRY-GO-ROUNDS

It is one of football's unexplained mysteries why one manager can be a failure at one club, and then have unparalleled success at another. This was the case for Bob Stokoe. Sacked by Charlton after a poor start to the 1967/68 season, the Northumberland-born manager then took over at three other clubs in succession (Rochdale, Carlisle and Blackpool), before joining Sunderland in 1972. Appointed manager in November of that year, Sunderland were down towards the bottom of the Second Division and not only did Stokoe save the club from relegation, he also took them to a Wembley FA Cup final to beat First Division Leeds United 1-0 and win the trophy. A bronze statue of Bob Stokoe was later erected outside Sunderland's new ground, the Stadium of Light, depicting him in the famous celebratory run he made across the Wembley turf at the final whistle, arms outstretched, with raincoat flapping and wearing his trademark trilby hat.

Before the Charlton board had dispensed with the services of Bob Stokoe in September 1967, towards the end of the previous season Eddie Firmani had been resigned for the second time as a Charlton player, scoring six goals in nine appearances. Only playing one match at the beginning of the 1967/68 season, Firmani was then appointed as acting-manager when Stokeo left the club. Immediately retiring from playing, he set to the task of guiding his teammates away from their fourth-from-bottom

League position after gaining just three points from five games. Attendances at The Valley soon improved after Firmani had taken over managing the side, despite the club losing talented young fullback Billy Bonds who moved to West Ham United for £49,000, and star player Lenny Glover who was sold to Leicester City for £80,000.

The appointment of one of the club's legendary football heroes to acting-manager may well have been an attempt by the board to appease the fans outraged over the sale of two of the club's most important players, which affirmed supporter's opinions that the Charlton board were more interesting in making money from player sales, than attempting to win promotion to the First Division. Despite the feeling of doom and gloom among the older supporters of Charlton Athletic who remembered the glory days when Charlton were competing in the top division and playing in Wembley Cup finals, the much younger Charlton fans took it upon themselves to show their support for the club and new manager by marching on mass, Charlton Athletic banners held high, from The Valley to Loftus Road for Firmani's first away match of the season at Queens Park Rangers on 23 September 1967. En route, the Charlton fans stopped off at a meeting place for supporters attending away matches in London, the bronze statue of Sir Henry Irving, erected outside the National Portrait Gallery just off Trafalgar Square, where they paid homage to the seventeenth-century dramatist by chanting out in passing 'Enry, Enry Irving, Ooh, Ooh!'.

Although Eddie Firmani won his first match as Charlton manager at home the week before, beating Aston Villa 3-0, his team lost 3-2 at Queens Park Rangers. This became a famliar pattern for the remainder of the season, Charlton's good home record keeping the club away from relegation zone to finish the season in fifteenth place. This result earned manager Firmani a three-year contract as full-time manager. During that season, a percentage of the transfer money received from the sale of Bonds and Glover was used to bring into the squad England Schoolboy and youth international defender, Paul Went; Welsh international defender Grahame Moore and Republic of Ireland international forward Ray Treacy. With the three new signings joining Charlton full-backs Brian Kinsey and Bob Curtis; 'keeper Charlie Wrightl; midfielders Alan Campbell, Keith Peacock, Harry Gregory and Peter Reeves and forward Matt Tees, manager Firmani had the makings of a strong team in which he could build upon, and develop going into the 1968/69 season.

SING-ALONG ON THE TERRACES

At the modern day Valley you will often hear a chorus of 'Valley Floyd Road', sung to the tune of Paul McCartney's 'Mull of Kintyre'. This song was not the first time that a composition written by a member of the Beatles had been made use of by the Charlton fans.

During late 1950s and into the 1960s, teenagers, free from the constraints of post-war austerity, were becoming less dependent on adult supervision when pursuing their own leisure activities. For many teenage boys, and a few girls, this included going along with your friends to watch your local football team play.

Before they found this independence, young football fans would be taken along to matches by an older relative, having been indoctrinated at an early age into supporting a club through family ties. In the 1960s, the all-standing terraces, once the domain of working-class men, were now becoming filled by hundreds of younger football fans, usually congregating behind the goals and making up football chants to sing out in support of their club or a favourite player. The most innovative of young supporters also made up alternative verses to old or contemporary popular songs of the day, a tradition which fans of Liverpool Football Club insist originated from the Merseyside beat music scene. In September 1968, one of those Merseybeat groups, the Beatles, released the ballad 'Hey Jude', which the young Charlton Athletic supporters adopted and sang along to when celebrating Charlton going top of the Second Division. They changed the last line of the ballad to 'Na, na, na, top of the League, top of the League, Charlton ... Na, na, na, top of the League, top of the League, Charlton'.

In the first match of the 1968/69 season Charlton had gone down 4-3 at home to local rivals Millwall, where there was plenty of singing and chanting exchanged between both sets of fans. Charlton then went on a nine-match unbeaten run to take them to the top of the division with fifteen points. Even though it was early in the season, there was a belief among those younger fans that their team, under the management of Eddie Firmani, had a chance of challenging for promotion. After two successive draws in the first weeks of October, Charlton dropped into second place and Blackburn took the top spot. Charlton then fell further away after losing 3-0 away to Bolton Wanderers.

Throughout the rest of the season, Charlton were unable to get the results necessary to go back up into top place. With the two highest placed teams going up, Charlton were still in contention of winning promotion, by securing the second spot, with three matches of the season to go. Derby County, then top of the table, had practically secured promotion as champions and Charlton, in third place with forty-seven points, were only four points behind second placed Crystal Palace. In the final three fixtures, Charlton only won four points, ending with fifty in total. This was not enough to overtake Crystal Palace, promoted to second place with fifty-six points. It had been an extremely exciting time for young Charlton supporters, and although the season had finished in disappointment, they were all expecting their football playing heroes to make another challenge for promotion next season.

The young Charlton supporters had plenty of opportunities to meet their football idols during the 1960s, as the players would make their way up to the Star Café on Old Dover Road for a late morning fry up after training. They would then sign autographs for the local schoolchildren waiting outside during school lunch breaks. A few players would linger on after breakfast and drop in at The Royal Oak public house, just along the road from the café, for a couple of pints and a game of darts.

Full-back Bobby Curtis enjoyed a game of darts and was one of several Charlton players who regularly spent time at the Royal Oak. Curtis had come into the side to take over from supporter's favourite full-back Billy Bonds, after he left to join West Ham United. Soon, Curtis became just as popular as the man he replaced. The talented right-back may well have gone on to win international honours if he had not picked up a bad injury halfway through his career and then, on his return, decided to dye his brown hair blond. The FA establishment were apparently disapproving of this fashion statement, which may well have hindered Curtis's chances of selection to play for England after he did well at under-23 level.

6

RAISING PRICES AND LOSING SUPPORT

Attendances at The Valley had increased on average by 4,000 each game during the promotional chasing campaign, the biggest gate of 33,000 coming against promotion rivals Crystal Palace. Although gate receipts for the season totalled £78,000, the club made a loss of almost £27,000. To bring in some much needed revenue, the board made the decision to increase admission prices for the coming season, hoping to cash in on the expected rise in match day attendances after the previous seasons excellent performances.

Manager Eddie Firmani was given very little money to spend in the transfer market after he paid out £12,500 for veteran forward Ray Crawford, and brought back former player Mike Kenning from Wolves for £20,000 (the winger having been sold to Norwich for £27,000 in November 1966). With no further quality signings coming in to help build upon the previous season's achievements, Charlton made a relatively poor start to the season. Struggling to find any sort of form, Firmani found himself under extreme pressure to get immediate results. Two years after retiring from playing, and in his first managerial position at the age of just thirty-seven, people at the club believed his managerial inexperience was beginning to show.

With just five matches of the season remaining, Charlton were third from bottom in the table with twenty-seven points, one more than Preston North End, and five points more than bottom-placed Aston Villa, but both clubs had a game in hand over Charlton. To ensure any chance of surviving relegation, Charlton may well have needed to take maximum points from those final five matches, three at home, and two away. The first match, against Leicester City, took place at The Valley on 28 March 1970 and by half-time Charlton were losing 4-0, City's third goal scored by former Charlton winger Lenny Glover. Conceding another goal in the second half, Charlton lost the match 5-0 and two days later Eddie Firmani was sacked. Undoubtedly one of Charlton's most popular and skilful players, football management might have came too soon for Firmani, as towards the end of his managerial term with the club he began making some surprising team selections, which were not well received by the players or the supporters. Two years later, Firmani would prove his managerial qualities in the North American Soccer League and later in the Gulf, which brought him a long, successful and distinguished coaching and managerial career.

Two days after Eddie Firmani lost his job, his assistant, Theo Foley, was appointed as acting manager by the Charlton board. Two draws, a loss and a vital win on the final day of the season ensured Charlton survived by just three points. Many of Charlton's celebrating supporters then headed for the new Valley Club behind the North Stand, officially opened in November 1969 by club chairman Michael Gliksten, where celebrations continued long into the night. Two weeks after the season ended, the Charlton board appointed Theo Foley as full-time manager. With the board reluctant to spend too much money in the transfer market, there was little change in the club's playing staff during the close season. Foley was required to build a successful team using very little money, relying on players from the previous season and a few youth team players to make up the squad. Charlton failed to win a single match during the first nine matches of the 1970/71 season. The new manager lost several of his key players through injury, including one of the players Foley was able to sign, forward Bobby Hunt, who required a cartilage operation after only playing one match.

The first victory of the season came on 3 October 1970 in a 2-1 win over Swindon Town. The Valley was sparsely populated with only 10,052 supporters in attendance, a figure which included a number of opposition fans. Theo Foley was then forced into carrying out some dealings in the transfer market, selling two of the supporters' favourite players on. Alan Campbell went to First Division Birmingham City for £70,000, and Harry Gregory transferred to Third Division Aston Villa for £7,777. Gordon Riddick, who made nine appearances that season, was also sold for £7,777 to Second Division Leyton Orient. The money from the transfers was then used by Foley to bring in four new signings, defender Dietmar Bruck, midfielder Dennis Bond, 'keeper Derek Bellotti and forward Barry Endean. Although the player changes had improved team performances, the wins needed to move Charlton up the table continued to be elusive.

With an increase in admission charges and the team's bad start to a season, which left Charlton down at the foot of the table, it was hardly surprising that home attendances fell away for a second consecutive year. By late March, with only ten fixtures remaining, Charlton were still at the bottom of the table, one point behind both Blackburn Rovers and Bolton Wanderers, but with a game in hand over Rovers and two over Wanderers. Drawing 1-1 with Sunderland in the penultimate match of the season, Charlton once again narrowly escaped relegation, much to the delight of the 10,520 Charlton supporters in attendance at The Valley. The result sent Blackburn Rovers and Bolton Wanderers down to the Third Division for first time in both clubs' history.

At the end of the season, Theo Foley made further player changes by selling home produced midfielder Dennis Booth and fans' favourite 'keeper Charlie Wright, whose place was taken by Derek Bellotti. Although the loss of so many of the club's favourite players had been very unpopular with the Charlton fans since Foley had taken charge, his dealings in the transfer market would later prove to be exceptional and far reaching for the club, both on and off the pitch.

When decimalisation took place in February 1971, the Charlton board took the opportunity to raise extra revenue by converting admission prices from *£sd* into the new decimal currency system for the 1971/72 season. This meant the supporters faced another increase in admission prices for the third year in succession. Understandably, the board needed to keep the club running on a stable financial footing, however, the expectation that the long-suffering Charlton fans would contribute in bailing out the club through an increase in admission prices, as it was evident that the board of directors were responsible for the ongoing financial misfortunes of the club.

To further aid the board's attempt to balance the books, freehold properties owned by the club were sold off. This included an area of land to the rear of the south terrace occupied by a row of turnstiles, with a proposal to build new houses. Even with this expected income, manager Theo Foley was given little to spend in the transfer market, resorting to signing two players on free transfers, forward Mike Flanagan, an amateur player from Tottenham Hotspur recommended to Foley by chief scout Les Gore, and 'keeper John Dunn from Aston Villa. Although Mike Flanagan only played eighteen League matches during the season without scoring a goal, Foley's free transfer signing proved to be the greatest financial dealing in the history of the club.

Charlton Athletic supporters had no expectations for the coming season and would have been content if performances ensured a safe mid-table position after fighting off relegation over the previous two seasons. After a relatively sound start, Charlton gradually dropped down the table to fourteenth place midway through the season, with eight wins, three draws and ten losses. A 3-1 win over Swindon Town at The Valley in March gave Charlton thirty points, and with ten matches of the season to play, the team should have been well capable of gaining enough points to ease supporters' fears that the season would be another fight for relegation survival. Going into the last match of the season, Charlton had already lost seven and drawn two of those final games, and were facing Blackpool away, needing a win at Bloomfield Road to stay up. Blackpool went 1-0 up after 8 minutes and although Charlton held out until half-time without conceding another, the team capitulated completely in the final 45 minutes, letting in four goals without reply to lose the match 5-0. The defeat ensured that Charlton's fight against relegation was finally over and Third Division football would be returning to The Valley for the first time in thirty-seven years.

DOWN IN THE THIRD DIVISION

Once again the Charlton supporters were faced with the loss of more players after the club's relegation. Defender Paul Went moved to Fulham, Dietmar Bruck to Northampton Town, Derek Bellotti was exchanged for Peter Hunt from Southend United and Ray Treacy transferred to Swindon Town, with forward Arthur Horsfield coming to Charlton in return plus £20,000. The proceeds from transfer fees ensured the club made a profit at the end of the financial year which helped reduce the bank overdraft, but the lack of investment in new playing staff for the 1972/73 season gave supporters little encouragement to pay Second Division prices to watch Third Division football at The Valley.

Thousands of once-loyal fans were conspicuous by their absence at the beginning of the new season, attendances dropping by half compared to the same period during the previous campaign. After losing the first match of the season 3-2 away to Walsall,

Charlton then lost 2-1 at home to Shrewsbury Town, conceding two late goals after taking a 1-0 lead. Supporters' frustrations were made obvious during the second half when they began chanting 'Gliksten out!'.

Even though performances and results would later show some improvement with Charlton forwards Mike Flanagan and Arthur Horsfield beginning to score plenty of goals, support continued to fall. The lowest home attendance of 3,015 came against Halifax Town in the latter half of the season. Charlton, failing to make any competent challenge for promotion, finished the season in an unimpressive eleventh place, the average Valley attendance plummeting to 5,685.

In January 1973, Theo Foley had signed non-League winger Colin Powell from Barnet, a player whom the manager had wanted to sign two years before, but failed to receive the backing of the board. Although Powell did not feature in any matches during that season, he proved his worth during the 1973/74 season, creating goals from the left wing for the forward line-up of Arthur Horsfield, Mike Flanagan and new signing Derek Hales. Joining Charlton on a three-month loan from Luton Town, Foley signed Hales on a permanent deal in October 1973 after the lively striker had scored seven goals in nine games. Charlton's strike force of Hales, Flanagan and Horsfield would go on to score thirty-eight League goals between them during the season.

At the start of that current campaign, the Football League brought in new promotion and relegation rules. Three would go down and three would go up between the First, Second and Third Division, and four down, four up between the Third and Fourth Division. This gave Charlton supporters hope that promotion back into Division Two may be more achievable for the club with the extra promotion place available. Although Charlton finished the season as fourth highest goalscorers, with sixty-six goals, they were fourth worse for goals conceded and finished the campaign down in fourteenth place.

Although winning £4,000 in a Watney's brewery competition for finishing as one of two non-promoted, highest-scoring clubs, Charlton's failure to contend for a promotion place had cost Theo Foley his job, three matches before the season came to a close, chairman Michael Gliksten appointing chief scout Les Gore as caretaker manager. Just three days before his removal, at a home match against Watford, the Charlton Athletic Supporters' Club had presented Foley with a cut-glass rose bowl in recognition of four years service as manager.

Theo Foley's exceptional dealings in the transfer market would later be recognised when the club went on to make over £1 million on players he brought to the club for a total outlay of just £29,000. These included Arthur Horsfield, Colin Powell, Mike Flanagan and Derek Hales. On leaving Charlton, Foley had an extremely successful career in football management, especially when assistant to George Graham at both Millwall and Arsenal.

Although it was another season where Charlton conceded more goals than scored, the supporters voted 'keeper John Dunn as their player of the year, as without his exploits in goal during the season, Charlton may well have finished much lower in the division. Attendances at The Valley had now fallen to an average of 5,306, the lowest in the club's Football League history, a huge drop in support for a once-great club which, at one time, had been the sixth best-supported club in English football.

Charlton's new manager, Andy Nelson, came in to take over from Les Gore after winning promotion with Gillingham in 1974, where he had taken the Kent-based club up from the Fourth Division to Third as runners up. A robust, former-professional defender, Andy Nelson had played at the highest level of football, winning the First Division Championship in 1961/62 with Ipswich Town, managed at the time by Alf Ramsey, who would reach the pinnacle of football management himself when guiding England on to winning the World Cup in 1966. Andy Nelson's tough approach to football management had worked well at Gillingham and the Charlton board were expecting his firm managerial style to bring success for Charlton too.

To raise finances to assist in Charlton's attempt at winning promotion back to the Second Division after two unsuccessful attempts since relegation, The Valley was hired out for a rock concert just over a week after the season ended. The Who was top billing and warm up acts included Lou Reed, Bad Company and Humble Pie. Two years on, in 1976, The Who were back again, and made it into the Guinness Book of Records for the loudest ever musical performance, measured at 120 decibels – the threshold of pain. The attendance was officially recorded as 75,000. Thousands more, however, got in with forged tickets to what is still considered as the group's finest ever rock performance. The band was managed by Bill Curbishley, whose teenage brother Alan helped out on the day, selling The Who T-shirts to the fans of the band. The young West Ham United apprentice would later return to The Valley as a Charlton player in 1984.

The 1974/75 season began with Charlton drawing 2-2 away to Halifax Town, followed by a 2-0 win at The Valley over Hereford United. With an attendance of 6,398, it was a big improvement when compared to the previous campaign. Charlton went on to win twenty-two of forty-six fixtures, drawing eleven, losing thirteen and finishing the season as the division's second highest goalscorers. More importantly, success on the pitch brought the club promotion at The Valley on the last day of the season in a 3-1 victory over Preston North End. The average attendance at The Valley had doubled to 10,444 during Charlton's promotion-winning season, which had brought in just over £94,000 in gate receipts. The club, however, made a trading loss of £90,473 from a turnover of £187,332, leaving the club with a bank overdraft of almost £150,000, a debt incurred through the club spending three seasons in the Third Division.

GOALS GALORE

Two matches into the 1975/76 season, Andy Nelson sold Arthur Horsfield to Watford for £20,000, leaving Derek Hales as the club's main striker. Although Mike Flanagan had played in a forward position, his main role had been making goals for his teammates, rather than scoring himself. In his goal-assisting duties, Flanagan had provided forward Hales with plenty of opportunities to get on the scoresheet and the exceptional striker had his best ever season for the club, which not only brought him to the attention of the media, but also to the attention of several First Division clubs.

Going into the last game of the season, Derek Hales was two goals short of winning the £10,000 prize money offered by the *Daily Express* to the first player in the top two divisions to reach the target of thirty League goals. Unlike today, where supporters can check clubs stats and figures, results and League positions instantly, back in the days before satellite broadcasting and the internet, the only interactive media resource available to fans came from the daily newspaper sports pages. Over their breakfast tables Charlton supporters would scour the results and goalscoring tables to check up on the goal records of their striker's rivals. Blackpool forward Mickey Walsh, expected to be one of the competition challengers, had been openly dismissive of Hales' chances of taking the prize money and a great rivalry grew between both strikers during the season. It would be Southampton's Mick Channon, however, who came closest to matching the Charlton striker's scoring rate.

Safe in ninth place by the last game of the season, Charlton's match against fourth-placed Bolton Wanderers at The Valley on 24 April 1976, attracted an attendance of 14,451. All Charlton supporters were expecting Derek Hales to score the two goals required to win the £10,000 prize. Bolton, with one more game still to play and needing a win to keep up their hopes of promotion, took the lead in the first half, and scored three more times in the second half. Unable to get on the score sheet, Hales missed out on picking up the Daily Express prize money, which went unclaimed. Hales finished the season with thirty-one League and Cup goals, seven in front of England and Southampton forward, Mick Channon.

Derek Hales attained legendary status among Charlton supporters, earning the nickname 'killer'. This was not just because of his lethal finishing in front of goal and aggressive style of play, but also because the Kent-born striker came from a family of butchers. Unfortunately for the Charlton supporters, the exploits of their goalscorer brought further unwanted interest from several First Division clubs at the season's end, and with the board more than willing to sell on their prize assets, the fans were understandably concerned that Hales may not be around for the start of the 1976/77 season.

Surprisingly, the only movement out of the club during the close season was defender Bobby Goldthorpe, who moved to Brentford on a free transfer. To the relief of the Charlton supporters, Derek Hales ran out alongside his teammates at The Valley for the first match of the season to loud cheers and a huge round of applause. Although Hales failed to get on the score sheet that day, in Charlton's 2-1 loss to Cardiff City, the striker went on to score sixteen goals in fifteen appearances. The board of directors could hold out no longer and the prolific striker was sold to Derby County in December for £333,333, a huge transfer fee at the time. In Hales' last match for the club, he was unable to sign off with a goal against Blackburn Rovers but Mike Flanagan, who would take on the striking role, scored two in Charlton's 4-0 win.

After the sale of Hales, Charlton were only four points off a place in the top three of the Second Division, but were unable to keep up with the clubs battling it out at the top of the table, even with Mike Flanagan scoring twenty-three goals in forty-two matches (his first hat-trick coming towards the season's end at The Valley in a 4-0 win over Chelsea).Any realistic chance Charlton may have had in challenging for promotion had, by then, gone.

The board had accomplished their task of balancing the books at the season's end through the sale of the club's most prolific goalscorer since the days of Stuart Leary and Eddie Firmani, but it left supporters speculating where the team might have finished if Hales had stayed until the end of the season, where his goalscoring abilities may well have turned a few of the eleven matches Charlton drew, after he left, into wins. As far as the supporters were concerned, the season had ended in failure, reflected in the drop in attendances after the sale of Hales. Charlton supporters were also confronted by their first serious incident of hooliganism at The Valley, which occurred during the 4-0 win over Chelsea. The West London club's unruly supporters began smashing up the North Stand when Charlton's third goal was scored and then set newspapers alight in the back of the stand. After the match, the riotous Chelsea supporters then targeted the turnstiles and The Valley Club, smashing in the windows and causing £12,000 of damage.

Hooliganism had first raised its ugly head around the country during the early 1970s, when visiting supporters deliberately began causing needless damage to rival clubs' grounds, local shops, pubs and houses, as well as taking pleasure in fighting with each other inside and outside the stadia, behaviour which resulted in supporter segregation in football grounds and security fencing erected around the perimeter of pitches. Even the usually mild-mannered Charlton fans had been warned in a 1973 matchday programme that hooligan behaviour would not be tolerated by the club. This was after a group of Charlton Athletic supporters had been reported causing problems at some away matches.

Now debt free, after the fee from the sale of Hales had gone some way to solve the club's ongoing financial difficulties, the next step forward for Charlton should have been for the board to make funds available for the manager to use in the transfer market to bring in a few quality signings. For many years Charlton supporters held suspicions that the board of directors never actively sought promotion into the top division. If First Division football ever returned to The Valley, promotion would have brought an increase in the club's financial outlay.

In one supposedly lucrative business opportunity, brokered by the board of directors during the 1977/78 season, was the twinning of Charlton Athletic with the North American Soccer League club New England Tea Men, in a deal taking at least three of Charlton's top players out to the United States towards the season's end, Charlton receiving a substantial financial reward in return, a proportion of which would go to manager Andy Nelson to use in the transfer market. The deal however did not go as well as the directors and manager had planned.

Leading up to the Christmas of 1977, Charlton were seventh in the Second Division and only three points off third place in the table. After a poor run of results they then dropped down to fourteenth place. Manager Andy Nelson, confident that Charlton would be safe from relegation, released Mike Flanagan, Colin Powell and Lawrie Abrahams in April, five matches before the end of the domestic season, to fly out and join up with the New England Tea Men for the start of the North American Soccer League season. This transatlantic transaction was not well received by the Charlton supporters, or the football clubs involved in relegation and promotion battles, as Charlton would be playing a weakened team in the remaining fixtures of the season which may well have distorted results, affecting the final placing in the division. The Football League refused to uphold official complaints made by those clubs affected and Charlton lost the services of three influential players for the remainder of the season.

After securing one win from four games, Charlton only required at least a point in the last game of the season, away to Leyton Orient, to stay clear of relegation, with two clubs at the bottom of the division, Hull City and Mansfield Town, already down. In the midweek fixture, postponed on two previous occasions due to bad weather, Charlton's East End opponents were positioned third from bottom, two points behind Charlton with a game in hand. The match ended in a goalless draw and although dropping down into seventeenth place, Charlton escaped relegation by just one point.

The gamble taken in allowing players to leave before the season came to a close may have paid off financially, but it almost cost the club its place in the Second Division. During the close season, while Mike Flanagan had been making a name for himself playing in the United States, scoring thirty goals and named as the most valuable player in the North American Soccer League, Andy Nelson had delved into the transfer market spending £75,000 to bring Derek Hales back to The Valley from West Ham United, the club he joined after leaving Derby County nine months before.

Although his short stay at Derby County was considered unsuccessful by the sporting media, Hales joined a club with a poor team where their style of play limited the striker's goalscoring opportunities. While at West Ham United, Hales scored ten goals in twenty-four games, finishing as leading scorer. There was no doubt that Hales' goalscoring ability had not deserted him and, on his return, Charlton supporters were delighted to welcome him home. One player, however, who was not too pleased to see his former striking partner back was Mike Flanagan, now an England B International and global football star.

Flanagan had taken on the role of main striker at Charlton after the sale of Hales, and now found himself back in the role of goal supplier instead of goalscorer. Seven matches into the 1978/79 season, with both Flanagan and Hales back on the Charlton forward line together and in what should have been a lethal striking partnership, Hales suffered a serious groin injury which put him out of the game for five months. While Hales made his recovery, Flanagan took on the main striker's role once more. Coming back into the side for a 3-0 away win over Oldham, Hales scored one and Flanagan got two, and both players gave the impression they were working well together. However, the supporters were unaware that a certain amount of bad feeling had been growing between the pair since the start of the season, which came to a head during a third round FA Cup tie at Maidstone United.

With just under 5 minutes of the match to play, the tie level at 1-1 and Flanagan scoring Charlton's equaliser in the 77th minute, both players had words when Hales was caught off-side from a through ball from Flanagan, each blaming the other for the lost opportunity to win the tie. Suddenly blows were exchanged, as well as words, and the referee had no other option than to send both players off. Three days later the Charlton board took the decision to sack Hales but keep his League registration, and fine Mike Flanagan £250. The incident between both players and Charlton's actions in dealing with the situation brought repercussions for the club, with the board criticised by the Players' Football Association for the way the affair had been handled.

Subsequently, Flanagan, who did not agree with the fine imposed on him, put in a written transfer request while Hales appealed to the Football League management committee over the decision by the Charlton board to retain his League registration, depriving him of a means to earn a living. When Hales turned down a proposed move to Cardiff City and was then reinstated with Charlton, but fined two weeks wages, Flanagan walked out on the club, deciding to spend a holiday out in the Caribbean while negotiations for a move away from Charlton took place. The whole long, drawn-out episode undoubtedly affected team morale, as Charlton, tenth in the table before the Maidstone affair, dropped down to nineteenth place by the season's end, two points off relegation. The Valley was not a happy place to be, neither for the players, or supporters, as reflected in the season average attendance which fell to 9,563.

Mike Flanagan eventually left the club before the start of the 1979/80 season, transferred for £650,000 to recently promoted First Division Crystal Palace, with a majority of the transfer fee used to keep Charlton financially sustainable.

7

GROUNDS FOR CLOSURE

During the previous twenty-two years, the average season attendances at The Valley had never been higher than 20,000. Once regularly filled with 50,000 enthusiastic football fans, this huge ground would never hold such numbers again, caused by an act of government, rather than years of under underachievement, since the club had been relegated from the First Division in 1957.

In 1975, the Safety of Sports Grounds Act came into force, giving local authorities the powers to inspect and, if necessary, restrict sport stadia capacity if there were any serious crowd safety concerns. The act had been passed after a serious incident occurred at an Old Firm derby between Glasgow Rangers and Glasgow Celtic at Ibrox Park in January 1971, where sixty-six spectators were killed and over 100 injured when crushed on leaving the stadium at the end of the match.

The act provided a guide for local authorities to follow when dealing with matters such as the provision of adequate entrances and exits, means of escape, the slope of terracing, the strength and positioning of crash barriers, construction of staircases and measures to ensure the safe movement of spectators under normal and emergency conditions. The Valley, after more than fifty years of neglect, failed these guidelines on several counts and the maximum attendance was reduced by more than any other League ground in the country, from an official capacity of 66,000, to 20,000. The enforcement of the act and the subsequent reduction of The Valley capacity forced the Charlton board of directors into action, and major ground improvements were made between 1978 and 1981. This was to bring the ground up to the required modern-day football ground safety standards, which cost approximately £350,000. A majority of the funds were raised through an extremely successful lottery supported by the Charlton fans.

The improvements included refurbishing the North Stand and putting in seats, building a new covered and seated South Stand and replacing the iconic multi-span roof of the West Stand with a much more modern but plain structure. As for the high-banked old East Terrace, nothing significant changed and area was left in a poor state of repair.

Charlton's indifferent run of form carried on into the 1979/80 season, the after effects of the Hales-Flanagan incident seemingly continuing to have a negative influence throughout the club. With only two wins in the first fourteen League matches played, Charlton dropped to fourth from bottom of the Second Division, on ten points. In October 1979, former Charlton midfielder and England International

Mike Bailey returned to the club as chief coach, with Andy Nelson taking on the role of general manager. For supporters this became a confusing situation, unsure of who was acting as team manager, Bailey or Nelson.

Derek Hales was now back in the side, but then picked up an injury during the first game of the season, which kept him out of the side for the next two matches. On his return, Hales scored in each of Charlton's next two games but was then missing from the team through injury until mid-November. Derek Hales finished the season as the club's top League goalscorer with eight goals in twenty-three matches, his partner up front, Martin Robinson, and midfielder, Steve Gritt, both finished just one goal behind with seven each. Overall, Charlton's goals for the season totalled just thirty-nine, the lack of goals contributing to Charlton's drop down the division. In February, Andy Nelson had taken over the selection of the team from Mike Bailey. This resulted in Charlton supporters, dissatisfied with how the club was run, protesting against manager Nelson and club chairman Michael Gliksten and gathered outside the main stand after a 1-0 loss at home to Birmingham City, protesting for over an hour and calling for both to resign. Nine matches before the end of that disastrous season, Nelson's contract was terminated by mutual consent, and the board appointed chief coach Mike Bailey as first-team manager three days later. By then it was too late for Bailey to save Charlton from the drop. Charlton conceded seventy-two goals by the season's end and although the club had been relegated with the worst defence in the division, Charlton supporters voted defender Les Berry Player of the Season, his solid performances undoubtedly saving the team from letting in many more goals than they did.

Even though average attendances at The Valley had fallen by 2,000 during the relegation season, the club made a profit of just under £190,000. With the club operating on a turnover of almost £500,000, the transfer fee received from the sale of Mike Flanagan saved the club from going into serious financial debt. As it was, going into the 1980/81 season as a Third Division club, Charlton still had an overdraft to service of well over £200,000.

In an attempt to take Charlton straight back up, Mike Bailey was faced with a much smaller playing squad to select a team from. Several players had moved on and only two came into the first-team squad, veteran defender Terry Naylor, signed from Tottenham on a free transfer, and young local boy Paul Lazarus, moving up from the reserves since having been on the club's books as an apprentice. With limited resources available, Bailey's first full season as manager of Charlton Athletic was an undeniable success, the team winning twenty-five of forty-six League matches, which included eleven victories away.

Derek Hales finished the season as leading scorer, with seventeen League goals, and forward Paul Walsh, a player who had broken through from the youth team the previous season to become a first-team regular, scored eleven. Not only were the long-suffering Charlton supporters able to celebrate a good run in both domestic cup competitions, going through to the third round of the League Cup and fifth round of the FA Cup, on the last day of the season they were celebrating promotion after a 2-1 away victory at Carlisle United.

With fifty-nine points, Charlton finished the season in third place, on the same number of points as second-placed Barnsley, who had a better goal difference, and were only two points behind League winners Rotherham United. Mike Bailey had earned a well-deserved place in the club's history. He received a financial bonus and an increase in his wages for the forthcoming season, but not an extension to his contract, which he was hoping for and expected. For the supporters, everything now seemed to be progressing well at the club. However, after the promotional celebrations were over and the fans were looking forward to Second Division football once more, they were faced with the news that Mike Bailey had accepted an offer to take over the managerial post at First Division Brighton and Hove Albion, the position made vacant after manager Alan Mullery resigned. As soon as Mike Bailey handed in his resignation the Charlton board appointed Mullery as his replacement.

In the local media, Charlton chairman Michael Gliksten made an announcement to supporters that there were going to be some exiting plans underway to bring in much needed funds for the development of Charlton Athletic Football Club. This included the running of a Sunday market in the club car park, and bringing Rugby League football to The Valley. Andy Nelson was re-appointed by the chairman to oversee these commercial opportunities, Gliksten making it clear that the former Charlton manager would have no involvement with the playing activities, as Nelson would be based at the training ground in Eltham.

Although the new Charlton manager had been comfortable with this arrangement, the involvement of a new prospective club sponsor, who introduced himself to Mullery before the start of the new season, would later become a problem. The sponsor, Mark Hulyer, a local businessman, told Mullery in their first meeting at the training ground that he had been supporting Charlton ever since he was a young boy. He proposed helping the club out by offering £50,000 in exchange for allowing him to place his company name across the front of the West Stand, a proposal which chairman Michael Gliksten later readily accepted.

Alan Mullery made a start on reshaping the team by letting three of the promotion-winning players go and bringing in six new signings, which he brought straight into the starting line-up for the first match away to Luton Town, which Charlton lost 3-0. At The Valley, Charlton went five games unbeaten, until they were defeated 2-1 by Queens Park Rangers at the end of October. Mullery's team were competing well throughout the early part of the season and by March, after going twelve matches unbeaten, moved up into to sixth place. The run ended at Loftus Road on 20 March 1982 in a 4-0 loss to Queens Park Rangers.

Alan Mullery was confident that, after the team's impressive run of form, they had a realistic chance of winning promotion, repeating what Mullery and his assistant Ken Craggs had achieved when at Brighton together, provided funds were made available to strengthen the Charlton playing squad. The finances Mullery required, however, was never made available, as the Charlton chairman, who was now spending more time overseas dealing with his business interests rather than at the club, had been out of the country when Mullery needed to deal in the transfer market. When Gliksten returned, he told Mullery he was not aware the manager had made any request to buy players and, even if he did, the money was just not available.

With Gliksten away for much of the season, one person spending more time at the club – much to the annoyance of Mullery – was young Kent businessman Mark Hulyer, who was turning up in the boardroom on matchdays, mingling with the players at the training ground in Eltham and even travelling with them on the team coach. Both Mullery and his assistant Craggs were becoming increasingly troubled by the lack of support they received from the board regarding the purchase of players, the directors unable to make any decisions while Gliksten was out of the country. The Charlton manager was also concerned over the amount of involvement Hulyer appeared to have in the club's affairs.

With only one win and two draws coming in the final eleven matches of the season, it seemed as if the managerial unrest had affected the players and their performances. Charlton finished in a disappointing thirteenth place, and while manager Alan Mullery and his assistant Ken Craggs deliberated over their futures during the close season, chairman Michael Gliksten, whose family had been involved with Charlton Athletic over the previous fifty years, had been negotiating the sale of the football club. Resigning from the board of directors, Gliksten announced he had sold his shares in Charlton Athletic Football Club to Mark Hulyer the Kent based entrepreneur. The young businessman Hulyer took over the role of club chairman and Gliksten, despite having no future role to play in the football club affairs, brokered a deal to retain ownership of The Valley.

Alan Mullery, who had made it clear he was not prepared to work with Hulyer, having doubts about the businessman's motives for becoming involved with the club in the first place, decided he had no other option than to resign after the takeover. He made a statement that he had taken the decision because he did not believe the potential was there to make Charlton a top-division club, especially for a club with such low attendances.

Charlton Athletic Football Club was now under the control of the youngest chairman in the Football League, although the club was actually owned by Hulyer's company Marman Ltd. Ken Craggs, who had a good working relationship with Mullery and had become a very close friend, accepted when offered the Charlton manager's position, rather than resigning in support of his colLeague, which caused a rift between the two men that lasted for many years. The new club chairman, made good use of the local and national media to publicise his takeover and development plans, Hulyer proposing to make Charlton Athletic a First Division football club again, assuring the Charlton supporters, whose numbers had dropped to an average attendance of 6,649 at the end of the previous campaign, that the future of the club was safe and secure in his hands.

Ken Craggs was given £280,000 to spend in the transfer market, and bought midfielder Terry Bullivant and forward Carl Harris, offering several of Charlton's most valuable and promising players new improved contracts, which gave Charlton supporters a sense of optimism for the coming season. This optimism would not last long, however, as a month before the 1982/83 season kicked off, Charlton's outstanding young forward, Paul Walsh, was sold to First Division Luton Town for a fee of £250,000, with forward Steve White coming in exchange. Of those three new players brought into the club, only Carl Harris would stay with the club for longer than a season. If it had been up to the Charlton supporters, they would rather have kept Paul Walsh, the talented youngster going on to play for England, than bringing in players who would not improve the team.

Charlton began that season with a fine 2-1 away win over Leicester City, then lost four matches in succession. In a 1-0 defeat by Grimsby Town at The Valley, the attendance of 4,361 was one of the lowest home turnouts in over forty years.

8

ARRIVAL OF A FOOTBALL SUPERSTAR

To boost attendances at The Valley, Hulyer was determined to bring at least one big name signing to the club, whatever the cost, and first attempted to sign Southampton's Kevin Keegan before the start of that season, a player previously recommended to Charlton by former Charlton player Charlie Revell while working as a scout, when Keegan was unknown and playing for Scunthorpe Town. The ambitious signing of the England international failed to materialise. Then, in September, Charlton supporters were astounded by the news that their club was in the processes of signing Danish international and two-time European Footballer of the Year, Allan Simonsen, from Spanish giants Barcelona for a fee of £320,000.

With seasonal operating losses far in excess of yearly income, it was questionable how such a financial deal would ever be funded. Nevertheless, on 15 October 1982, the national press were invited along to a London hotel to witness Allan Simonson sign a two-year contract to become a Charlton Athletic player, making him the most expensive signing in the history of the club. With the Charlton supporters waiting in anticipation for Allan Simonsen to make his debut in the next match at The Valley against Burnley, frantic negotiations were taking place between the board of Charlton Athletic and their counterparts at Barcelona, the Spanish club's administrators holding up the deal and refusing to release their former player's international clearance certificate, until receiving guarantees from the bank the £320,000 transfer fee would be paid.

Charlton's fans were left disappointed when it was then reported in the national press that the transfer deal may well fall through if Barcelona's demands were not met. Eventually, Hulyer negotiated a deal to pay off the transfer fee over three years, which was against Football League transfer rulings. Hulyer somehow managed to get around this matter of detail. In the personal terms agreed between Simonsen and Hulyer, an arrangement was made where the forward would be released on a free transfer if the club were unable to keep him on at the end of the season, a clause in the contract which apparently no one, especially the Charlton supporters, were aware of. Through the Charlton chairman's overseas business dealings, a new member of the board was later appointed as a non-shareholding director, Nigerian businessman Chief Francis Nzeribe, whose company was reputed to have a £70-million turnover. Hulyer, however, refused to reveal the chief's financial involvement in the affairs of the football club.

When at last Allan Simonsen was cleared to play for the club, his debut came as a substitute against Swansea City in a combination fixture at The Valley on 9 November, where almost 2,000 fans were in attendance, a remarkable turnout for a reserve match. Four days later, there were over 10,000 supporters in attendance at The Valley for the Danish International's first-team appearance in a 3-2 loss against Middlesbrough, Simonsen scoring one of Charlton's two goals. Missing the next two fixtures through injury, by the time the forward returned to the side, for a home match against Newcastle United broadcast live on Danish television, Charlton had a new manager in charge after Ken Craggs left the club five days earlier, assured by club chairman Hulyer only the night before his sacking, that his job was safe.

The man Hulyer put in place as caretaker manager was reserve-team coach Lennie Lawrence, who joined the club at the start of the season. Lawrence, a former PE teacher at a Blackheath school, moved into football management as an assistant to former Charlton player Malcolm Allison (then manager of Plymouth Argyle). Lawrence later joined Lincoln City under Colin Murphy, before moving back to South East London to take up a coaching position at Charlton.

Fifth from bottom of the division when Lawrence took over, and with a European and international superstar reportedly on £1,500 a month to contend with, a figure far in excess of the wages earned by the rest of the Charlton players, and the club unquestionably now in serious financial difficulties, the new manager was thrown straight in at the deep end. The club's only hope of financial salvation would be by winning promotion to the First Division, an impossible task to expect of a man taking on a managerial position for the first time in his career. The best the supporters could hope for was in Lawrence keeping Charlton safe from relegation.

Once again, over 10,000 supporters were in attendance at The Valley for the Danish forward's second home League match of the season. Simonsen's inspiring performance throughout the match proved he was a class above the rest of his teammates, leaving the television viewers in Denmark and the supporters at The Valley to wonder why such an exceptional footballer was playing for a club struggling to survive in the Second Division of the English Football League.

The Danish forward scored Charlton's second goal in the 2-0 win, which gave supporters some hope that their club would begin to move up the table, and away from any relegation worries, with Simonsen in the side. However, these hopes were soon dashed as Charlton could only manage one victory in the following six games, dropping down the table into nineteenth place, one point off a relegation position.

To compound the difficulties Lennie Lawrence faced in attempting to guide the team away from trouble, the board, in desperate need to bring in funds, made the decision to sell another of the club's outstanding young talents, defender Paul Elliot, transferred to Luton Town for £95,000, the player worth far more than the transfer fee Charlton received. Soon after Elliot left the club, Charlton supporters were faced with even more devastating news that Allan Simonsen had played his last game for the club with eleven matches of the season remaining. After making only sixteen appearances for Charlton, Simonsen was heading home to Denmark to join club Vejle Boldklub. Although the presence of Allan Simonsen in the Charlton team had given supporters the opportunity to watch one of the world's finest players in action, the signing of such a player would cause far-reaching and serious financial consequences for the club.

Going into the last game of the season, Charlton were up against Bolton Wanderers, where the losers of the match would be relegated to the Third Division. With the score 0-0 at half-time, Bolton Wanderers took the lead 15 minutes into the second half. Seven minutes after conceding, Derek Hales scored Charlton's equaliser and then with 20 minutes of the match remaining, the striker was brought down in the Bolton area. Hales got up, shook himself down and scored nonchalantly from the spot to make it 2-1. With further goals coming from Steve Gritt and Carl Harris, Charlton won the crucial relegation decider 4-1. Bolton were relegated and Charlton finished in seventeenth place. Later, Derek Hales would tell Charlton supporters that the penalty, which turned the match, was the most important goal he had ever scored for the club.

Even though there had been a slight rise in attendances at The Valley during the season after the signing of Allan Simonsen, resulting in an increase in gate receipts, the overall financial situation at the football club had now reached crisis point. Before the dramatic season had ended, former club chairman Michael Gliksten made threats to take the current club chairman Mark Hulyer to court over outstanding debts he was owed over the sale of the club.

When Hulyer disputed such claims, Gliksten issued a bankruptcy order against him, but later agreed to delay proceedings while Charlton were fighting off relegation. It later emerged that the deal arranged between Hulyer and Gliksten had left the club with a £300,000 debt. When Gliksten sold his shares in the club, Hulyer paid an initial £1,000 up front, agreeing to pay off the rest, with interest, through a four-year loan deal. With Hulyer also making arrangements to rent The Valley from Gliksten on a thirty-year lease, the whole situation had become a financial fiasco.

While manager Lennie Lawrence was preparing his team for the start of the 1983/84 season, claims and counter claims were being issued through the courts by both Hulyer and Gliksten. Leeds United then joined the foray by seeking a winding-up order over the club for an outstanding debt owed on the transfer of Carl Harris. If that was not all, the Inland Revenue made claims against the club for £145,000 of unpaid taxes. Hulyer made an announcement he was going to attempt to buy The Valley from Gliksten, financed through the Charlton chairman's undisclosed business dealings. His proposal also included the involvement of Greenwich Council in the redevelopment of the ground, to include new sports and leisure facilities for the use of the community.

One of the prospective backers of Hulyer's bid to buy the ground was local property developer Ron Billings, who had previously approached Michael Gliksten with an offer to buy The Valley and the Eltham training ground. The deal had fallen through because of the unresolved financial issues outstanding between Hulyer and Gliksten. The new bid to buy The Valley, where Hulyer was acting as the figurehead, also failed to materialise when Ron Billings and a consortium of businessmen involved in the proposed purchase, pulled out, deciding that the deal was no longer an advantageous proposition due the complexities of the financial agreements made between the current and former chairman of Charlton Athletic.

With doubts about the club's future, and Lennie Lawrence unsure if he would have a team to manage going into the new season, the club was offered a reprieve at a court hearing. The Inland Revenue agreed to postpone the enforcement of the winding up order for three months, providing the club were prepared to pay the outstanding debt in full, through instalments, by the date of the next hearing. During the close season, all of the players' wages had been paid by Hulyer's company Marman Ltd. Going into the new season, however, Charlton's financial troubles were far from over. Lennie Lawrence had very little money to spend in the transfer market and only had a small squad of players to select a team from, ready to take on newly promoted Cardiff City at The Valley in the first fixture of the season on 27 August 1983. When the players ran down the tunnel and out onto the pitch, with the tune of the Red-Red-Robin playing in the background, they were met with a moderate round of applause from the Charlton supporters inside the ground.

The low attendance of 4,590, which included a few hundred travelling Cardiff fans, was a miserable turnout for Charlton's first home game of the season. Winning the match 2-0, Lawrence's team would then go on a six-match unbeaten run, climbing up to third in the Second Division. Just as things were looking good on the pitch, Charlton were beaten 7-0 away at Brighton and Hove Albion. A week later, after Hulyer had apparently resolved the club's Inland Revenue issues, he was faced with another court action taken out by Gliksten, who claimed he was now owed a total of £573,000. When supporters arrived at The Valley for the home game against second in the division Manchester City on 15 October 1983, it was highly likely this may well have been Charlton's final match in the Football League, the financial debts threatening to cause the club's demise. Although there was an impending feeling of doom among the home fans, spirits were lifted through the outstanding performance of the team Derek Hales scored the only goal of the game to give Charlton a 1-0 victory. At the final whistle, the Charlton supporters gave the players a rousing cheer as they left the pitch, very possibly for the very last time. On the following Monday morning, the hearing to decide the fate of the club was adjourned and Charlton were given just under a month to put in place a financial rescue package to save the club. Negotiations with several interested parties followed the proceedings, including Greenwich Borough Council.

Immediately after Charlton extended their unbeaten run, with a 2-2 draw at home to Swansea City on 22 October 1983, Mark Hulyer handed in his resignation as chairman, continuing as a member of the board and director Richard Collins was appointed as the new club chairman. Charlton supporters formed their own action committee immediately after the game, raising just over £400 from a collection to aid the club's financial woes.

Richard Collins then set out on the task of attempting to acquire a buyer willing to service the club debt, which was an almost impossible undertaking. The Charlton board then took out an action against Michael Gliksten over irregularities in his dealings in the sale of the club. This left supporters in a state of utter bewilderment, with rumours beginning to spread that if a buyer could not be found, Charlton may need to move away from The Valley to groundshare with another club. The Charlton supporters, although now few in number, began to protest against their club's plight, putting forward a proposal to form a company run by the Supporters' Club to raise funds, with the intention of buying an interest in Charlton Athletic. Although well intentioned, in reality this optimistic proposition would not be achievable due to the size of the club's mounting financial debt.

The Football League had brought in a new rule before the beginning of that season, which allowed clubs to keep all home gate receipts. With Charlton in such a serious financial situation, this new ruling hit the club hard financially when playing away fixtures with no further share of gate receipts. The home fixture against Chelsea, scheduled to take place in February 1984, which would have attracted a large number of fans from both sides, was moved forward to November 1983, with full support of the West London club, in an attempt to help Charlton's financial predicament. With an attendance of over 14,000 turning out for the match, an exceptional number for a midweek fixture at The Valley, Charlton took £40,000 in gate receipts. On the night, Charlton 'keeper Nicky Johns played an outstanding game, ensuring his team held on to a 1-1 draw to take a well earned point in a gripping encounter.

After the court hearing listed for November was adjourned until early the following year, Richard Collins unexpectedly resigned from the role of chairman and from the board, making it clear he held no hope of attracting new buyers while Mark Hulyer was actively involved with the club. Hulyer took over the chairman's position again to become the only active member of the board, as by then all the other club directors had resigned. Hulyer's first task back in the role of chairman was facing a Football League hearing relating to the club defaulting on a transfer fee which brought striker Ronnie Moore from Rotherham United, to Charlton, in September for £30,000. The club was fined instead of a deduction of points and the Supporters' Action Committee donated £8,000 towards the transfer fee, paid directly to Rotherham United.

Against the background of financial misdemeanours, winding up orders and court hearings, the Charlton team continued on their impressive unbeaten run at The Valley, ended in a defeat to Huddersfield Town 2-1 on New Year's Eve. Even after the loss, Charlton were still third in the Second Division. At the beginning of the New Year, with Charlton's financial crises on hold, Lennie Lawrence took a gamble to bring Mike Flanagan back to the club from Queens Park Rangers, a move which did not go down well with former teammate Derek Hales, who immediately made his views known through an article published in a national newspaper. Dropped from a forthcoming FA Cup tie, and then put on the transfer list for the comments he made, Hales was back in the team alongside Mike Flanagan for a home League match against Cambridge United on 21 January 1984. Charlton won the game 5-3, Hales scored two goals, the first, a penalty, won from a Flanagan corner directed into the box.

Two days after the match, Charlton were back in court to face the Inland Revenue ,who were seeking a winding up order over the outstanding tax arrears. As talks between the club and potential buyers were apparently in progress, the hearing was adjourned until a later date. Under all the circumstances it was remarkable the team were performing so well on the pitch, while off it, the club continued to move from one financial crisis to another. When Charlton played Swansea away on 25 February 1984, there was now a real possibility the match would be Charlton Athletic's last as a Football League club. It was widely reported throughout the media, in the local and national newspapers, on television and radio, that if the club were unable to put the required financial rescue package in place in time to fulfil the club's next fixture, Charlton Athletic Football Club would be expelled from the Football League.

Back in court the following Tuesday, Mark Hulyer attempted to give the presiding judge assurances that the Inland Revenue debt would be paid through instalments, once he completed a business transaction involving a shipment of rubber on a container ship and a Swiss bank. The judge, however, decided that enough was enough and that Hulyer had been given too many opportunities to come up with a plan to resolve the outstanding financial issues and Charlton Athletic was ruled as insolvent. Two days later, Hulyer gave up all interests in the club, writing off a £300,000 debt, the sum which his company Marman Ltd had initially invested in the club. The official receiver took charge of the club's financial affairs, locking The Valley gates shut.

Now Mark Hulyer was no longer involved, Richard Collins was free to begin negotiations with two long-term Charlton fans who showed interest in coming to the aid of the club. Mike Norris, a chartered surveyor from Eltham, and John Fryer, managing director of Sunleys (a property development company based in Beckenham), held talks with Charlton representative Richard Collins, to discuss proposals to put together a financial rescue package to present to the official receiver at the High Court hearing on Friday 8 March 1984, the day before Charlton were required to fulfil the fixture against Blackburn Rovers to continue playing in the League.

While negotiations took place with the Official Receiver, Lennie Lawrence had based the team at The Valley Social Club, which was next to the ground where he waited with the players and a gathering of journalists for news to come through from the court over the fate of the football club. At the High Court, which was packed out with Charlton supporters, the official receiver requested more time to study the new consortium's proposals, and the hearing was adjourned until the following Monday. The Football League postponed the forthcoming fixture to give the new consortium an opportunity to obtain approval through the High Court for the rescue package to proceed, setting a new deadline for 5.00 p.m. on Tuesday 5 March. Subsequently, the court hearing was adjourned twice more before a final hearing was set to be heard at 3.00 p.m., on the same day as the Football League had set their own deadline date.

Once again, Charlton supporters turned out in force for the hearing, where the new consortium, under the banner of Sunleys, consisting of John Fryer, Mike Norris and Richard Collins, put forward their financial proposal to the presiding judge. It was revealed that the club had mounting debts of almost £1 million, and the rescue package would go some way to resolving the club's financial predicament.

Former club owners Mark Hulyer and Michael Gliksten agreed to drop their legal actions and would forgo any debts owed by the club. It was later revealed that an offer to purchase The Valley, made to Michael Gliksten by Sunleys, was rejected. Greenwich Borough Council had also come to the club's aid by offering the prospective new owners a grant of £250,000 in return for use of The Valley for community activities, provided the consortium's rescue proposition was accepted in the High Court. The judge, on reviewing the financial package, agreed to the proposals, which ensured the club would continue as an ongoing financial concern, and the new owners formed Charlton Athletic Football Club (1984) Ltd, ready to take the South East London club onwards into a successful new future. The Football League gave their approval for Charlton Athletic to carry on playing League football and the news was reported back to Lennie Lawrence, the players, club staff, members of the press and groups of supporters, all of whom had been waiting expectantly in The Valley Club to find out whether the club had survived or died. On receiving the good news, everyone in The Valley Club began celebrating the football club's survival.

The following Saturday, Charlton's saviours, John Fryer, Richard Collins and Mike Norris, came out onto the pitch at The Valley before the League match kicked off against Grimsby Town, to an enthusiastic and heartfelt welcoming round of applause from the Charlton Athletic fans. In an exciting game, which finished 3-3, one of the highlights of the match was the debut of former apprentice Robert Lee, making his first appearance as a senior player, scoring his first League goal for the club. Finishing the season just below mid-table, a fantastic achievement given the dilemmas surrounding the club throughout the season, Charlton's home League record was only bettered by five other clubs in the division. With the financial future of the club secured, Lennie Lawrence now had the task of bringing Charlton success on the pitch.

The 1984/85 season started off well with a 3-0 win away over Cardiff City, a hat-trick from Derek Hales equalling Stuart Leary's all time Charlton League and Cup goalscoring record of 163 goals. After a reasonable start, Charlton's form throughout the season became inconsistent. Derek Hales, however, had a good reason to celebrate in what would be his last season with the club.

Settling his differences with teammate Mike Flanagan, the Hales and Flanagan partnership resulted in the supporters' all-time favourite striker becoming Charlton's all-time record goalscorer, with 168 League and Cup goals. The poor run of form had an inevitable effect on Valley attendances, even with Lawrence appealing to the fans to stick with the club as there were good times coming, the board having plans underway to invest money into the team. By the season's end, Charlton finished seventeenth in the Second Division and Valley attendances had dropped to an average of 5,108.

The board of Charlton Athletic Football Club (1984) Ltd, comprising of chairman John Fryer, directors Richard Collins, Michael Norris, John Sunley and secretary Graham Hortop, were joined by three new directors, Greenwich councillor Bill Strong, appointed as part of the council's financial deal, former Charlton player Derek Ufton and television pundit and former Fulham player Jimmy Hill, who became acting chairman between December 1984 and May 1985. As part of the board's progressive new development programme, Hill and Norris came up with the idea to form a Junior Charlton Supporters' Club, which was given the title Junior Red. This was the first opportunity young Charlton supporters had to join a dedicated club membership. For just £4, members received a team photograph, badge, scarf, pen, newsletter, membership card and a chance to be selected to run out with players at The Valley as a match mascot.

True to their word, the board gave Lennie Lawrence a substantial amount of money to invest in the transfer market during the close season, and with Charlton's legendary striker Derek Hales moving on to Gillingham on a free transfer, Lawrence signed England youth international forward John Pearson for £100,000. Lawrence brought in seven new players for the start of the 1985/86 season for a total outlay of £235,000.

9

A MOVE TOO FAR

Unbeaten after four matches, and with Charlton fourth in the table, supporters were full of optimism for the season ahead when making their way to The Valley for a derby match against local rivals Crystal Palace on 7 September 1985. On paying their entrance fee at the turnstile, each one the supporters on that day received a single sheet of A4 paper, where printed upon one side were the details of Charlton's impending move away from The Valley, to groundshare with their opponents on the day, Crystal Palace, at Selhurst Park. There was also a list of travel recommendations for supporters journeying from South East London, to South Norwood, for Charlton home matches.

The Charlton supporters were aware that the board of directors had been facing problems surrounding safety issues at The Valley, prior to a pre-season friendly against visitors Liverpool, the Greater London Council taking out summons against the club to have the old East Terrace closed down. After years of neglect, the East Terrace was in a sorry state of repair, the long high concrete series of stepped terracing, which at one time could accommodate 20,000 spectators alone, were now beginning to crumble away.

The Greater London Council had already attempted to have the East Terrace capacity limited to 3,000 in 1979 after the introduction of the Safety of Sports Ground Act, but agreed a compromise to reduce capacity down to 10,000, provided the club then made the necessary repair work to bring the terrace up to the required safety standards. As the club had not carried out these repairs as required, this gave the GLC the opportunity to have the East Terrace closed down altogether, and with Valley attendances dropping to an average of around 6,000, it was debatable whether the loss of use would have had much impact on the club's seasonal operations in staging matches at the ground. On the assumption that the work required would in time be carried out to bring the East Terrace up to the required safety standards, supporters would have been content to carrying on watching football in a three sided stadium.

The closing of the East Terrace, however, was not the main reason the board had made the decision to move the club away from The Valley. In chairman John Fryer's statement, printed on the A4 sheet of paper, he claimed that the owner of the land behind the West Stand had given notice to terminate the club's right to use it and that through a court order, the club would have been evicted from the land. Under these circumstances, the decision had been made to move from The Valley by September. Michael Gliksten, owner of the piece of land in dispute, later refuted these claims, giving his own side to the story published in a local newspaper. In Gliksten's version, he laid the blame upon the Charlton board. He explained that after the club had been bought by the Sunley consortium, they renegotiated the lease on The Valley and, in an attempt to reduce the rental costs, decided the club no longer require the use of this large area of land.

After the lease of The Valley had been renewed with Gliksten's holding company Adelong, the Charlton board believed that Gilksten may well have taken over this piece of land at any time. When it was reported that the owner had intentions to build houses on the land, although no planning applications had been presented to the authorities at the time, this gave the board an ideal reason, and opportunity, to move the club out of The Valley and away from Charlton.

The supporters were informed that although the board had endeavoured to locate a new home in the borough, with the help of the local council, adequate facilities could not be found and the move to Selhurst Park would give the supporters superior facilities to those at The Valley, even suggesting that supporters would be able to obtain a discount to watch both Charlton Athletic and Crystal Palace home matches. The next home fixture on 21 September 1985 against Stoke City would be Charlton Athletic Football Club's, and the Charlton supporters', last ever match to be played at The Valley. No consultation had been made with the fans, no other options and no recourse. As far as the board were concerned, the decision was made and the supporters could either back the move or walk away.

TO SOUTH NORWOOD AND THE FIGHT TO RETURN

The only consolation for supporters, on the day they received notification the club would be relocating to Selhurst Park, was in beating their prospective landlords Crystal Palace 3-1. During the match, supporters began showing the first signs of protest by singing out 'we shall not be moved'. At the final whistle, groups of young supporters hurriedly made their way towards the back of the West Stand ready to confront any directors who dared show their faces.

Richard Collins came out to explain the boards' highly controversial groundshare decision. Whether by chance or intent, Jimmy Hill then made a brief appearance and, upon encountering the assembling fans, made a vain attempt to appease them with reasons why they should support the move. Clearly ruffled by the intensity of passion shown by the supporters, Hill quickly headed back into the West Stand. Charlton Athletic supporters looked towards the official Supporters' Club to take action. Chairman Jack Lindsell described the move as a 'disgrace', agreeing to put his name to a statement written by long-time Charlton supporter, club historian and journalist, Colin Cameron, which condemned Michael Gliksten and demanded that urgent talks take place with the Charlton board of directors.

However, after a meeting with the Charlton officials, the Supporters' Club soon began toeing the party line, the chairman explaining to the members he understood the reasons for the move, realising there was no alternative. The lack of action and total capitulation by the Supporters' Club in condemning the move infuriated

Charlton's loyal supporters, who took it upon themselves to organise a protest at the match against Stoke City. Michael Gliksten then came back onto the scene, claiming Charlton would owe him £385,000 rental fees for the remaining years of the lease contract if moving out of The Valley, a claim which club Chairman John Fryer dismissed as out of hand.

Once receiving official sanction by the Football League for the groundshare between Charlton Athletic and Crystal Palace to take place, the board were determined that the move would go ahead. The once saviour of Charlton Athletic, John Fryer was now loathed by the Charlton supporters, who believed that under no circumstances should the club have been forced to leave its spiritual home The Valley. At the time, it was understood that the decision to vacate the old ground had been arranged within a week. Groundshare discussions had already taken place between Charlton and West Ham United, prior to any proposals that were made to Crystal Palace, the East London club turning the proposition down.

The concept of groundsharing had also been discussed with Greenwich Council sometime before Jimmy Hill and Derek Ufton met with John Fryer, when they were informed he had already struck up a deal with Crystal Palace chairman Ron Noades. Both Charlton directors, shocked by the chairman's revelations, made an attempt to talk him out of it.

Bill Strong, Greenwich Council's representative on the board, was never involved in any meetings regarding a groundshare and only found out about the move before the match against Crystal Palace. He made it clear when informed of the move that any such proposals should have been put forward to a board meeting and then voted on. Strong believed other members of the board had known of the plans to move from The Valley for months. Mike Norris, a member of the consortium which had saved the club from administration, on first hearing of the club's relocation, walked out, but was then persuaded to return. It later transpired that it was John Fryer alone who initiated the move to Selhurst Park with the board of directors forced to show unity among its ranks.

John Fryer made a statement to the press, after the match against Crystal Palace, that a partnership between Charlton Athletic and Crystal Palace would lead to a joint ownership of Selhurst Park that would cost Charlton £1 million.

The supporters were left feeling betrayed by the way the board had deliberately conducted the negotiations in secrecy, without any form of public consultation, leading many fans to write to the local newspapers and have their views made public. In an edition of the *Greenwich & Eltham Mercury*, which went to press prior to the match against Stoke City, a selection of supporters' letters the newspaper received were published and if the Charlton directors had cared to read the fans' views, they would have come to the obvious conclusion groundsharing was not supported, many vowing they would never follow the club to Selhurst Park. The haste in which the Charlton board of directors pushed through the club's relocation to Selhurst Park, under the guidance of chairman John Fryer, gave the Charlton supporters and the local media no realistic opportunity to make an intensive and collaborative effort to challenge, block or postpone the board's decision.

On a sombre day for all Charlton Athletic supporters, the last match to be played at The Valley on Saturday 21 September 1985 was hardly a day for celebration. The board of directors, however, made the day just that, publishing a special souvenir edition of the official matchday programme containing articles and features reminiscing on Charlton's past glories and historic matches played at The Valley. Supporters around the three-sided ground sang out in protest against the move, as fans laid red-and-white flowered wreaths on the pitch, and before the match kicked off, an assembly of former Charlton Athletic players were paraded out to wave a fond farewell to the ground where they had all once played.

A fairly ordinary first half passed without incident, until the referee blew his whistle to bring the first 45 minutes to a close. Then, a band of Charlton supporters ran out onto the pitch to stage a sit down demonstration in the centre circle. One brave fan, who had decided to climb to the top of the north-west corner floodlight pylon, waved a fist towards the directors in the West Stand. The start of the second half was delayed as the fans sitting on the pitch refused to move and others attempted to pull the north-end goal down until manager Lennie Lawrence persuaded supporters to return to the stands to allow the match to continue.

In the second half, the 8,858 fans inside the ground, including a small contingent of Stoke City supporters, had to wait until the 78th minute for the first goal, scored by Charlton forward Mark Stuart, to make it 1-0. Five minutes later Robert Lee, who had once manned the turnstiles at The Valley as a young boy, scored Charlton's second. At the final whistle, supporters believed Lee's goal would be the last ever scored at The Valley.

As the players and officials made their escape down the tunnel, hundreds of Charlton supporters invaded the pitch, protesting against the board of directors and their decision to move to Selhurst Park. Politely requested over the ground's tannoy system to peacefully vacate The Valley, the supporters refused to move, many tearing up large patches of the pitch to take home as souvenirs. Later, when the directors and players managed to exit The Valley, supporters lingered on, many taking items such as club signage and fire safety posters from around the ground as mementos, before they were chased off by a small posse of police.

Club chairman John Fryer labelled those protesting fans on that fateful day as 'idiots'. As far as the Charlton supporters were concerned, it was the Charlton board who were the idiots, if they believed that the move to groundshare with Crystal Palace would ever be accepted. When the removers came in to pack up the club's goods and possessions, there was plenty of speculation among the supporters on the fate that would befall The Valley. Rumours of Welling taking over the ground were quickly denied, and any assumptions that this historic football arena would now become the site of a housing development were soon dismissed when Greenwich Council made it clear they would oppose any plans to turn the ground into a building plot, making assurances that The Valley could only be used for sport and recreation.

On 5 October 1985, Charlton Athletic were up against Sunderland for their first match as tenants of Crystal Palace. One lone Charlton supporter, Rick Everett, took it upon himself to stand outside the ground and hand out his own single sheet of paper to supporters arriving at Selhurst Park (a newsletter which became the origin of 'Voice of The Valley') in an attempt to rouse the supporters to come together and constructively campaign against the move from The Valley.

With only 5,552 in attendance on the day, including a small contingent of Sunderland fans, all those inside the ground could well have been attending an away match. Even with the club offering free travel to the ground from South East London to make the journey easier, the Charlton supporters refused to acknowledge Selhurst Park as their club's new home and chanted for the return to The Valley. Winning their first Selhurst Park match 2-1, the team of tenants began on an impressive run of results, both away and at their Selhurst Park home, despite poor home matches' attendance figures. At the Supporters' Club AGM, held at The Valley Club, supporters were left disappointed when none of the club's directors made an appearance. It was left up to manager Lennie Lawrence to face a barrage of questions from the floor, which he did his very best to answer.

There was now discontent growing between the Charlton fans and the official Supporters' Club, and when a member asked for a show of hands to re-elect the committee, only a third of those in attendance raised their hands in support. A week later, Supporters' Club chairman Jack Linsdell resigned, along with his wife, who had been acting as treasurer. Newly appointed Supporters' Club chairman Bill Treadgold made an appeal for the fans to stop the demonstrations and back the team, with secretary Roy King telling supporters there was nothing much which could have been done about the move. The Supporters' Club stance did not go down well with the Charlton fans, many deciding they would never attend so called home matches at Selhurst Park. Even though the club was heading for promotion into the First Division, attendances continued to be poor, only showing gradual improvement towards the season's end.

With two matches of the season remaining, Charlton were sitting comfortably in second place, three points ahead of third placed Wimbledon, and eight points behind already promoted Norwich City. A win in their next match at Carlisle United on 3 May 1985 would guarantee Charlton promotion. Around 2,000 Charlton Athletic supporters journeyed north for the crucial away match, which was hardly surprising, as large numbers of Charlton supporters refusing to attend matches at Selhurst Park had began following the club away.

Although going 2-0 down with just over 20 minutes played, Charlton were back in the game before half-time through a Carlisle United own goal. Charlton then drew level in the second half with a goal from Mark Stuart, before centre-half Mark Aizlewood scored the third and final promotion-winning goal. At the end of the match, Charlton supporters jumped the pitch-side fencing to run over and celebrate with the players. Upon finding manager Lennie Lawrence among the crowd, several fans hoisted him up high onto their shoulders and paraded him around the pitch in celebration. After twenty-nine years, Charlton Athletic had finally made it back into the top division of the English Football League. Despite the League success, there was mixed emotions among those jubilant fans, knowing their club would be playing First Division football at Selhurst Park, rather than their home, The Valley.

In Charlton's last game of the season, visitors Wimbledon, promoted the previous Saturday, needed a win to ensure a second place finish, leaving Charlton to finish third. The attendance of 13,214 was the highest of the season at Selhurst Park, for both tenants Charlton, and landlords Crystal Palace. At the final whistle, the game ended in a 0-0 draw. Charlton finished second and Wimbledon third, and a mass of

Charlton supporters ran out onto the pitch, not only in celebration, but to chant towards the directors' box 'We want our Valley back'.

Charlton chairman John Fryer reinforced the club's position after the match, stating there would be no return to The Valley, and with Charlton now playing First Division football, the club's future would be at Selhurst Park. The club made a substantial financial loss of over £500,000 at the season's end, leaving manager Lennie Lawrence with very little to spend on new players. Always economical in the transfer market, Lawrence made several shrewd signings by bringing good, solid, experienced players into the squad for a relatively small financial outlay, including centre-half Peter Shirtliff, midfielders Andy Peake and Colin Walsh and 'keeper Bob Bolder.

As Charlton Athletic began their challenge of competing in the First Division, The Valley was left to deteriorate, with the owner's intended usage for the empty football ground remaining unclear. Groups of Charlton supporters continued to make pilgrimages to The Valley, standing outside the locked main gates and peering in through the red-and-white, wrought-iron railings towards the overgrown pitch and huge East Terrace, now covered with tall weeds and bushy shrubs, refusing to give up belief that one day they would return to this historic old ground.

Charlton's first match back in the First Division on 23 August 1986 against Sheffield Wednesday attracted a modest attendance of 8,501 to Selhurst Park. Forward, Robert Lee, scorer of the last goal at The Valley, scored Charlton's first goal back in the top flight of the Football League in a 1-1 draw. The attraction of watching Charlton Athletic playing First Division football at Selhurst Park did not have a strong enough appeal to encourage Charlton fans to come out in force to support the club, playing at a ground which was not their own. Charlton away support however was remarkable, fans who refused to travel to Selhurst Park took to journeying the length and breadth of the county to follow the team away in the First Division.

Competing against the very best club's in the country, and up against teams with line-ups which included a multitude of international class players, Charlton made a respectable start to the season. Although well beaten 4-0 away to Brian Clough's Nottingham Forest after drawing the first game, Lennie Lawrence's team would go on to record victories over several of the division's top clubs. These included away wins over Chelsea, Manchester United, Queens Park Rangers and West Ham United, with wins at Selhurst Park over Everton, Leicester City and Newcastle United.

There were the inevitable losses during the first few fixtures of the season, but the team's performances showed that Charlton were capable of competing against the elite of the Football League. Charlton's First Division match reports were now featuring in the national newspapers, usually covered over a few column inches, or at least half a page, after an unexpected victory over one of the big clubs. In the local papers delivered throughout South East London, although Charlton were now playing their football outside the Borough of Greenwich, the club's supporters were able to read in-depth reports of all Charlton's matches in the First Division. One local newspaper, the *Greenwich & Eltham Mercury*, had been championing the Charlton cause, giving the club extensive match coverage within the sports pages as the publication's reporters were supportive of the Charlton fans' grievances regarding their treatment by the club directors and the decision to move to Selhurst Park.

On attending Charlton's 3-1 Littlewoods Cup tie win over Fourth Division Lincoln City, a match which only attracted a gate of 2,319, *Mercury* sports editor Peter Cordwell decided something needed to be done. It was obvious that with such low gates, Charlton Athletic would never survive as a football club playing at the home of Crystal Palace. Almost a year after Charlton had left The Valley, Cordwell took up an idea, first suggested by supporter Reg King, to launch a petition to bring the club back home , devoting the whole back page of the *Mercury* to the campaign.

Just two weeks after going to press, the petition had received 15,000 signatures supporting the *Mercury's* 'Our HOME is The VALLEY' campaign. In one edition of the *Mercury*, former Charlton 'keeper Charlie Wright was pictured on the back page signing the petition while sitting at one of the tables in his café in Lassell Street, Greenwich. One of the fan's favourite Charlton 'keepers, Wright, still a passionate follower of the club, would always be ready with an interesting story about his playing days for supporters coming to his café, Charlie's Place, for one of his famous big, hearty breakfasts early on a Saturday morning before the fans set off on the road to a Charlton match.

The Scottish-born 'keeper, who had once been voted Hong Kong footballer of the year, an honour he earned when representing the former British territory while stationed there on national service, built up a great rapport with the Charlton supporters behind the goal while playing for the club. His constant conversations with the crowd during matches lead to his manager at the time, Eddie Firmani, banning him from talking to the fans while playing. The *Mercury* petition, endorsed by Charlie Wright, was the beginnings of a constructive and well fought campaign to bring the club back home.

Supporter Rick Everitt, who a year before had stood handing out copies of his own newsletter condemning the move, wrote to Peter Cordwell, suggesting the petition could be handed over to Charlton director's attending the Supporters' Club AGM on 20 October 1986. Taking the letter to be an invitation from the Supporters' Club, Cordwell made the announcement on the back page of the *Mercury* which was published four days prior to the AGM, that all were welcome to attend.

The Supporters' Club committee attempted to stop supporters turning up in numbers by informing fans over the tannoy system during a match at Selhurst Park, that the AGM was for members only. The national newspapers picked up on the story of the petition to bring the club home, quoting several Charlton players in the article who were also of the opinion that the club should return to The Valley.

On the night of the Supporters' Club AGM, hundreds of fans began turning up at The Valley Club, where the AGM was held, well before the proceedings were due to begin. This led to a lock out, with hundreds of supporters left gathering outside in the dark and the police called in to manage the increasing difficult situation. Fans locked inside The Valley Club, deciding this may not be safe, opened all the fire exits, which allowed more supporters to get inside. Charlton fans that came from outside the *Mercury's* distribution area, and had not had an opportunity to sign the petition, now put their signatures down on printed copies of the petition, adding even more names to the campaign. Former Charlton player and manager Mike Bailey, who was now running The Valley Club, made more money in that one night's trading than during the whole week, serving up pints of beer to some thousand or more Charlton Athletic supporters who were now crammed inside the club, while awaiting the arrival of the Charlton directors.

The Supporters' Club committee, who in the fans' opinions had done nothing to actively oppose the groundshare and move from The Valley, appeared to be in collusion with the directors of the football club had to fend off questions and accusations from the hostile crowd over the role they played in the Valley-Selhurst affair. Directors' representatives Derek Ufton and Michael Norris, along with Tony Shaw, the football club's chief executive, were loudly jeered on their arrival to take centre stage. Club captain Mark Aizlewood also joined the board members to act as mediator when proceedings began to get heated. It had become clear to the fans during the discussion that none of the club representatives could give any constructive answers to questions surrounding the club's financial situation and survival prospects or any likely attempt to buy The Valley.

Derek Ufton, a former Charlton player and now director of the club, did tell the attending supporters the club had attempted to buy The Valley from Adelong, the company owned by Michael Gliksten, but that an offer of £1 million had been turned down. Unsatisfied with the answers received, which failed to appease the supporters, the meeting fell into chaos and the Supporters' Club AGM, hijacked by the fans, was abandoned before any official proceedings began. The meeting, which had turned into a supporter's demonstration, had at least given fans an opportunity to face club officials head on.

Backed by the presentation of the *Mercury* petition, the meeting had left those directors brave enough to attend the AGM in no doubt that the steadfast Charlton supporters were never going to abandon all hope that the club should make a return to The Valley. Just over two weeks later, club directors, members of Greenwich Borough Council and a party of Charlton supporters met up to discuss the possibility of finding the club a new home within the borough.

An announcement made by the club's vice chairman, Richard Collins, encouraged supporters who had so far remained resolute in boycotting home matches at Selhurst Park to come to South Norwood and support the team now that the directors objective was to bring the club back home, and if not to The Valley, then at least to a new site in the borough. Supporters, however, were left unconvinced, as the statement was nothing more than an expression of intention and attendances throughout the season continued on a downward spiral.

Out of the FA Cup in the third round, Charlton progressed further in the Littlewoods League Cup to reach to the fourth round, where they were beaten 2-0 by Arsenal at Highbury. In the Full Members Cup, a competition introduced for First and Second Division clubs after the Heysel Stadium disaster when English clubs were banned from competing in Europe, Charlton progressed all the way through to the final. Entering the competition in the second round, Charlton beat Birmingham City 2-0 and then Bradford City 2-0, with both ties played at Selhurst Park. Charlton then travelled to Goodison Park in the next round, knocking out Everton 6-5 on penalties, after drawing 2-2 over 90 minutes and extra time. Towards the end of a one-off semi-final, played at Selhurst Park, opponents Norwich City took the lead with only a minute of the match to go, Colin Walsh then scored a late equaliser before a Norwich own goal scored in injury time made it 2-1 to Charlton which saw them through to a Wembley final for the first time in forty years.

Charlton's opponents for the Full Members' Cup, played on 29 March 1987, were mid-table Second Division Blackburn Rovers and although Charlton were down towards the bottom of the First Division, they were favourites to lift the cup. Although not at their best, Charlton dominated for a majority of the game but were unable to take the few chances created to score a goal. It was the underdogs on the day who eventually took the lead through a goal scored by defender Colin Hendry in the 85th minute. Unable to break through the opponents defence in the last 5 minutes of play, Charlton lost the final 1-0.

The Full Members' Cup final had attracted a Wembley attendance of 43,789. The Charlton support in the minority with barely 7,500 making the trip to the National Stadium. For a club such as Charlton, the opportunity to play for a cup at Wembley did not come along often, and the lack of support at the final was an indication of how the club had lost generations of fans. Five days before the cup final, the Tuesday night League fixture against Oxford United at Selhurst Park attracted an attendance of just 4,205, the lowest gate for a First Division match since the Second World War.

If the Charlton board of directors were truly intent on encouraging fans to come to Selhurst Park with the promises of an eventual return to South East London, the message was clearly not being communicated to the fans. Down in eighteenth place, with nine matches of the season to be played, Charlton were just two places above relegation on goal difference. Four wins and two draws in those final fixtures saved Charlton from immediate relegation, but, by finishing fourth from bottom, they were in the dreaded play-off position.

The play-offs had been introduced for the first time that season, in an attempt to make the fight to stay out of the bottom three relegation places even more competitive, and supposedly more entertaining for the clubs' fans. In a tortuous series of ties, the team from the higher division would compete with the three highest-placed teams from the Second Division missing out on automatic promotion by finishing in either first or second place. Each team played in a home and away semi-final, the team from the First Division playing the team placed fifth in the Second Division and the third and fourth placed teams playing each other.

The winners of each semi-final would then play home and away in the play-off final. Charlton beat Ipswich Town 2-1 on aggregate to go through to meet the other semi-final winners Leeds United. Lennie Lawrence predicted that the final could well go to a three match conclusion, and he was proved right. Beating Leeds 1-0 at Selhurst Park, Charlton went to Elland road needing just a draw to stay in the First Division. Charlton lost the away leg 1-0 to set up a final replay decider played on 29 March 1987, at the neutral venue of St Andrews, the home of Birmingham City. With Leeds playing in all white, Charlton could have played in the home red kit with a change of shorts. Nevertheless, to the surprise of the attending Charlton supporters, their team ran out wearing blue, the same colours of host club Birmingham City, a likely ploy by manager Lennie Lawrence, who anticipated that any impartial spectators would support the team wearing the home club's colours.

With neither club scoring after 90 tension-filled minutes of play, the final went into extra time and if the match finished as a draw, the winners would be decided by penalties. Within 9 minutes from the start of the first period of extra time, Leeds won a dubious free kick which lead to a goal scored by midfielder John Sheridan. It seemed at this point that Charlton were on their way to losing their First Division status. In the second half of extra time, trailing 1-0 with only 7 minutes of the match remaining, Charlton captain Peter Shirtliff scored two goals for the first time in his professional career to make it 2-1.

At the end of the match, the heroic performance of Shirtliff and his teammates ensured Charlton survived as a First Division club. In what was one of the most dramatic ends to a season that supporters and players of Charlton Athletic football club had ever been involved in, the dramas on the pitch had been matched by those happening off it.

The day after the Full Members Cup final, director Jimmy Hill resigned to take on the chairman's role at Fulham, a club which was also enmeshed in a groundshare fiasco. Charlton chairman John Fryer also stepped down, while Charlton were fighting for First Division survival in the play-offs, to take up a role as the club's joint president, alongside John Sunley.

Director Richard Collins took on the chairman's position once again and chief executive Tony Shaw was succeeded by Ernie Warren. Former Charlton owner and Chairman Michael Gliksten was also back in football when he became president of non-League Clapton Football Club in East London. Along with other members of the committee he attempted to secure ownership of his new club's ground from the landlords, while his company Adelong continuing to hold ownership over The Valley.

One additional member who joined the Charlton board of directors at that time, Roger Alwen, a Kent based farmer, Lloyds broker and supporter of the club since the late 1940s, would eventually become the central figure in the proposed move back to The Valley. Charlton's first season in the top division had not brought the financial stability the board had expected and the club made a loss of £690,997, almost £100,000 more than the promotion-winning campaign. Lennie Lawrence was once again given little money to spend in the transfer market to strengthen the squad. His skill in finding quality players for a modest financial outlay did pay off once more in the transfer of former England Under-21 midfielder Steve MacKenzie from West Bromwich Albion for £200,000, a bargain at the time.

Although MacKenzie took a while to settle into the team, he became an influential member of the squad during his time with the club in the top division. Apart from midfielder Alan Curbishley moving on to Brighton and Hove Albion, there was hardly any change to Charlton's squad of players, which included former Tottenham Hotspur star forward Garth Crooks, who had joined late the previous season. While Lawrence had been preparing his squad of players for another season in the First Division, directors Roger Alwen and Michael Norris were negotiating the purchase of the Aires Sports Ground in New Eltham for £500,000, where the players were training after the club had lost the use of the previous training ground facilities.

Once the deal had gone through, plans were put into place to completely refurbish the old club house to include a manager's office, dressing rooms, medical room, training and kit rooms, a laundry and a kitchen. The training venue also included three full-size grass pitches, car parks and plenty of room for further development. For Charlton supporters, the purchase of the new training ground, which became the club's South East London headquarters, gave them further hope that this was the first step towards bringing the club home.

Four matches into the 1987/88 season, Charlton were down at the foot of the table with no goals and no points. The previous season's top scorer Jim Melrose left the club, after playing just three matches, to join Second Division Leeds United for a modest £50,000 fee. Short on strikers, Lawrence persuaded the board to spend a club record fee of £350,000 on Welsh International forward Andy Jones, signed from Third Division Port Vale. This delighted the Charlton supporters as Jones' performances for both Wales and Port Vale had brought him to the attention of several top First Division clubs who were interested in securing the goalscorer's services.

Although results improved, with the new striker finding the target four times in ten games, Charlton were unable get away from the bottom of the table. When First Division champions Everton visited Selhurst Park on 5 December 1987, the fixture should have brought in a bumper home crowd, but a modest attendance of just over 7,000 turned for the match which Charlton drew 0-0.

For Charlton supporters it did not matter who the visitors were, Selhurst Park was not the club's home and the fans continued to stay away in their thousands. Going into the new year, Charlton had moved up from bottom by one place, but after two good consecutive away draws, 0-0 against third placed Manchester United followed by a fantastic 2-2 draw with second in the division Nottingham Forest, Jones scoring Charlton's equaliser in the 84th minute, they were back down at the foot of the table on twenty points. To stay in the top division it was estimated that a club required at least forty points to have any realistic chance of survival, and with over half of Charlton's fixtures already played, the prospects of gaining enough points to retain First Division status was looking decidedly unlikely.

Charlton supporters, who travelled up by train to the Nottingham Forest match, had the their first opportunity to buy a new football fanzine entitled *Voice of The Valley*, written and produced by Charlton fan Rick Everett, the lone supporter who had handed out the single sheet newsletter at Charlton's first home match Selhurst Park.

Football fanzines had first become popular during the early 1980s, evolving from imaginative and influential underground style publications produced for enthusiasts of science fiction, television, film, music, politics and even sex and religion. The first football fanzines were produced as a direct response to the growing discontent felt among the fans regarding the evolution of the domestic game and the detrimental effect this was causing financially and socially for the clubs they supported. Produced in direct opposition to professional club publications, the fanzines were free to openly criticise or challenge the way clubs were run, which did not go down well with club officials, owners and board of directors.

The emergence of football fanzines had given supporters a means to have their voice heard, and the *Voice of The Valley* was produced in direct opposition to the Charlton Athletic Supporters' Club own publication *Valiants Viewpoint*. Although produced as an independent publication by the Supporters' Club, articles appearing in *Valiants Viewpoint* were submitted to the football club for approval before going into print. This was after a falling out between the football club board and the Supporters' Club committee over articles published in earlier editions that had been critical of the board and the running of the football club.

The independently published *Voice of The Valley*, however, free from any constraints of seeking club approval for articles published, became an immediate success with the Charlton supporters. As a means to put pressure upon the board to push forward plans for a return to South East London, the contributors to the publication promoted a mass boycott of a home match after it became evident the football club couldn't survive on the income generated through the gates at Selhurst Park.

A boycott initiative, which had been well received by the supporters, was planned to take place at the home match against Oxford United on 26 March 1988, one of the less attractive remaining fixtures of the season. The proposal was for all Charlton fans to travel to The Valley instead of Selhurst Park when the match was played. The boycott had been fervently condemned by Supporters' Club chairman Bill Treadgold, declaring the boycott would get no backing from the Supporters' Club. Steve Dixon, who had supported the boycott and had been writing articles for *Valiants Viewpoint*, transferred his allegiance to the rival *Voice of The Valley*, after the Supporters' Club refused to publish several of his submitted articles in their own publication.

Just over three weeks before the planned boycott, Charlton supporters received news which they had all been longing to hear, Michael Gliksten was no longer owner of The Valley and club directors Roger Alwen and Mike Norris had taken over control of his company Adelong. Now the Charlton Athletic fans had genuine expectations the club would be making a rapid return to The Valley, the proposed boycott was promptly called off.

These latest developments seemed to have had an encouraging influence over the players too, the team only losing one match in ten since the announcement had been made, Charlton moving from second to bottom on twenty-four points up into seventeenth place with forty-two points, going above their opponents Chelsea on the last day of the season by goal difference. Charlton only needed to avoid a defeat at Stamford Bridge to save them from competing in the play-offs and preserve their First Division status for a second season in succession.

In the last vital match of the season between Chelsea and Charlton, the home side took the lead after just 15 minutes through a dubious penalty awarded against full-back John Humphrey, who was booked for contesting the referee's decision, claiming the foul was made outside the area. In a video replay it was later proved that Humphrey had been correct.

Charlton trailed 1-0 up until the 65th minute when a speculative shot from Charlton defender Paul Miller was deflected into the back of the Chelsea net to make it 1-1. During the second half, young Charlton forward Carl Leaburn, who had come through the club's successful youth development programme, was virtually knocked unconscious from a challenge by Chelsea defender Steve Wicks. After Leaburn had recovered, his teammates needed to hold the big striker back from taking on the Chelsea player who committed the foul, endearing him to the Charlton fans for the passion he showed after the incident and his battling performance throughout the match. It was hoped that Carl Leaburn, or Carlo as he would affectionately be called by the Charlton fans, would develop into a tough and aggressive striker similar to the likes of Wimbledon's John Fashanu.

Never a prolific goalscorer, Leaburn always gave his best for the club and was well respected by his teammates, where his tireless work rate created many goalscoring opportunities for his playing partners up front. When the referee blew for full time, the 1-1 draw kept Charlton in the First Division, condemning Chelsea to the dreaded play-offs and later relegation, when the their place was taken by Second Division Middlesbrough, who beat the West London club in the play-off final.

Towards the end of Charlton's second season in the First Division, a group of life-long fanatical Charlton Athletic supporters began attending a class at the Thamesside Adult Education Institute in Woolwich, organised by tutor Andy Soloman, under the title the Charlton Athletic Reminiscence Class. The tutorial class had been formed after Soloman organised a Charlton Athletic history exhibition at Plumstead Museum in February 1988.

At the first meeting there was only one member in attendance, long-time Charlton supporter Archie Star. However, as word spread, more supporters began attending meetings with some of the older Charlton former players, who would come along as guests to talk about their days playing for Charlton. These former stars included 1947 FA Cup final winner Peter Croker, Welsh International George Green, wartime cup winner Charlie Revell and England International and club director Derek Ufton, all of whom had marvellous stories to tell about their days playing for the club.

A majority of the group's members were old enough to remember Charlton's glory years of the 1930s and 1940s and one of those older members, Percy Greenwood, was present when Charlton first played in the Third Division South in the early 1920s. The reminiscence class, run independently from the football club as an educational programme, was open to any football fan whatever their age or whichever club they supported. One fan who regularly attended classes was a self-confessed Millwall supporter! During those early days of the '30s and '40s it was not unusual for some Charlton and Millwall fans to attend each other's home matches when the team they supported where playing away.

The reminiscence class members made regular trips to The Valley to look over the old ground. With the pitch and terraces overgrown with weeds, they recalled times gone by and the days when Sam Bartram, Stuart Leary, Eddie Firmani and Johnny Summers entertained the crowds which regularly reached attendances of 50,000 or more. The reminiscence class then put together a self-published booklet, assisted in the project by a local news agency the News Shopper Group. It was entitled 'Memories are Made of This' and contained articles and photographs supplied by the members of the class, with archive images supplied by Andy Soloman. Sold for £1, all profits were donated to the Back to The Valley fund, which had been formed by fans to assist in financing the club's move home. As the Charlton reminiscence group grew in numbers, they were invited to hold classes, which by then, had evolved into group meetings and get-togethers at the club's New Eltham training ground. A second successful booklet was produced with support from the Charlton Athletic Supporters' Club and *Voice of The Valley* founder Rick Everitt, who edited the publication.

After the club's First Division status had been secured and the supporter's survival festivities were over, Charlton fans were celebrating once more during the close season, when the club broke the news that Valley owners Roger Alwen and Mike Norris had taken over ownership of the football club. The Supporters' Club and *Voice of The Valley* activists were invited to attend a meeting with one of the new Valley owners Mike Norris, and club director Derek Ufton to discuss the proposed move back to the borough of Greenwich.

Once Mike Norris and Roger Alwen had acquired equal controlling shares of the club from Sunley Holdings, at a cost of £3.25 million, the board were keen to bring harmony between the supporting groups, which had opposing views surrounding the move from The Valley. This was to ensure the anticipated move back to the borough of Greenwich would run as smoothly as possible with the full support of all Charlton Athletic followers. Joint club shareholder Mike Norris had preferred a move to a new purpose-built football stadium, close to the site where the Millennium Dome would later be built on the Greenwich Peninsular, whereas Roger Alwen preferred a move back to a refurbished Valley.

With all factions of supporters groups now working together with the Charlton board, negotiations began on relocating the football from South Norwood, back home to South East London. With the news of the club's tenancy of Selhurst Park coming to an end, the first match of the 1988/89 season against the previous season's First Division champions Liverpool attracted an attendance of 21,389 and, although Charlton lost the match to a John Aldridge hat-trick, thousands of previously missing Charlton supporters had come back to cheer their team on.

Towards the end of the previous season, manager Lennie Lawrence brought former non-League forward Paul Williams into the first team. Although he had not found the target in his first six League appearances as a substitute, the quick young striker scored twice during his full appearance in Charlton's 3-1 away victory over West Ham United in the second fixture of the season. After joining Charlton from non-League Woodford Town in August 1986, Williams had spent a season adjusting to League football by going out on loan to Brentford, where he hit six goals in eight matches. In Charlton's first team he proved to be another of Lawrence's inspirational signings, scoring eight goals in nine games.

In October, Lawrence brought in Chelsea central-defender Colin Pates for a club record fee of £430,000 to help shore up the Charlton defence, and for a time the team looked comfortable in a mid-table position. However, Williams picked up an injury against Wimbledon at Plough Lane in November, which put him out until the end of the year, and with the team's top scorer unavailable, Charlton dropped down to nineteenth place. The First Division had now been reduced down to twenty teams and, with relegation via the play-offs gone, the bottom three teams would go down automatically and Charlton would now have a battle on to stay safe from automatic relegation.

The day after losing 3-0 to Manchester United at Old Trafford on 3 December, as a welcome break from the pressures of playing First Division competition, the Charlton players stayed over in Manchester to take part in a two-day midweek Guinness sponsored Soccer Sixes tournament. In the televised coverage, Charlton won through the first day's series of matches and a play-off, to go through to the next stage played the following day. Charlton were in one of two groups made up of three teams, where the group winners would play each other in a final. After beating Liverpool 6-3 and then West Ham United 4-2 in two extremely competitive and ferocious matches to win the group, Charlton went through to the final to meet Nottingham Forest. In an exciting finale to the tournament, Charlton beat Forest 2-1 to win the trophy and take £51,000 in prize money.

Heading towards the final stages of the season, at an open meeting held at Greenwich Town Hall on 23 March 1989, Roger Alwen, now chairman of the club, announced to the supporters packed into the hall that Charlton Athletic would be returning to The Valley, a statement greeted with cheers of approval from the jubilant fans.

Although Paul Williams had returned to the side at the beginning of the new year, Charlton continued to find it difficult to pick up enough points to move away from the bottom of the table, and with only nine matches of that season remaining, Charlton were fifteenth on thirty points, only one point off a relegation place.

EARLY RETURN BUT THE GROUNDSHARE CONTINUES

Before the end of the season, Charlton Athletic supporters made a nostalgic return to The Valley when the gates were opened up on in April for a mass ground clear up. Hundreds of fans went along on a wet Sunday morning to clear the overgrown pitch and terracing of weeds and accumulated rubbish, some of which had been left behind by a small band of travellers who encamped in the vacated ground before moving on to pastures new.

Both the club chairman and football manager were on hand to lend support. Roger Alwen walked around the ground chatting to the fans, and Lennie Lawrence held an impromptu press conference for the attending media, while the tune of 'When the Red, Red, Robin' could be heard playing from a portable cassette as a group of youngsters kicked a ball around on the overgrown Valley pitch. The supporters set about their task full of enthusiasm, in the belief that football would soon be played at this historic old ground once more.

While plans were underway to bring football back to The Valley, the football club were attempting to ensure they remained as a First Division club, accumulating thirteen points from the last nine matches, Charlton moved up into fourteenth place, four points off relegation, and the club was safe in the top division after another eventful season.

One of the first stages in the plan to bring the club home was in making an appeal for supporters to join a new membership scheme, Valley Gold. This fund was set up to provide financial support to aid the return to The Valley. For £10 a month, members were entitled to a discount on club merchandise, season tickets and money vouchers, which supporters were able to use in local shops, restaurants and stores supporting Valley Gold. Each week, members had the opportunity to win cash in a prize draw and at the end of each season £20,000 in a grand prize draw.

This innovative membership scheme was well received and hundreds of Charlton fans signed up, with membership rising throughout the year. Four matches into the 1989/90 season, with Charlton still residents at Selhurst Park, the grand redevelopment plans for The Valley were unveiled at the club's New Eltham training ground open day on 20 August 1989. The impressive set of plans on display showed an all covered stadium with three wrap-around stands to the west, north and east of the ground. Only the existing South Stand was retained. Once all the stages were finished (which had a five year completion plan) The Valley would eventually hold up to 25,000 fans.

At first, the board were proposing to move back to a refurbished ground by February 1990. A new West Stand would be built, the North Stand refurbished and the lower half of the East Terrace re-concreted for use as a standing area. The plans also incorporated proposals to build flats and houses on club-owned land, towards the south-east corner of the ground off Lansdowne Mews. The planning application was presented to Greenwich Borough Council two weeks after the open day, and the Charlton supporters waited in expectation for the council planners to go through the due processes before granting permission for the work on The Valley to proceed. In the meantime, the Charlton board attended a public meeting held at The Valley Club to discuss the club's ground development plans with local residents, who were raising concerns over an increase in traffic and parking on match days. There were also objections to any plans the club might have to hold rock concerts in the stadium again, remembering back to when the Who appeared there twice in the 1970s.

As the new season progressed, there was a unnerving lack of activity by the council over the listing of a date for hearing the planning application, and the supporters, many of whom had purchased season tickets in the expectation that club would be returning to The Valley in February, began having understandable concerns the council were stalling over the planning application. With local residents not only raising concerns around the traffic and parking problems, they now had fears surrounding the threat of football hooliganism on the streets in close proximately to The Valley.

The council, once fully behind the homecoming, now appeared to be hesitant in showing support for the club's return since the appointment of a new body of councillors, which included planning committee chairman Simon Oelman and council leader Quentin Marsh, two men whom Charlton fans would later blame over the ever-increasing planning delays. Then, in October, a series of consultation meetings were held with representatives of the club and local residents, to discuss the proposed move back to The Valley and the concerns residents had regarding an increase in traffic on non match days from the commercial activities the club were intending to organise as a means to ensure the football club would be financial sustainable. After the council planners then raised objections over these commercial activities, Greenwich and Woolwich MP Rosie Barnes, elected to the role in 1987 while Charlton were playing in South Norwood, chose to get involved in the planning application saga, concerned for her constituents and the repercussions a return of the football club would have over those living in the vicinity. She came to the conclusion, following six months of canvassing her constituents, that there was a relatively even split between those for and those against the club's return.

While the board were dealing with the planners at council level, Lennie Lawrence was more concerned about ensuring the team gained enough points to keep the club in the First Division for a fourth consecutive season. With a majority of the transfer fund already used up, and the ongoing planning delays causing serious financial operating difficulties for the club, there was very little money left for Lawrence to bring in the players that he needed to shore up the defence. Then, when defender Peter Shirtliff wanted a move so he could be closer to his home, Lawrence sold him to Sheffield United for £500,000 and bought Chelsea defender Joe McLaughlin to replace him for a new club record fee of £600,000, the manager also signing 'keeper Mick Salmon for £100,000 as understudy to Bob Bolder.

By the time the Greenwich planning committee met at Woolwich Town Hall on 31 January 1990 to review the planning application, Charlton were at the foot of the First Division table with just sixteen points from twenty-three matches played, seven points behind fourth-from-bottom Manchester United. In what at first had been perceived as a straightforward return to The Valley, the ongoing planning delays and residents' objections were now putting a prompt homecoming in doubt. Although planning permission was not required to allow football to be played at The Valley, Charlton required a safety certificate before football could be played in front of a paying public, and with the order that had closed the East Terrace still in force, any return would need the full support and approval of Greenwich Borough Council. After the catastrophic Bradford City stadium fire in May 1985, where fifty-six fans lost their lives and more than 250 were injured, followed by the tragedy at Hillsborough in April 1989 which led to the deaths of ninety-six Liverpool fans and injured over 700 more, the redevelopment of existing grounds and development of new football stadia were required to meet ever-increasing stringent levels of safety.

TAKING THE COUNCIL TO THE POLLS

On the day of the council planning committee meeting, which was open to the public, hundreds of Charlton Athletic supporters marched from The Valley to the town hall, filed in through the doors and took their seats alongside the much smaller contingent of residents in the council hall. With around 600 packed inside, the town hall doors were then closed, leaving hundreds more supporters locked outside.

There was no doubt the council would have preferred the planning meeting to have taken place in a closed session, which could still have happened if the proceedings became disorderly, however the impeccably well behaved Charlton fans gave the committee chairman no opportunity to take such a course of action. The council planners' report had been made available to the *Mercury* the week before and the newspapers reported that the planning outcome was not expected to be favourable in support of the club's immediate return.

With the meeting underway, chief planning officer Sandra Hunt brought into question the suitability of The Valley as a football ground, citing Lord Justice Taylor's report on Hillsborough, which called for safer all-seated stadia. The planning officer then laid out the reasons for the planning committee's case for rejection, which mainly related to access, traffic congestion on matchdays, parking and, specifically, the effect crowds would have on the local residents with the club's proposal for an increase in commercial activities.

There followed an exchange of viewpoints between representatives of the club, Greenwich Borough Council members, Charlton supporters and local residents, conducted in a moderately restrained manner. However, when opinions between parties became overtly heated, causing heckling from those seated in the hall, councillor Simon Oelman threatened to take the planning meeting to a private session until the proceedings came to order.

Councillor John Austin-Walker spoke in favour of the club's return to The Valley, fully supporting the efforts to bring Charlton home, while councillor Peter King, appearing not to be in favour of the planning application but pertaining to be a Charlton fan, informed those attending that he had been supporting the club since they won the FA Cup in 1948. This caused an outburst of laughter to break out among the seated Charlton fans in the hall, with several members of the planning committee also joining in, all aware that this historic football event actually took place in 1947.

Supporters' Club secretary Roy King and representatives of the *Voice of The Valley* fanzine Steve Dixon and Rick Everitt, after addressing the committee, encouraged supporters to walk out on the planning meeting, as in their view, the planning officers were not going to support the club's planning application, and hundreds of fans made their exit before a vote was taken. Meanwhile, up on the stage, fourteen members of the planning committee were asked to raise their hands by the chairman to vote on Charlton's planning application. The application was rejected by ten votes to two, one committee member abstained and another, former director and Charlton supporter Bill Strong, by declaring an interest, decided not to vote.

On leaving the stage the planning committee members opposing the application were booed by the supporters who had stayed on. Several councillors exited through a side door rather than face any hostility directed towards them by the crowds of angry Charlton fans waiting outside. Planning chairman Simon Oelman made a quick escape as he was confronted by fans in the town hall, in an attempt to avoid facing a barrage of questions from the Charlton supporters dissatisfied with the outcome. As more unhappy fans gathered outside the town hall on that dark and wet Wednesday evening, defiant club chairman Roger Alwen came out to ask supporters to leave in an orderly manner, ensuring them that the fight to bring Charlton back to The Valley was not over.

Once informed of the planning application rejection, Woolwich MP John Cartwright, a Charlton supporter since the mid-1940s and one of many fans who chose to boycott Charlton's home matches at South Norwood, issued a statement in support of the club's return urging both parties, council planners and club members, to compromise on a plan to ensure football would be played at The Valley again.

The decision to reject the application was criticised by a majority of people throughout the borough, even by those with no affiliation to the club. The local press publications concluded that the decision had already been made behind closed doors, and that democracy had been ridiculed in Greenwich. One dedicated Charlton fan wrote to Prime Minister Margaret Thatcher expressing concern at the way Greenwich Council had handled the application, receiving a reply from the Department for the Environment on the PM's behalf, which outlined the correct procedures for making planning applications. The football authorities had raised the issue with the Secretary of State regarding the difficulties clubs were having in the redevelopment of existing grounds or building new stadia. However, although the government were aware of the problems football clubs were facing in ground development after the Taylor Report, it did not help Charlton's immediate predicament. Charlton supporters had to take the initiative and they did so by proposing to form their own political party to fight Greenwich Council in the coming local May elections.

A proposal to form a supporter-led political party was first suggested a year earlier by the secretary of the independent Hayes and West Wickham Supporters' Group, Richard Redden. Fans of the club then decided to take the idea further. The concept of the fans forming a political party came to the attention of the *Mercury* and *South London Press*. Both publications printed the story, which led to Thames Television featuring the Valley Party campaign in a regional news programme.

On the morning of the planning meeting, BBC News South East were covering the proceedings as a local interest story, and were outside the town hall at the end of the meeting waiting for any newsworthy statements. Steve Dixon immediately gave them a story by making his intentions known that he would be standing against the council in the local elections.

While the supporters began making plans to form a political football party, the first ever group of football fans to attempt such a venture, the club directors made several unsuccessful attempts to arrange talks with Council Leader Quentin Marsh and Councillor Simon Oelman to discuss how the planning application could be revised to allow the club to return to The Valley. With the council unresponsive, the board appealed against the decision to reject the original planning application and a date for the appeal meeting was scheduled to take place on 20 February 1990 at the town hall in Woolwich. Once again the *Mercury* rallied to the Charlton cause, backing the formation of a supporters' political party. It urged all Charlton fans to put their vote to the names of candidates standing as members of the Valley Party in the coming elections, with a back page headline proclaiming 'Vote Valley'. The day before the appeal, Charlton beat Luton Town 2-0 at Selhurst Park and, although the result did not improve the position in the table, the win was the first since a 2-0 victory over Manchester United back in November, which put Charlton fans in good spirits leading up to the appeal meeting.

There had been much speculation over other options available to the club after Charlton's planning application rejection, from building a brand new stadium in Greenwich to moving the club out of the borough and into the neighbouring borough of Bexley. Playing at Selhurst Park proved financially unviable and, with the Taylor report calling for all-seated stadia, giving up on a return to The Valley and continuing the tenancy would have cause further economic difficulties if Crystal Palace chairman Ron Noades increased Charlton's financial groundshare contribution to pay towards the stadium redevelopment costs. The alternative of building a brand new stadium in he borough also proved impractical, as no suitable site had ever been located since the club announced an intention to return. Even if such a venture could be financed, the only way Charlton Athletic could survive was by returning to a refurbished Valley, an outcome now dependent on the result of the appeal.

While the Charlton board were optimistic that the appeal would be successful, members of the newly formed Valley Party were less hopeful and, unsurprisingly, they were proved right when the appeal was refused.

The Valley Party campaign now went into full swing with meetings organised throughout the borough to promote the party that were contesting sixty, of the sixty-two, wards in the local May elections. The wards not contested were those of the councillors who had not voted against the planning application. Supporters' Club social secretary Barry Nugent was appointed Valley Party leader, and was joined in the political fight by Charlton supporters living in the borough and volunteering to stand in the elections against the current elected councillors. Many other supporters, living outside the boundaries of the borough, joined the cause by assisting with the party administrative duties.

Charlton fan Richard Hunt, the director of a London-based advertising agency, chaired the first party meetings. Hunt went on to produce a well conceived, hard-hitting and emotive 'Vote Valley' advertising campaign, evoking the club's heritage and community spirit to promote the party values and the central issue of the council acknowledging the supporters' opinions and reconsidering their seemingly irrational opposition towards the club's move back to The Valley.

The five uniquely designed Vote Valley posters went up on display hoardings around the borough. Accompanying leaflets, reflecting the poster designs, were handed out to Charlton supporters, their friends and relations, to put up on display in the windows of their homes or in pubs, clubs and shops they used throughout the wards. The members of the Valley Party were under no illusion that the campaign would probably not secure enough votes to win positions on the council. The hope was for enough of the club's fans living in the borough to go along and put a cross next to the name of a Valley Party candidate, proving to the council the depth of support there was for the football club's return.

Labour-led Greenwich Borough Council did not give the Valley Party much credibility, dismissive of their chances of persuading the people of the borough to support a party whose sole objective was to bring a football club back to a football ground vacated five years before, when attendances barely reached higher than 6,000. However, the Vote Valley campaign stirred up the emotions of the residents of the borough of Greenwich. The inspirational poster promotion brought plenty of publicity for the party, not only in the local papers but in the nationals too, winning Richard Hunt's advertising agency a prestigious industry award.

The Valley Party received extensive news coverage throughout the whole television and radio broadcasting industry, prompting a Thames Television current affairs programme to carry out an investigation into the council's opposition to the club's planning application and potential move back to the borough. Channel 4's head of broadcasting, Michael Grade, a Charlton supporter since the early 1950s, wrote an article in *The Guardian*, wholeheartedly endorsing the Vote Valley campaign.

With the Vote Valley campaign in full swing, the Charlton team were on the verge of relegation. After an initial good run of form brought fourteen points in eight games, after two straight defeats and four matches of the season still to play, Charlton required a win over Wimbledon at Selhurst Park on 17 April to keep up any slender hope they had of surviving the drop. Within 8 minutes of the match played Charlton conceded two goals and, despite pulling one back through an own goal with 20 minutes of the match remaining, a win was looking exceedingly unlikely. At the final whistle, Charlton lost 2-1 and were relegated after four hard-fought, eventful and memorable seasons in the First Division.

After the club's relegation fight came to its conclusion, the fans now put all their effort into supporting the Valley Party's assault on the local elections by distributing leaflets to homes in all the contested wards. On the day of Charlton's final home League fixture of the season at Selhurst Park against Sheffield Wednesday, six days before the election, members of the Valley Party outmanoeuvred their rival ward contenders by travelling around the borough in a decorated double-decker open-top bus, handing out Valley Party leaflets and calling out to the local population through a megaphone, as the bus passed by, to 'Vote Valley on 3 May'.

Three days later, Valley Party members and supporters met in The Valley Club to finalise their plans, before taking to the streets of each ward and targeting all the borough railway stations to distribute party leaflets and encourage the voting public to support their cause. When election day came, the Valley Party candidates and supporters were in an extremely positive mood after carrying out an election campaign far superior to those of the opposition.

On the day of the election, the Woolwich Town Hall was crowded with supporters and candidates from all parties, with more arriving when the polling stations closed after the residents of the borough had cast their votes. Although the two main parties, labour and Conservative, were competing for a majority of the wards, as the results began to come in, it was clear that the Valley Party were taking many more votes than either had expected. Labour party candidates, many of whom were expecting to retain their seats, began to lose out to the Conservative party opponents, after the constituents changed their allegiance from Labour to the Valley Party.

In Kidbrooke, the Labour member lost out to the Conservative candidate by just thirteen votes, which had been the result of the Valley Party member polling 326. Labour Party councillors and supporters, many of whom had previously ridiculed a political party formed by the fans of a football club, were left aghast as Valley Party votes continued to rise.

Valley Party members, representing Charlton Athletic and the supporters of the club, behaved in an extremely dignified manner throughout the whole of the historic campaign and in Woolwich Town Hall during election day, despite much unwarranted provocation received from the opposition party members and their representatives.

Then, when news came through that Simon Oelman, the planning committee chairman and one of the councillors opposing the planning application, had lost his seat, a great cheer of approval rang out through the political arena as Valley Party members and club supporters within the town hall celebrated his downfall. Although the Valley Party did not win any seats on the council, which in reality had not been the party's objective, all sixty candidates had amassed an astonishing 14,838 votes between them. Quentin Marsh, leader of the council, came within 369 votes of losing the seat of Sherard ward in Eltham to the Valley Party candidate.

The day after the election, Valley Party candidates and campaigners, supporters and club directors, along with the people of the Borough of Greenwich, celebrated a triumphant victory for democracy after the uncooperative actions of the local council forced the passionate fans of Charlton Athletic to take matters into their own hands through political campaigning and the ballot box. Although the battle to return to The Valley was not yet over, and even though the club had lost First Division status,

Charlton supporters travelled to Manchester United for the last game of the season, many wearing fancy dress and faces painted in the club colours of red and white, in a mood of joyous optimism.

On the terraces of Old Trafford, a lively rapport built up between both clubs' football fans during the match, with supporters of Manchester United singing out 'You'll be back, you'll be back, you'll be back'. Although Charlton lost 1-0, there was no doubt who the club's fans would be supporting in the following Saturday's FA Cup final between their landlords Crystal Palace and Manchester United, and it would not be the club from South Norwood.

A WELCOME BACK TO THE BOROUGH OF GREENWICH

In what had become an exceptionally eventful season, attendances for Charlton home matches averaged 10,748, the best since the club had played at Selhurst Park. Even though match revenue for the season totalled £842,383.50, the club still made a substantial loss of £239,196. This was proof, if proof was needed, that even though support had been at its highest since the late 1970s, the move to Selhurst Park had been a financial failure, leaving the new board and the supporters who had opposed the move to speculate on what the club may have achieved if playing First Division football at The Valley. But this was now all in the past and Charlton would soon be on their way back home to compete, once more, in the Second Division of the Football League.

During the close season, the club began on a widespread campaign to strengthen Charlton's community position within the borough. There was another successful open day at the training ground, a tour of local schools and the club attended the Bexley summer show at Danson Park, where they erected a large promotional marquee in collaboration with Woolwich Building Society (the club's sponsors once again). This was to promote the partnership between both organisations, Valley Gold and the club's revised plans for the refurbished Valley, the club hoping to return at the start of the following season.

The club had by now closed its offices at Selhurst Park and moved back to renovated buildings situated on Harvey Gardens towards the front of The Valley, housing a new club shop, the commercial office and Junior Reds and Valley Gold departments. The offices dealing with football club administration were already based at the Sparrows Lane training ground at New Eltham. Former club groundsman Maurice Banham, who retired when the club moved away, was also back in action at The Valley. He assisted the current groundsman Collin Powell in returning the playing surface to its former glory, as seen in the days when 'Paddy' Powell was running down the left wing with the ball at his feet. Former player Powell, after hanging up his boots, spent a period in non-League management and playing cricket for Stevenage, where his interest in groundskeeping began. He then returned to Charlton to take up a groundsman position at the training ground, later becoming head groundsman of The Valley.

With rising interest in the club generated through the Valley Party campaign, and the community activities Charlton were actively involved with throughout the borough, an opportunity came along to raise the profile of the football club over the airwaves when the Radio Thamesmead soul music presenter, Clive Richardson, a keen Charlton

Athletic fan, came up with the novel idea to run a Charlton Athletic chat show. The DJ's Sunday evening music show went off air at 8.00 p.m., leaving a couple of hours of free airtime between 8.00 and 10.00 p.m. Contacting the club's commercial manager Steve Sutherland, who was always ready to take advantage of an opportunity to promote the club, Richardson proposed the innovative idea for the dedicated club radio show, and 'Charlton Chat' soon began broadcasting on Radio Thamesmead.

The two-hour radio show gave Charlton fans the opportunity to call in and talk about all matters relating to the football club, listen to interviews with club directors, manager and players as well as having the opportunity to speak to guests appearing on the show. The football club's commercial department also began producing an official twenty-four page bimonthly magazine, titled simply *Charlton*, the first edition featuring an interview with club vice chairman Mike Norris, where he laid out details for the new planning application to be submitted to the council, explaining he was confident the new plans would meet general approval.

By then, a number of consultation meetings had already taken place between the club directors and the latest members of the borough council. After the Valley Party's success at the ballot box the club had come up with a revised working plan for the proposed Valley redevelopment. Along with the refurbishment of the North and South Stands, the planning application included the construction of a new, four-level, cantilever West Stand along the whole length of the pitch, incorporating executive boxes, a fitness centre, conference and function facilities, offices, a new Valley Club for the supporters and a bowling alley. The somewhat controversial proposal to build houses had been dropped.

The old East Terrace would be open for standing spectators in a lower area only, but would eventually become an all-seated covered stand. Once these revised plans received planning approval, the club now expected football to return to a 20,000-capacity stadium for the start of 1991/92 season. The new plans had been submitted to the council in September 1990, for review in October. However, an industrial dispute within the council, which was drawn out for almost five months, put the planning application meeting back until the beginning of the following year. Meanwhile, the Charlton team carried on playing home fixtures at Selhurst Park as a Second Division club, while the supporters waited for a conclusion to the strike before they knew if, and when, the first match would be played back at The Valley.

After the club's relegation, manager Lennie Lawrence had lost the services of several of the squad's better players, who were sold to help stabilise the club's financial situation, including full-back John Humphrey, defender Joe McLaughlin, forward Paul Williams and, later on in the season, Gordon Watson, a young forward who had made a successful transition from the youth squad into the first team the previous season and was sold to Sheffield Wednesday for £250,000, with an extra £100,000 expected depending on number of appearances he made.

The sale of these players brought in over £1.5 million and Lennie Lawrence spent £320,000 to bring in defenders Simon Webster, Stuart Balmer, and forward Alex Dyer. Losing the first four matches of the 1990/91 season, Charlton dropped to the bottom of the division and although two draws and a win put a halt to the poor run of form, all was not well within the club. Former player and now first-team coach Mike Flanagan was suspended and later sacked for criticising the manager's tactics during an interview on Charlton Chat, and there was speculation surrounding the future of Lennie Lawrence after the team's disappointing start to the season.

The Charlton manager gradually began to turn the club's fortunes around, now assisted by Alan Curbishley, who moved up from the position as reserve team coach to first-team coach. Former player Curbishley returned to the club to take on a role of player/coach, along with another former Charlton player and teammate Steve Gritt, who then took over the role of reserve team coach on Curbishley's promotion.

As the season moved onwards, and with the council industrial dispute with officers of the planning department seemingly coming no closer to a conclusion, the Charlton Supporters' Club made enquiries into town council planning procedures. After taking professional advice, Supporters' Club secretary Roy King discovered Greenwich Council could, if they chose to do so, process the application without the planning officers who were still on strike, raising further concerns over the council's commitment to the development of The Valley and the return of the club.

By January, with Charlton moving up into seventeenth place, there seemed to be some indication of progress between the council and the union in regards to the ongoing strike. Any hopes of the planning application being processed, however, were soon dashed when the union rejected proposals which could have ended the strike.

With the amount of work still required to get The Valley ready by start of the following season, the Charlton supporters were left in no doubt that the proposed return date would be met. Even if planning was soon granted, fans were faced with the prospects of travelling across south London to Selhurst Park until the end of the year at least, leaving everyone feeling frustrated and disappointed. Then, with just a few weeks of the current season to go, the council set the date for the planning meeting for 2 April 1991.

Although the revised planning application had been submitted after previous consultation with the planning officers, there continued to be concerns regarding the proposed commercial activities (including the addition of a bowling alley). The club board and the Charlton supporters grew increasingly uneasy about the planning outcome as the day of the meeting drew nearer.

Only selected parties were permitted to attend the planning meeting, which was held in the council committee room. Representatives of the club and their advisors, along with a number of supporters and local residents, were given a limited 100 tickets to attend the meeting. The public hall was open to all, with the proceedings relayed via a speaker system to around 500 fans packed inside, with many more waiting on the streets outside the town hall.

The planning committee heard from all parties in attendance. Those speaking on behalf of the residents told the committee their concerns over the planning application were more to do with an increase in traffic and crowds around the area on matchdays, rather than an opposition to the football club returning to The Valley. While the planning committee deliberated over the application, supporters inside and outside the town hall waited nervously for the verdict. All those fears, however, were soon cast aside, as those more than patient Charlton fans, both inside and outside the town hall, celebrated in joy and in relief when the news came through that the planning application had been approved by seventeen votes to one. At long last, Charlton Athletic Football Club would be returning home to The Valley.

The team were now safe in a mid-table position and had performed beyond all expectations during a season of uncertainty. Playing the last League fixture at Selhurst Park, in the penultimate game of the season, Charlton drew with visitors West Ham United 1-1 and, although losing the last match 2-0 to Plymouth Argyle away, finished the season in a respectable sixteenth place. Before the season had come to a close, club chairman Roger Alwen had invited Richard Murray and Martin Simons, two business associates, to join the board of directors.

Not only would both of these successful businessmen introduce much needed funds into the club, they would also be influential in bringing the club back home. Work on The Valley began almost as soon as the season came to a close, the contractors moving in to start on the process of making the site ready for the groundwork to take place. Then, just two weeks into the project, with work well underway, the contractors went into administration. Undaunted by this development, the Charlton directors soon secured the services of Beazer Construction to take over the project.

BUILDING A NEW FUTURE

The Valley plans now incorporated the erection of a temporary West Stand at a cost of £100,000, for use while the permanent stand, which would take too long to build in time for the start of the coming season, was constructed around it.

Funds from the Football Grounds Development Trust, granted to the club before the move to South Norwood, were now released to help finance the ground refurbishment. The supporters also played their part by raising funds to assist the club in financing the redevelopment of the ground during the months which followed. The building of the temporary West Stand should have increased the capacity for the start of the coming season, but had been reduced down to around 10,000 when problems were encountered with the turnstiles situated to the south end of the East Terrace, which restricted the standing area to 3,000. While work carried on steadily, in readiness for the first game of the season, supporters were shocked by the news that Charlton manager Lennie Lawrence was leaving the club to join Middlesbrough United, a most unexpected and disappointing development for the club.

A great diplomat, as well as a magnificent football manager, Lawrence eloquently put his case forward for why he decided to make the move to the North East in an article written for the *Mercury* newspaper. He explained that after years of operating on insufficient funds, resulting in the sale of the club's best players, fighting relegation and the ongoing preoccupation by the board and supporters to get back to The Valley, he believed the team had come second and felt it was now time to move on. An approach had first been made by Middlesbrough to secure his services after Lawrence had been negotiating with the club over the permanent transfer of Alan Kernaghan to Charlton after a successful period on loan.

When Middlesbrough manager Colin Todd then resigned, the club's board, impressed with the way Lawrence had conducted the player transfer negotiations, offered him the position of manager. Lawrence would win promotion with Middlesbrough at the end of the coming season, receiving a respective round of applause and cheers from the Charlton supporters when both teams met home and away during that season.

FOOTBALL REGENERATION

Without a manager, Charlton supporters were left to speculate on who could ever follow in Lennie Lawrence's footsteps and emulate the success achieved during his time with the club. Even after suffering relegation the previous season, the vacated managerial position at Charlton Athletic was an exceptionally attractive proposition for any experienced, or up-and-coming manager to take on.

As a London-based football club with long-term plans in the area for commercial and residential growth, the potential was there to make Charlton great again, and bring back the missing thousands of fans which had once filled The Valley. The area of Thamesmead, covering some 1,000 acres of marshland which included part of the old Royal Arsenal armaments works, was undergoing a sustained period of redevelopment. A vast social housing project that began in the late 1960s and was planned to continue into the next century would increase the local population by almost 60,000.

The properties built within the Thamesmead estate would not only be occupied by people moving in from outside of the local area, but also by thousands of working-class families relocating from the old Victorian and Edwardian terraced houses of South East inner London, many existing, or lapsed, supporters of Charlton Athletic. The club's return to the borough saw an opportunity to not only bring back Charlton supporters who had lost interest in attending matches before and after the move to Sellhurst Park, but also, attract a new generation of fans from the masses moving into Thamesmead with The Valley located only 4 miles to the west.

Beside the development of Thamesmead for housing, the whole Thames frontage, from the west of Greenwich to Woolwich and onwards out towards Kent, would eventually undergo complete regeneration and transformation. The majority of the old redundant riverside industries, including those on Greenwich Marsh, which was the site of a prospective new stadium before the issues surrounding a return to The Valley had been resolved, were to be replaced by modern commercial properties, leisure facilities and residential developments. This gave the club further opportunities to draw prospective fans from the communities evolving along the riverfront, and potential income created through sponsorship deals and commercial activities with local emerging trades and industries.

FROM PLAYER-COACHES TO MANAGERS

The Charlton board of directors had made no indication to the supporters of a favoured candidate to take on the role of Charlton manager. Before leaving the club, Lennie Lawrence recommended the directors make the appointment from within. Charlton fans would not have been surprised if former player Keith Peacock had been offered the position, after returning to the club in a scouting capacity and then taking over as youth team coach with his experience as manager of Gillingham and later Maidstone United.

The board's choice however was a complete surprise to the Charlton supporters and football media, when the club released a statement announcing that first-team coach Alan Curbishley and reserve team coach Steve Gritt had been appointed joint first-team coaches, later becoming joint managers, with Keith Peacock taking over the reserve team coaching role. There was initial cynicism among football journalists regarding the effectiveness of having two coaches in charge of the first team, suggesting it was as short-term low-cost measure, taken by the board until the right man could be found.

When the club first advertised the managerial post, Curbishley, Gritt and Peacock all applied, along with several experienced coaches and managers and a number of former Charlton players. The board eventually decided to follow Lawrence's suggestion to appoint from within, going with the two younger, less experienced men over the older, but more experienced, Peacock. With hardly any funds available to spend in the transfer market, Curbishley and Gritt continued to be registered as players, with the possibility both may have needed to play during the season.

As time was running out to get The Valley ready for the first game, Curbishley and Gritt were busy attempting to bring new players into the squad, without spending too much of the limited amount of funds that had been made available for use in the transfer market. Chelsea midfielder John Bumstead had already signed before Lennie Lawrence had left for Middlesbrough. The former manager's last acquisition was soon to be joined by the new managerial duo's own signings, defender Steve Gating and forward Garry Nelson, both moving from Brighton and Hove Albion, two players Curbishley knew well from when all three were at the same club together.

The ongoing development of The Valley had by then run into further delay, and the board negotiated a deal with West Ham United to share Upton Park for the first few matches of the coming season, until Charlton could return to The Valley for the scheduled fixture six matches into the 1991/92 season against Portsmouth on 14 September. The expected move home to a limited capacity Valley resulted in a big increase in season ticket sales, bought by supporters to ensure they would be at the club's first game back since leaving six seasons before.

The first match at Upton Park was played on a Sunday because West Ham's home fixture had taken place the day before. Attracting an attendance of just over 9,000 for the game against Newcastle United, hundreds of Charlton supporters arrived late for kick off, caught up in traffic delays at the Blackwall Tunnel river crossing. Charlton beat Newcastle United 2-1 with goals from Robert Lee (the player who scored Charlton's last goal at The Valley and the first at Selhurst Park) and Carl Leaburn, the first time he had scored a game at home, as all his previous goals had been scored in away fixtures. The new management duo had got off to a flying start and the excellent run continued with Charlton only losing once in the first six games. The last match in that run, a 3-0 win over Portsmouth, should have been the first match to be played back at The Valley, but two days after the start of the season, the contractors downed tools when the project required a further investment of £500,000 from the club, incurred through the unexpected safety work required as specified by Greenwich Council under the Taylor Report.

The pitch was ready to be played upon and the new floodlight pylons were in place, but the temporary West Stand was still a shell and there were growing concerns about how the club would be able to continue financing the remainder of the work required. Supporters' Club member Roy King, giving up his own contracting business to take on the role of stadium manager, had the unenviable task of trying to manage all of these ongoing constructional setbacks. He was not helped in his task when vice chairman Mike Norris, who had been overseeing a majority of the development work resigned due to issues arising with club chairman Roger Alwen and the rest of the board.

As joint owner of the club, training ground and The Valley, the resignation of Mike Norris, whose property development company was in financial difficulties through the recession, could well have resulted in further serious financial difficulties for the club. By October, work on The Valley had come to a complete standstill and Mike Norris's share in the club had been diluted by a rights issue after his company went into voluntary administration. This presented directors Richard Murray and Martin Simons with an opportunity to acquire a 12.5 per cent share each of club ownership. As one of the football club's saviours, the departure of Mike Norris in such unfortunate circumstances was an extremely sad end for a genuine Charlton fan who had done so much to bring the club back home to the borough.

Richard Collins, whose company were project architects, took on the responsibility of overseeing the continuation of the work at The Valley, which was now seriously behind schedule with debts mounting daily. Project builder Kier Construction Group were working relentlessly, along with Richard Collins and the Charlton board, to find any means possible to bring the contractors' standstill to an end and allow the construction work to continue, while safeguarding the financial interests of Kiers. As the weeks went by, Charlton supporters were unaware of the financial problems the board were facing, receiving little positive news on the ground's progress or any date for a return. The fans made regular trips to The Valley to see for themselves how much work had, or had not, been completed.

To assist the club in financing the required work at The Valley, midfielder Andy Peake left to join up with his former manager Lennie Lawrence at Middlesbrough, for a transfer fee of £150,000. With the majority of any income that the club secured going towards financing the work at the ground, Curbishley and Gritt were unable to spend any significant amount of money on new player purchases, midfielder Alan Pardew joined on a free transfer from Crystal Palace as a replacement for Peake. Despite the unusual joint managerial partnership, Alan Curbishley and Steve Gritt soon developed a good working relationship together, travelling throughout the country on scouting missions looking for new prospective signings for very little financial outlay, and checking out the opposition teams.

The pair had an understanding that team selection would be carried out behind closed doors and, if one of them had a difference of opinion over which players to use, these differences and outcome would be kept between themselves. They also agreed not to contradict each other over team or club affairs and would share training and coaching sessions at Charlton's Sparrows Lane training ground. The partnership certainly seemed to be working better than many had expected, as by the end of the year Charlton were in the top half of the table, performances giving supporters hope that even if there was going to be no return to The Valley that season, then at last there might be a realistic opportunity in pushing up into a play-off place and possibly even promotion. In February, Plumstead-born American businessman Mike Stevens, joined the board and invested £300,000 into the football club. This meant the club required a further £1 million to finalise the refurbishment of The Valley.

With Charlton fourth in the table, one place above Lennie Lawrence's club Middlesbrough, there was now a feeling of positivity throughout the football club, the optimistic supporters ready to assist when an appeal was made by the directors for help in raising the £1-million shortfall. The supporters were offered the potential of investing from £25, up to £3,000, in an investment plan. The proposal of an investment scheme had first been raised by fans during discussions on the Charlton Chat radio show, the idea then appeared in Charlton fanzines and *Mercury* newspaper articles. The initial reaction to a share scheme had been extremely positive, with more than 2,000 supporters pledging over £1 million. However, the share plan came to a shuddering halt when the insurers found themselves in difficulties over the legalities of guaranteeing repayments to the prospective shareholders, and the scheme was put on hold.

Going into the final few weeks of the season, Charlton were positioned comfortably within the play-off places. For the three clubs promoted at the end of the season, they would be playing football in the recently created FA Premier League, which would bring huge financial rewards for all twenty-two clubs in the division. The formation of the FA Premier League had taken place in February 1992, following a decision by clubs in the First Division to break away from the Football League and form an independent division, in order take advantage of the lucrative global television rights on offer.

Subsequently, after protracted negotiations between the FA, Football League and television broadcasters (included the new satellite stations) a compromise was agreed where the top division would break away from the Football League and come under the direction of the FA, retaining promotion and relegation throughout all four divisions. The three divisions below the FA Premier League were then retitled as First, Second and Third Divisions of the Football League. Before the last game of the season, Charlton had dropped out of the play-off places into seventh place, when Blackburn Rovers won a game in hand to go sixth on goal difference. Charlton needed to win away against Bristol Rovers, another club forced to groundshare and playing home fixtures at Bath City's Twerton Park. Charlton also had to rely on results against Blackburn Rovers and Cambridge United going their way to take them back up into a play-off place.

The attendance of 7,622 in Bath City's compact ground, the highest recorded all season, included several thousand Charlton supporters, travelling west to cheer on the team. At 0-0 with just over 10 minutes of the match to go, Bristol Rovers scored, and Charlton's chances of going back up into a play-off place were all but over. Although Charlton lost the match 1-0, even a win would have made no difference as both Blackburn Rovers and Cambridge United secured the points required to ensure their own play-off place. Charlton finished the season in a credible seventh position, a fantastic achievement for the club, the players, the managerial duo and, especially, the directors, who had taken a chance on appointing Curbishley and Gritt as joint managers. Throughout the close season, the Charlton board of directors worked unwaveringly in their attempt to reduce the financial deficit that was preventing completion of work at The Valley.

IN FINANCIAL SUPPORT OF THEIR CLUB

In June, the club launched The Valley Investment Plan, which offered supporters the opportunity to make a financial contribution to help finish the refurbishment of the ground. Fans could invest between £50 to £2,000 into the scheme, the funds deposited into a separate account and released by solicitors when the total £1.2 million that was required had been reached. Each £50 invested in the scheme gave the VIP member a vote to elect a VIP candidate onto the football club board of directors, and all investors received a personalised VIP certificate and a discount on season tickets.

By the time of the opening game of the season against Grimsby Town on 15 August 1992, Charlton taking up residence once more at Upton Park, the VIP scheme was heading towards a figure of £1 million. With the funds' release date fast approaching, the total required was short by around £200,000. The Charlton directors had no other option than to make up the difference themselves, and on 28 August 1992 club chairman Roger Alwen made the announcement that Charlton Athletic would be returning to play football at The Valley for the fixture against Portsmouth on 5 December 1992.

Work re-commenced at The Valley towards the end of September, after a group of Charlton supporters volunteered to help clear away undergrowth which had reappeared while the work on the site had come to a standstill. Once the constructors were back on site, the final groundworks were carried out, cables laid, drainage installed and a new police control centre was built in the south-west corner of the ground. While work carried on to get The Valley ready for the big day, the team had risen to second in the division, going ten games unbeaten since the beginning of the season.

As perimeter fencing was erected around the ground and seats installed in the temporary West Stand structure by November, a series of large, portable cabins were erected towards the rear of the West Stand on the main car park area. The portable cabins housed the changing rooms, hospitality areas, store rooms and a room for the matchday stewards. The directors asked for volunteers with any specialist skills, from painting and decorating, to carpet laying, to come and help prepare The Valley for the big day.

Although the supporters and directors had financed the final instalment of funding through the VIP scheme to get the ground completed for the match against Portsmouth, the football club continued to struggle in financing the operating costs. This resulted in the sale of Robert Lee, the last member of the Charlton team still with the club who played in the last match at The Valley, to Newcastle United for £700,000. Also leaving at the same time was young prospective fullback Anthony Barness, who was transferred to Chelsea for £350,000. Most of the two transfer fees was used to pay off debts incurred while playing at Upton Park and money owed to the Inland Revenue.

Club secretary Chris Parks was responsible for ticket allocation for the first game back with season tickets holders first in line, followed by Valley Gold and VIP members and any remaining tickets offered to season ticket holders for their guests. After the sale of both Anthony Barness and Robert Lee, the board assured supporters there would be no further sale of players, and club director Martin Simons was quoted in the *Charlton* magazine stating 'the not-for-sale signs are up'. Curbishley and Gritt brought in midfielder John Robinson, a Welsh Under-21 international from Brighton and Hove Albion, for a nominal fee of £75,000, which was decided by a Football League transfer tribunal. Robinson became one of the supporters' favourite players through the enthusiasm and passion he showed while wearing the Charlton Athletic shirt.

COMMUNITY PRESENCE

When Charlton first made the announcement that the club would be returning to South East London while groundsharing at Selhurst Park, a plan was devised to raise the profile of Charlton Athletic throughout the Borough of Greenwich through a community scheme programme, which began with one member of staff taking a bag of footballs out around the local community to engage children in some fun football activities. Gradually, as more coaches were employed in the Charlton Athletic community scheme project, the club took the football activities out into the boroughs of Bexley, Bromley, and Dartford and, later, throughout the whole of Kent to deliver football coaching for girls and boys. This successful project would go from strength to strength, with a disability development officer then employed to organise and deliver football opportunities for people with physical and learning disabilities.

The Charlton Athletic community scheme worked in partnership with many various organisations and authorities within education and local government. The interest created through the club's work in the community had also given more girls the opportunity to become involved in playing football. A group of enthusiastic, female football fans then came together to form the first ever Charlton Ladies football team.

One of the first ladies' teams to play at the Charlton training ground was organised by Supporters' Club social secretary Marilyn Rooke, who took a group of female fans for a training session with Steve Gritt and Alan Curbishley as part of a fundraising event. After the ladies had finished their training, they then took on a team of Charlton first-team players, including Garry Nelson, Stuart Balmer, Colin Walsh and Simon Webster, the ladies team victorious over the men.

The Charlton Ladies football team, which had formed with the intention of eventually competing in a local women's Football League, had no official affiliation with the main football club, although the team's results and fixtures would regularly feature in Charlton Athletic publications. The ladies team began organising regular training sessions and then selected a squad of players, aged sixteen and over, to enter the Second Division of the South East Counties Women's Football League. The Charlton Ladies competed against Hastings, West Sussex College, Crystal Palace reserves and even a team from Leeds.

When the Football Association took over direct control of English women's football in 1993, the game became more structured, organised along the lines of the men's game with local and national, divisions and cup competitions. Although the women's game became extremely popular during the early 1990s, women had been playing football before an FA ban in 1922 prevented them from playing at any grounds or clubs affiliated with the governing body of the men's game, a ban which lasted forty years.

Dick, Kerr's Ladies FC, a women's works team from Preston formed in the early 1920s, played matches at Goodison Park, the home of Everton football club. In a match against St Helen's Ladies on Boxing Day 1920, they attracted an attendance of over 50,000. Despite the FA ban, the women's game continued to be played regularly on non-FA affiliated football grounds throughout the country. The Dick, Kerr's Ladies works team went on to become Preston Ladies FC, before disbanding in 1965, six years before the FA finally officially recognised the game of women's football.

While the Charlton Ladies set out on their own campaign in the Second Division of South East Counties Women's Football League, the Charlton men's team were waiting for the day when League football would return to The Valley.

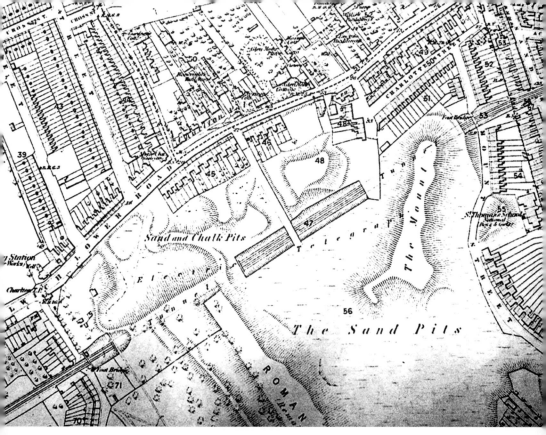

1. Charlton sand and chalk pits, the site of The Valley, 1880.

Above left: 2. The author (*front, second from right*) with fellow Charlton Athletic supporting friends in the upper North Stand of The Valley 2014. Their support, from oldest to youngest, spans a period of fifty years.

Above right: 3. A ritual pre-season friendly at Park View Road, 6 July 2013. Welling United 0 – Charlton Athletic 6.

Section of Robins Club members on an away visit.

Some happy members at Stoke City.

Club members en route for West Bromwich.

Above left: 4. The great Sam Bartram in his sports goods shop situated opposite the junction of Valley Grove and Floyd Road, Charlton SE7, opened during the early 1950s. On retiring from playing and managing, Bartram had by then closed his shop and taken up a successful career in sports journalism.

Above right: 5. On the road with the Robins Club. Travelling supporters during the 1950s following the team to away matches by coach or, as they were known, charabanc.

6. Charlton former player Harold Hobbis (*far left*) on holiday with his wife in Spain, out for a drink at Paddy's bar, meets up with friends including local Greenwich resident and Charlton fan Sid Gallagher (*centre*). From footballer to pub licensee, in 1960 Hobbis became the first landlord of The Valley public house on Elliscombe Road, just a short walk from ground after which it was named.

Above: 7. A fire at the top of the West Stand during the late 1960s, where forty years previously a fire had destroyed the club's account books and financial papers following Charlton's return from a financially unsuccessful period playing football at Catford Mount.

Right: 8. Forward Bobby Ayre (*right*) takes some advice from Jimmy Trotter, Charlton trainer and then manager after Seed, when suffering another of several injuries that blighted his football career while at Charlton between 1951 to 1958. A fast and tricky player, Ayre scored 72 League and cup goals in 166 matches for Charlton. Years later he returned to The Valley, becoming a popular and welcome member of the Former Players' Association.

9. Playing with a smaller ball, Charlton teammates compete in a round of golf during the late 1930s, a sporting activity popular with footballers from all eras carrying through to this day. The Former Players' Association organised charity golf days annually, regularly attended by a host of former Charlton players, guests and supporters.

10. Players keeping fit outside The Valley gym during the late 1950s. From left to right: Willie Duff, Eddie Werge, Billy Kiernan, Johnny Summers, Gordon Jago and first-team trainer Jack Shreeve being shown how to lift weights by a member of the Charlton staff.

11. Anyone for tennis? Sam Bartram takes up the racket for a workout behind the West Stand, where the club's main car park is now situated.

12. Although the facilities at The Valley were somewhat antiquated during the 1950s, with no substantial improvements made to the ground until the late 1980s, the Charlton team would train at The Valley and keep fit by running around the pitch, up and down the terracing and long runs out on the street surrounding the ground.

13. Charlton midfielder and England international Mike Bailey receives some advice from the local garage maintenance expert on taking good care of his car. He was soon off on the road to Wolverhampton Wanderers in 1966 for a fee of £35,000, as the directors were in need of some funds to keep the club solvent. Bailey returned to Charlton, first as head coach then as manager, winning promotion from the Third to Second Division in the 1980/81 season.

14. Out for a night on the town during the late 1950s, when players mingled freely with the local population and football fans for a social drink in the neighbouring pubs, clubs and dance halls of the borough. Charlton players in the foreground from left to right: Fred Lucus, Marvin Hinton, Stuart Leary and Sid O'Linn.

15. A fine looking athletic team of Charlton Athletic players poolside after taking a dip during some alternative keep fit activities in the 1957/58 season.

16. Three of Charlton's top strikers from the 1950s and early 1960s. From left to right: Stuart Leary, Roy Matthews and Dennis Edwards. Together, they scored a total of 260 League goals for the club.

17. Charlton strike partners Eddie Firmani and Bobby Ayre taking some tips from two very flexible dancing girls. In 1953, forward Firmani took up ballroom dancing with the sole intention of asking the daughter of former Charlton player, and at the time assistant manager George Green, out on a date, when he discovered the young lady enjoyed dancing at the Embassy ballroom in Welling. The rendezvous went very well and two years later they married.

18. A promotional parade outside the club shop, situated at the rear of the old West Stand before closure in 1985. The shop sold all the branded club merchandise a young Charlton fan could ever need to show support for his club, although the boy in the image seems more interested in the immaculately dressed ladies than what the shop had on offer.

19. Charlton No. 9 Harry Gregory embraced by the adoring young Charlton fans, when jumping up on the pitch perimeter fencing after scoring an equalising goal in a 3-1 at The Valley on 2 December 1968. Gregory soon became a firm favourite with the Charlton supporters after joining the club in 1966, through the passion and commitment he showed on the pitch.

20. Blonde full-back midfielder Bobby Curtis may well have lost his chances of England selection after he decided to dye his hair, which was frowned upon by the FA hierarchy during the '60s. He was a magnificent player while at Charlton, worthy of an international cap. Curtis scored twenty goals from penalties for Charlton, which still stands as a club record today.

Above left: 21. The main Valley entrance railings prior to groundshare of Selhurst Park in 1985, the old West Stand and East Terrace in the distance. After the club moved out the tops of the railings were the target for souvenir hunters. All the sword motifs gradually disappeared, cut through and removed, never to be seen again.

Above right: 22. Charlton joint manager Steve Gritt at one of the Bexley summer shows in Danson Park, after the club's return to The Valley in 1992. He was promoting the club and raising funds for the British Brain & Spine Foundation.

23. Guess the Charlton players? Members of the squad at the Sparrows Lane training ground prepare for a 1970s themed Christmas party, an annual event that took place after the club took over the training ground before the return to The Valley in 1992. From left to right, back row: Chris Powell, young Lee Hales, son of former player Derek, Martin Pringle, Carl Tiler, Dean Keily, Shaun Newton and Steve Brown. Front row: John Salako, Keith Jones, John Robinson and Mattie Holmes.

24. Alan Curbishley (*back row, second from left*) taking a break with the Charlton Vets on a tour to Spain in 2001, after two seasons managing Charlton in the Premier League.

25. Charlton Vets, Bob Bolder and Colin Walsh, at the Camp Nou, home of Barcelona, with the Champions League Cup, 2001.

26. Keith Peacock (*far left*), pre-match team talk with John Humphrey, Alan Pardew, Colin Walsh and Peter Hunt.

27. A charity match at Welling United's ground before Charlton returned to The Valley in 1992. Along with Charlton Athletic former players, Charlton Vets often had stars from television guesting in the team; one, Karl Howman, was a Charlton supporter, often mentioning the club during his sit-com *Brush Strokes*, where he played 'Jacko'.

28. Charlton manager Alan Curbishley makes his way out of the Portakabin changing rooms at The Valley for a Charlton Vets match during the mid-'90s, co-founder of the Vets Brian Kinsey is behind.

29. Charlton statistician and author of *Home & Away*, published in 1992, a comprehensive book listing all Charlton's match stats from 1920–92, at a book signing in The Valley shop with former player Colin Powell (*left*) and current players at the time, Simon Webster (*centre*) and Stuart Balmer (*right*).

30. Derek 'Killer' Hales taking some refreshment after a Charlton Vets match against former Chelsea players to raise funds for the British Brain & Spine Foundation in May 1994.

31. Charlton Vets trophies, plus a glass emptied of supplements, in Crossbars during a Charlton League match at The Valley in the 2007/08 season.

32. Celebrating another win after a charity match in 2001, the Charlton Vets team have been unbeaten for over two decades since formation in the late 1980s.

33. Charlton Vets line-up with their Italian opponents, the former players of Palma FC.

34. Former player John Hewie (*left*) with his son Adam and Former Players' Association chairman Bernard Wickham. Hewie, a regular visitor to The Valley after Charlton's return, presenting his Scotland International match shirt to the club.

35. Charlton match mascots with defender Paul Knochesky prior to 2-2 draw against Fulham at The Valley on 27 December 2006. As a member of the Junior Reds scheme, youngsters had the opportunity to run out with the team at both home and away matches.

36. The Charlton Community Trust, formerly the Charlton Community Scheme, started in 1992 under the direction of Jason Morgan, its manager, who later received an MBE for the work carried out in the club's award-winning community programme.

37. Crossbars Lounge in the North Stand where the Former Players' Association have entertained a host of players since 1992. From left to right: forward Tony Booth, defenders Peter Shaw and Phil Warman, forward Keith Tucker, FPA committee members Sue Copus and Mark Baines, and defender Mark Penfold.

38. Charlton Athletic were one of the very first football clubs to install a dedicated safe area for supporters with disabilities, promoted in the match day programme on 25 November 1978, twenty years before the Football Task Force report for improving facilities for disabled supporters.

39. The very popular burger, hot dog and tea bar, situated on the corner of Floyd Road and Harvey Gardens, run by husband and wife team Sean and Lorraine, has been on the same spot since the club returned to The Valley in 1992, an integral part of the Charlton Athletic community on match days.

40. The campaigning *Voice of The Valley* fanzine, devised and edited by Charlton supporter Rick Everitt, produced as a direct result of the club's relocation to Selhurst Park in September 1985.

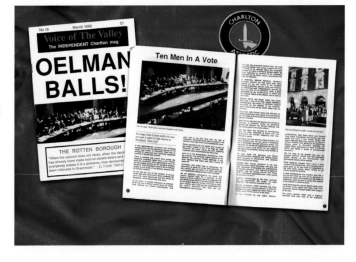

Left: 41. Former Players' Association committee member 'Rookie' in front of the trophy and memorabilia cabinet bequeathed to the association by former player Les Fell in 2012. Situated in the North Stand reception at The Valley, where supporters can view the many former player artefacts on display.

Below: 42. Charlton Vet's team line-up at The Valley for a match organised by the Former Players' Association in 2008. Back row, left to right: Luciano Masiello, Tony Booth, John Robinson, FPA guest player Bob Balder, Alan McLeary and Andy Jones. Front row: Richard Wilson, Mark Stuart, Garry Nelson, John Humphrey and John Bumstead.

10

THE VALLEY HOMECOMING

Just over a week before the first scheduled match at The Valley, Alan Curbishley and Steve Gritt took the players for a training session at the newly-refurbished ground for the first time, to try out the pitch and get used to their new home surroundings. The mayor of Greenwich arrived at the ground three days before the big event to hand over the safety certificate which gave the club permission to open the gates to the public, and play football matches at The Valley once more.

On 5 December 1992, supporters began arriving outside the ground on a bright, sunny Saturday morning, eagerly waiting in anticipation for the ceremonial opening of the Valley's main gates at midday. Many fans turned up dressed in red and white, while others wore fancy dress. The younger supporters, who had never seen the team play at The Valley, arrived with the club colours, badge, or sword painted on their faces. The supporters' group from Bromley hired an open top bus which came rolling down Floyd Road, festooned in red and white banners, balloons and bunting with the tune of 'The red, red robin comes bob, bob, bobbing along', played out loud through an amplifier positioned on the top deck of the bus.

A large group of Charlton supporters, marching on mass, made their pilgrimage back to The Valley after setting out from the town hall at Woolwich, the scene of so much disappointment, despair, jubilation and celebration throughout the six long years that Charlton Athletic had been away, a few fans stopping off at several public houses en route, before arriving at the ground. Stadium manager Roy King was still directing the contractors laying down tarmac, while club chairman Roger Alwen waited for the appointed time to unlock the gates and let the gathering fans inside. With the old East Terrace still out of commission, the ground capacity had been reduced to 8,337, less than the number in attendance for the supposedly last ever match at The Valley. With all the tickets sold for the first game back home, the day turned into a great street carnival, with bands playing and supporters celebrating with family and friends, young and old, along Floyd Road and into Harvey Gardens.

The media were in attendance to interview supporters waiting for the gates to open and the game to begin. Fans recalled the days of Jimmy Seed and Sam Bartram, Stuart Leary and John Hewie, Derek Hales and Mike Flanagan, remembering the greatest games and their favourite players from different eras throughout the club's illustrious history, many with a tear in their eye as they spoke about those great days past and many more still to come. When the clock struck twelve, it was time for Roger Alwen to unlock The Valley gates to let the awaiting supporters in.

As the supporters made their way to the seats in the North, West and South Stands, the atmosphere inside the three-sided ground began to grow as kick-off time fast approached. A host of former Valley heroes paraded out onto the pitch leading up towards 3.00 p.m., including everyone's favourite striker Derek 'Killer' Hales, FA Cup final winner Peter Croker, wartime cup winner Charlie Revell, legendary 'keeper Charlie Wright, old Charlton stalwart 'Sailor' Brown, midfielder Peter Reeves (who had travelled over from Spain where he lived to be there on the day) and one of the oldest former players, Eric Lancelotte, to name just a few, all receiving a great round of applause from both home and away fans. 5 minutes before kick-off, 2,632 red and white balloons, one for each day the club had been away from The Valley, were released from the centre circle to rise up high into the bright blue sky.

Then, out onto the pitch came the players, the Charlton team wearing the traditional colours of red and white, the shirts specially designed for that day, the Portsmouth team wearing all blue. The Charlton line-up for that historic match was Bob Bolder, Darren Pitcher, Simon Webster, Stuart Balmer, Scott Minto, Colin Walsh, John Robinson, Carl Leaburn, Garry Nelson, loanee Paul Power and joint team manager Steve Gritt, the only player in the team still with the club who had played at The Valley before the move. On the bench for Charlton were Kim Grant and Alan Pardew. One of the Portsmouth substitutes, former Charlton striker Paul Walsh, had also played at The Valley during the early 1980s.

When referee Alan Gunn blew the whistle to start the match, all those years of heartache and despair seemed to lift away. Charlton Athletic were home where they belonged, back at The Valley in the Borough of Greenwich, London SE7. Then, at 3.07 p.m., Charlton's Colin Walsh ran onto a pass from Darren Pitcher and struck the ball low, to the right of Portsmouth 'keeper Alan Knight, to score in the covere end goal, sending all Charlton fans jumping up from their seats in joyful celebration. On such an emotional and memorable day, Portsmouth were never going to get back into the game and, at the final whistle, Charlton had won the first game back at The Valley 1-0.

After the homecoming party was over, it was then back to reality. Although Charlton had moved into second place during the early part of the season, by December, the team had dropped to eleventh. The victory over Portsmouth then took them two places higher, up into ninth. The return to The Valley had cost the football club over £4 million, financed through directors' loans, the VIP fund, a Football Trust grant, a loan from the construction company Kier and sale of players.

Charlton drew the following six matches before recording their next victory in a 2-0 win away to Bristol Rovers. Charlton's inconsistent form continued throughout the rest of the season, resulting in a mid-table finish. At the end of the financial year, the club made a loss of over £600,000 and although attendances at the end of the season only averaged 7,029, this figure included the gates at Upton Park, which were lower than those at The Valley. During the season, the first VIP member had been voted onto the board. Supporters' Club chairman Steve Clarke won the most votes, finishing well ahead of the two other candidates, Jill Humphreys and former director Bill Jenner.

The VIP board member would not only be representing the investors, but all Charlton supporters, the first opportunity for the fans to have a representative voice in the boardroom. The club's move back to The Valley, and presence within the borough, had given the club opportunities to work in partnership with the council on several educational and community led projects, which also involved the Charlton Athletic Supporters' Club and Charlton Athletic Community Programme. In 1992, the Charlton Athletic Race Equality Partnership was founded to promote equality within the community, and to address issues surrounding the problem of racism at local and national level.

Although the CARE programme ran through the whole year, the football club and Supporters' Club celebrated Red, White and Black Day annually, holding a festival of events and activities to promote the diversity of the local community, and to encourage a much wider multicultural club fan base at The Valley.

EXPANSION AND INTO EUROPE

For the club to survive and prosper at The Valley, the directors were well aware that the capacity of the ground needed to be increased. With the football club and Supporters' Club working together to build up a larger club fan base, in August the club announced the approval of plans to build a 6,000 seated, covered stand on the old East Terrace, at a projected cost of £2 million, funded through the Football Trust. The work on the new East Stand was to start immediately with a completion date set for 2 April 1994.

Charlton made an excellent start to the 1993/94 season, only losing one League match in the first fourteen. Although knocked out of the League Cup by former landlords Crystal Palace, Charlton went through to the final stages of the Anglo-Italian Cup, first beating Millwall, and then Crystal Palace, to set up the club's first competitive venture into European competition.

The Anglo-Italian Cup had been brought into the English domestic game in 1970 for four seasons before it was disbanded, due to trouble between English and Italian fans. The tournament returned in 1976 as a semi-professional competition before going out of favour in 1986. It was then brought back for the 1992/93 season to replace the Full Members Cup. By making it through to the latter stages, Charlton would compete against four Second Division Italian teams, playing two home and two away, in a group which included three other English Second Division teams. Within the format of the competition, the English clubs would not play each other and neither would the Italians, the winners of the group going through to the finals of the competition.

First up in the series of ties were Serie B side Brescia. The Charlton team flew out to northern Italy for a midweek match on 12 October 1993 at the 16,000-capacity Stadio Mario Rigamonti, situated at the foot of the Italian Alps. The match attendance of only 1,174 spectators included just over 100 Charlton supporters who travelled the long distance to the match by coach. In an extremely antagonistic match, the Italians took the lead in the 19th minute through an own goal credited to Charlton's new signing defender Phil Chapple. Unable to get back into the game, Charlton conceded a second, in the very last minute of the game, to lose their first European Cup match 2-0.

Although an entertaining excursion during the season, for the small number of English club supporters journeying out to Italy to watch their team play, the Anglo-Italian Cup was considered an inconvenient interruption to the domestic League by the majority of both English and Italian clubs taking part. The competition involved a lot of travelling overseas and extra midweek games during an already busy League season.

Despite losing the first in the series of Anglo-Italian Cup matches, Charlton had the opportunity to progress into the next round through points accumulated over the next three ties. Just over three weeks later, a small band of Charlton supporters flew out to an industrial coastal port in north-east Italy for a match against Ancona, a club founded in 1905, the same year as Charlton Athletic.

Although not the most attractive of Italian towns, the Charlton supporters took in the local sites with a few drinks along the way while waiting for the evening kick-off, before they were transported on buses to the Stadio del Conero, which had been built on the outskirts of town in 1992. With a capacity of 26,000, the large, modern, oval-shaped open-air stadium was sparsely populated with 1,261 fans when both teams ran out onto the pitch on a cold November night, many of the Charlton and Ancona supporters swapping club scarves before the match began. Charlton were facing another Italian team not short of hard tacklers, resulting in defender Steve Brown being substituted just before half-time after sustaining a badly gashed knee from a high tackle by an Ancona player.

Three minutes into the second half, Ancona forward Eupremio Carruezzo scored what would be his only goal of the season, to put the home team into a 1-0 lead. Charlton's own low-scoring forward, Carl Leaburn, then levelled the tie with a well taken goal in the 60th minute and, at the final whistle, the match finished 1-1. On their return home, the Charlton supporters had an opportunity to mingle with the players, management and staff, all travelling together on the same flight back to Gatwick, where several of the Charlton squad gave supporters their boxed Italian panettone cakes, presented to them by the Ancona officials after the game.

The next match took place a week later on 16 November 1993, Charlton going 3-0 down to Ascoli at The Valley with an attendance of 3,646. The Italians' second goal was scored by future German International forward Oliver Bierhoff. Soon after the game, it was reported that the high-scoring, Serie B striker was interested in playing his football in England. Speculation and rumour grew among Charlton supporters that he was considering a move to Charlton, his father supposedly discussing a transfer. Whatever the truth was surrounding a possible move to England, Bierhoff would later join up with Italian side Udinese.

With just one point to show, out of three of the four Anglo-Italian group games, Charlton went into the last match knowing they could not go through to the final rounds. This was reflected in a poor attendance of just 1,452 at The Valley, four days before Christmas, for the match against Pisa. In another damaging affair, Charlton's Mark Robson was sent off after a clash with Pisa defender Gianni Flamigni. Roberto Muzzi scored a hat-trick for the Italians and Charlton lost the match 3-0. With Charlton's foray into Europe over, having only scored one goal in all four matches apart from a Phil Chappell own goal, forward Carl Leaburn entered the club's history books by becoming the first and only player to date to score for Charlton in European competition.

Carl Leaburn finished the season as top scorer with sixteen goals in fifty-two League and Cup matches, including a goal scored in the 3-1 FA Cup sixth-round defeat by Manchester United at Old Trafford, Charlton's first FA Cup quarter-final since the club had won the Cup in 1947. The attendance of 44,347 included 10,500 travelling Charlton supporters, which at the time was more than the capacity of The Valley.

Towards the end of the season, The Valley capacity increased to over 12,000 when the new East Stand was opened on 2 April 1994 for a match against Southend United. Charlton won 4-3 with the winning goal scored by Alan Pardew in the 89th minute. The club had received around £250,000 from the FA Cup tie at Old Trafford, however the funds were used to invest in the club rather than in the squad, which was a disappointment to the management duo, who were hoping to bring in a couple of new players to give the team a boost and improve the club's chances of staying in the play-off places, if not going for automatic promotion. Losing ten of the final fourteen matches, Charlton dropped out of the play-offs and down into eleventh place, an unsatisfactory end to what could have been a very successful campaign.

Towards the end of the season, the football club became a public Ltd company, with an operating turnover of almost £3 million. The club made a small profit of £112,766, resulting from the sale of Scott Minto to Chelsea for £875,000. The loss of the home-produced, talented young full-back proved to Charlton supporters that the board could not fulfil the promise that Charlton would not become a selling club, when players needed to be sold to keep the club financially stable.

SUPPORT FAR AND WIDE

Since Charlton's return to The Valley, the Supporters' Club had been active in establishing a network of branches throughout Kent in Medway, Maidstone, Canterbury, the Weald of Kent, Gravesend and even a branch across the county border in East Sussex to increase supporter membership, and fill the extra seats at ground. The Supporters' Club had also been busy running travel to away games by train and coach, including the two trips out to Italy for the Anglo-Italian Cup. The football club provided the Supporters' Club with a portable cabin at The Valley for a nominal installation fee, used as a base to run the travel service, and as a point of contact for its membership and for all Charlton fans.

One of the annual events organised by the Supporters' Club was the Player of the Year presentation, first won by defender Paul Went in 1971. For several years, the presentation had been held at the Meridian Sports and Social Club, before the venue changed to the Waterfront Sports Complex at Woolwich, a much bigger venue to accommodate an expected increase in attendees. A year after the club's return, the Supporters' Club also held a celebratory 'Back to The Valley' dinner, organised by supporter Peter Varney, charity director of the British Brain & Spine Foundation, an event which would go on to be celebrated every year during December, as close as possible to the date of Charlton's return.

From humble beginnings, the Charlton Athletic Supporters' Club had now become an integral part of the football club's ongoing development within the community, now working closely with the club and with Greenwich Council. With developments at The Valley continuing throughout the close season, which included improvements made to the West Stand by replacing the temporary seats with permanent seating, The Valley capacity would rise to around 15,000, which included 3,000 seats for away fans accommodated in the South Stand.

To assist the club in filling The Valley, Target 10,000 was launched by the Supporters' Club in partnership with the football club, an initiative aimed at attracting more people to Charlton home matches through a series of innovative marketing strategies. Charlton led the way over other clubs by offering special ticket deals and price reductions for children, promoted throughout the local media, leaflets distributed throughout the club's fan base and in the club programme.

In Charlton's first game of the 1994/95 season, a 5-2 defeat away to Oldham, Charlton striker David Whyte scored this first of nineteen League goals for his new club. Charlton had taken Greenwich born David Whyte on short-term loan from Crystal Palace in 1992, while Charlton were playing at Upton Park. After failing to get a regular place in the Crystal Palace team, Whyte made the move permanent, in exchange for highly-rated Charlton defender Darren Pitcher. Picther joined Palace after their promotion to the Premier League and Charlton receiving a transfer fee of £700,000, plus Whyte and former player Paul Mortimer, who moved back to Charlton as part of the deal.

Although both Curbishley and Gritt had been impressed with David Whyte during his loan spell with the club, his laid-back style, attitude and work effort would be an ongoing cause for concern for the managers, throughout his time with the club. Charlton supporters, however, gave Whyte a warm welcome to the club, believing they had got one over on their rivals Palace by exchanging a prolific striker for a defender, plus a fee and classy midfielder Paul Mortimer.

Although the board had indicated Curbishley and Gritt would be allocated £400,000 from the Darren Pitcher deal to strengthen the squad, after a majority of the transfer fee had been allocated to fund the club's infrastructure there was far less than expected left to spend in the transfer market. Even though the cash-strapped management team were restricted by the funds available to sign the players they wanted, they brought in two 'keepers, American Mike Ammann and Australian Andy Petterson, as backups for first-team 'keeper Mike Salmon. They also purchased a young striker from Edgware Town, Scott McGleish, and midfielder Keith Jones from Southend United, which proved to be one of their best buys. The club also had several prospective young players breaking into the squad from the youth team, including Lee Bowyer, Dean Chandler, Paul Sturgess, Jamie Stuart and Richard Rufus.

The Supporters' Club Target 10,000 scheme was beginning to show results. The average League attendance had risen to an impressive 10,216. Results on the pitch, however, were less than impressive, with the team only winning sixteen of the forty-six League matches throughout the season. There were, however, some fine performances by individual players. David Whyte finished top scorer with twenty-one League and Cup goals, and defender Richard Rufus was voted player of the year in his debut season. However, two young youth team prospects, Lee Bowyer and Dean Chandler, caused some controversy for the club when they were both suspended by the FA after failing a drugs test. The media had a field day, using the club nickname 'Addicks' in their headlines as a reference to drug taking. Both players were found to have been dabbling in recreational drug use and, after a period of rehabilitation, the suspension lifted by the last game of the season. Charlton finished the season in fifteenth place, the lowest position in the table since Curbishley and Gritt had been appointed as joint managers, but both had achieved much more than many had expected, especially operating on such a small budget. Nevertheless, after Richard Murray became chairman of the PLC, with Roger Alwen stepping down to take up a director's position, Murray decided the dual management role was not working and ended the partnership.

A PARTING OF THE WAYS

The loser in the management breakup was Steve Gritt, his dismissal coming as a great surprise to all Charlton fans, as well as his managerial partner Alan Curbishley. More than just a supporter's favourite player, Gritt was considered as Mr Charlton, a well respected and loyal player who had represented the club in every position on the field and, after a short period playing for Walsall, had returned to Charlton to become a coach and then joint manager. Unaware of the chairman's decision to let Gritt go, Curbishley was informed at a meeting with Murray before he was offered the job of managing Charlton on his own, the chairman assuring him that Gritt would be well looked after financially.

Steve Gritt later took on the manager's role with Brighton and Hove Albion, another club groundsharing after moving out of the Goldstone Ground which had been sold to pay off debts. Struggling at the foot of Third Division and playing home fixtures at Gillingham's Priestfield Stadium, the job of managing Brighton and Hove Albion seemed an almost impossible task to take on, even for someone with the experience of Steve Gritt, who had encountered similar situations during his time as player, and then manager, at Charlton. Gritt did a fantastic job at Brighton by turning the team's form around, successfully avoiding relegation to the Conference on the final day of the season before Gritt guided Brighton away from non-League football, Alan Curbishley had taken Charlton up into the play-off places at the end of his first year as manager.

At the start of the 1995/96 season, the prospects of the club reaching such a lofty position would have seemed extremely unlikely. Curbishley had received no significant sum of money to strengthen the squad and nearly lost the services of defender Richard Rufus when substantial offers came in for him, with Curbishley needing to persuade the board not to sell the team's prize asset. In preparation for the season ahead, Curbishley brought in Les Reed as his new first-team coach, to work with the squad of players. Relatively unknown outside the circles of football, Les Reed was a well-respected coach with the FA who Curbishley knew well, since their first meeting when Reed was an FA regional coach, and Curbishley was a young player at West Ham.

Moving several players on for nominal fees, including Alan Pardew, Mickey Bennett and Scott McGleish, the only player to come in at the start of the season was former Charlton defender John Humphrey, joined later in the season by another former Charlton player, forward Paul Williams. Losing the first game of the season 1-0 away to West Bromwich Albion, Charlton then went on a nine-match unbeaten run. In a 5-1 away win at Ipswich on 23 September, striker Carl Leaburn scored his first ever senior hat-trick, the third goal coming from the penalty spot.

Although there had been some objections among the Charlton supporters over the way the club had dealt with the managerial changes, by the end of September Charlton were fourth in the First Division, and the fans now recognised that the club's long-term prospects were now looking exceptionally promising under Curbishley.

Progressing through to the a third-round replay of the Coca-Cola Cup, losing 2-1 in extra time at home to Wolverhampton Wanderers and then reaching the fifth round of the FA Cup where they were narrowly beaten by Liverpool 2-1, after a relatively successful Cup campaign, Charlton were sitting comfortably third in the division. There was now a realistic chance of Charlton winning automatic promotion, with fifteen matches of the season still to go and a game in hand over second-placed Sunderland, and two in hand over top of the table Derby County. By the end of the season, Charlton had accumulated nineteen points from those final matches to finish with a total of seventy-nine. Although not enough points to win automatic promotion, it was enough to ensure a sixth place finish in the play-offs, where a win over Crystal Palace in the two-leg semi-final would take Charlton through to a Wembley play-off final.

Charlton played the first leg at home, which attracted a gate of 14,618, the largest at The Valley for over twelve years. Going into the lead through a Shaun Newton goal after just 55 seconds, Charlton held out for an hour before in-form Crystal Palace scored the equaliser and then a second goal with just under 10 minutes of the game remaining, to win the first leg 2-1. Charlton travelled to Selhurst Park three days later, needing to win by two clear goals to take them through to the final. Within only 4 minutes played, Charlton conceded a goal to give Crystal Palace an overall lead of 3-1, and Palace went through to the Wembley play-off final. Although it was a disappointing end to an excellent season, Charlton supporters later had the satisfaction of playing their rivals the following season, after Palace were beaten by Leicester City 2-1 in the First Division play-off final. Steve Claridge scored Leicester's winner from a ball which flew off his shin from 20 yards out and into the back of the Palace net, with just under a minute of extra time remaining.

With an operating turnover of over £3.6 million, Charlton made a record loss of just over £1 million at the end of the financial year. Huge financial burdens were now being placed on football clubs attempting to operate within the modern-day world of football, where clubs in the Premier League received a majority of the revenue generated through television rights deals, lower-League clubs like Charlton relied on balancing their books through the sale of their best up-and-coming young players. It came as no surprise to Charlton supporters that, during the close season, Lee Boyer was sold to Leeds United for £2.8 million. While a majority of the transfer fee was set aside for the development of The Valley West Stand, Alan Curbishley was allocated £400,000 to use in the transfer market, Curbishley signing midfielder Brendan O'Connell from Barnsley and bringing back former Charlton defender Anthony Barness from Chelsea.

To help Charlton's cash flow, director David Hughes, also a director for the London Broncos, brokered a deal to bring the rugby League side from West London to groundshare at The Valley, for which Charlton received a small rental fee of around £4,000. Since the formation as Fulham Rugby League Football Club in 1980, the London Broncos team had played home fixtures at Craven Cottage, before the move to The Valley, the nomads of London shared several other sports grounds. With the newly-formed Super Rugby League season running through most of the summer months, the rugby club and football club fixtures only overlapped at the start and end of the football season. Although it was not anticipated that the Rugby League club's presence at The Valley would be overly intrusive on the football operations, former Charlton winger and Valley groundsman Colin Powell had serious concerns over how the pitch would hold up throughout the calendar year.

Charlton assisted the London Broncos in promoting the game of Rugby League to the football club's supporters, offering free entry to London Bronco matches for all Charlton season ticket holders. The London Broncos carried out a trial period, playing at The Valley before the permanent move. However, although Super League Rugby at The Valley was something of a novelty at first, the Rugby League was never popular with South East London sports fans, who preferred union to League. With one of the founder members of Rugby Union, Blackheath, in the near vicinity, the London Broncos had a hard time enticing the local public to The Valley for Rugby League matches, even though games could often be highly entertaining. After playing a season at The Valley, the London Broncos were off again and relocated to the Stoop, home of Rugby Union's Harlequins, before returning to The Valley two years later for another season.

During the summer, Colin Walsh, the scorer of Charlton's historic goal on the return to The Valley, hung up his boots after an ongoing knee injury forced him to retire. The club organised a testimonial for the long-serving winger against Tottenham Hotspur, Alan Curbishley using the game as a pre-season friendly. The game attracted a gate of 10,000, the majority Charlton fans coming along in support of the club legend. One of the players in the Charlton squad on the day, Irish midfielder Mark Kinsella, who came in on trial during the close season from Colchester, would reach legendary status after making the move to Charlton permanent. Kinsella was recommended to manager Alan Curbishley by Keith Peacock and even though Curbishley was interested in signing him up, the talented midfielder was sent back to Colchester before the start of the 1996/97 the season as the club had run out of transfer funds.

The beginning of Curbishley's second year in charge did not start well, with Charlton losing three away and drawing one at home in the first four fixtures. Charlton's results, however, became the last thing on Curbishley's mind when first-team coach Les Reed collapsed at the training ground and was rushed to hospital after suffering a burst blood vessel in the brain, a life-threatening condition. Once Reed was out of danger, Curbishley turned his attentions back to football.

Although Charlton were second from bottom of the table with just one point, Curbishley had been linked to the vacant manager's job at Queens Park Rangers, the West London club having dropped out of the Premier League the previous season and then parted company with manager Ray Wilkins. While no official approach to Charlton was ever made, speculation continued surrounding Curbishley and the vacant managerial position until Queens Park Rangers appointed Stewart Huston.

With Les Reed making steady progress on the road to a full recovery, Alan Curbishley was busy in the transfer market, attempting to bring midfielder Kinsella to Charlton, beating Kent club Gillingham for his signature in September. Even though the club had no money to sign Kinsella during the close season, the financially resourceful chairman managed to put together a financial package for Colchester United worth around £150,000 to bring the influential midfielder to the club.

As results improved and Charlton gradually moved up from the bottom of the table, the club received some welcome funds, which came through two domestic cup competitions. After beating Burnley home and away in the Coca-Cola Cup, Charlton drew Liverpool in the third round at home on 13 November 1996, where an attendance of 14,796 brought in record receipts of £160,635. Drawing the tie 1-1 with the fourth-placed Premier League side, Charlton earned a reply at Anfield but lost the tie 4-1 on aggregate. In the FA Cup third round, Charlton were drawn at home against Newcastle United on 5 January 1997, the match covered by BBC Radio 5 and shown live on Sky satellite television broadcasting. Going 1-0 down through a goal from former Valley favourite Robert Lee, Mark Kinsella scored the equaliser with just over 10 minutes of the tie remaining and the game finished 1-1. Another big Valley attendance brought in a new club record of £163,864 in gate receipts. Before the replay at St James' Park, Newcastle manager Kevin Keegan lost his job and was replaced by Kenny Dalglish.

The match was played in extremely poor weather conditions, with the ground thick with fog leading up to the evening kick-off. Charlton were more than a match for a Newcastle United team that would finish the season second in the Premier League. Although going 1-0 down in the first half, Charlton midfielder Mark Robson scored the equaliser with a fantastically-taken free-kick, the Cup tie replay going into extra time. Newcastle went on to win the tie 2-1 through an Alan Shearer free-kick, the first time the England striker had ever scored against Charlton. Although Shearer's winning goal was a superb strike and received the television pundits' plaudits for the match-winning free-kick, there was no doubt Robson's was by far the best.

11

FOOTBALL BECOMES BIG BUSINESS

At the beginning 1997, the Charlton directors took the decision to list the football club on the Alternate Investment Market to raise up to £5 million, a majority of the funds going towards financing the ground developments and completion of the West Stand. The AIM was a sub-market of the London Stock Exchange, which gave smaller companies the opportunity to float shares with a much more flexible regulatory system than with the main market. For the purposes of the floatation The Valley was valued at £10,290,000.

Valley stadium manager Roy King, who had risen up through the ranks from Charlton Athletic Supporters' Club protestor to become part of the football club establishment, was appointed onto the board of directors, along with long-time fan, season ticket holder and media and television executive Michael Grade. Charlton supporter Peter Varney, who had joined the club in October as commercial director, was promoted to the position of managing director, one of the most important non-playing signings the club made in the modern era of football. With an ever-increasing number of members joining the board, the directors were now beginning to outnumber Charlton's first-team playing squad.

With club turnover increasing to over £4 million, the club's progress and development in both the playing side and redevelopment of The Valley had become evermore reliant on the directors and supporter investments in the club. The floatation raised net proceeds of £5.5 million and, by March, the share certificates were issued and then posted out to Charlton Athletic shareholders.

A week before the season came to a close, the club commemorated the fiftieth anniversary of Charlton Athletic winning the FA Cup by holding a celebration dinner and dance at the Café Royal in London on 27 April 1997. Supporters and former players mingled together at a venue where, fifty years before, the 1947 FA Cup winners held their own celebrations the day after the club's historic 1-0 victory over Burnley at Wembley. By the end of the 1996/97 season, Charlton finished fifteenth in the division, thirteen points off a play-off place.

FOOTBALL HERO MAKES HISTORY

With funds available to spend in the transfer market, Alan Curbishley had one player in mind whom he immediately wanted to bring into the club before the start of 1997/98 season. Grimsby Town striker Clive Mendonca had impressed the Charlton manager the previous year, after he scored two goals for his club in a 3-1 win at The Valley and in the return fixture at Blundell Park, Mendonca scored from the penalty spot in a 2-0 victory over Charlton. Curbishley persuaded chairman Richard Murray to part with the £700,000 asking price, and Clive Mendonca became Charlton's most expensive signing.

Towards the end of the previous season, Mark Bright came in on a free transfer from Swiss club Sion. The forward would go on to form a good partnership up front with new signing Mendonca. Midfielder Mattie Holmes joined during the close season, moving from Blackburn for £250,000, and non-League 'keeper Sasa Ilic joined up with the club for training, playing for expenses in the hope of impressing the manager and earn himself a contract. Welsh international full-back Mark Bowen was then signed up on a free transfer after playing in Japan, shortly after the start of the season. Several players moving on in the close season were Brendan O'Connell, Mark Robson and David Whyte. Curbishley now had a squad of players who would be more than capable of successfully competing against the best clubs in the First Division, and perhaps even challenging for promotion.

No one outside of the club, however, believed Charlton Athletic were credible candidates to win a place in the Premier League, especially after their less than impressive performances the season before. Although losing 2-1 away at Middlesbrough on the opening day of the season, Charlton beat Oxford United 3-2 at The Valley a week later. Defender Paul Konchesky made his debut in the match aged just sixteen, setting a Charlton record by becoming the youngest player to represent the club at senior level. In the following match against Bury away, Charlton fielded another sixteen year old, only slightly older than Knochesky. Midfielder Scott Parker was already well known by the burger eaters throughout the nation after appearing in a television advert for McDonald's. The young Parker was seen preferring to practice his football skills in the garden rather than go with his family to get the take away.

The team selections made by Curbishley, which combined youth and experience, began to produce results. The club's record signing, Mendonca, showed his class by scoring nine goals in his first fifteen games before he picked up an injury which kept him out for the side for three games. Although Charlton were progressing well in the League, one of the club's talented young players, Jamie Stuart, failed a club drug test and was found to have been taking recreational drugs. Although placed on the club's support programme, he later failed an FA random drug test and the club decided they had no option but to release him from his contract.

Clive Mendonca returned from injury for a live televised match against Swindon Town on 27 November 1997, where the viewing public had the opportunity to see Charlton's prolific striker score two goals in a comprehensive 3-0 win. The result took Charlton up to fifth in the table and for all those watching the match live, Charlton looked like credible promotion contenders. After then losing 3-0 away to Stockport Town, non-League 'keeper Sasa Ilic was given his chance in the side after impressing reserve team coach Keith Peacock with his displays on the training ground. Charlton beat their next opponents, Stoke City, 2-1 away and Ilic continued in goal for the rest of the season.

Alan Curbishley was invited to take charge of a Football League Under-21 side for a match at The Valley, against the Italian Serie B Under-21 team. Included in

Curbishley's squad of talented young players was right-back Danny Mills, who came through the Norwich City youth system but was unable to establish himself in the first team. Mills told Curbishley he would like an opportunity to join Charlton and, after impressing the manager during the Under-21 match, the full-back signed for Charlton in a deal worth around £350,000.

Dependent on the away team supporters taking up their seat allocation in the South Stand, matches at The Valley were close to becoming sell-outs. The highest attendance of the season, 15,815, came against the First Division leaders Nottingham Forest in March, the table toppers convincingly beaten 4-2. Charlton won the following six matches without conceding a goal and were up in fourth place going into the last match of the season away to Birmingham City.

In contention for automatic promotion, the 0-0 draw at St Andrews was 'keeper Sasa Ilic's seventh clean sheet in a row, which equalled a seventy-four-year-old club record set by Sam Bartram. Charlton missed out on automatic promotion but finished in a play-off place, with Nottingham Forest and Middlesbrough going straight up. Charlton now faced Ipswich Town in a two-leg semi-final, the first leg played at Portman Road was shown live on Sky.

During the highly-charged, competitive match, which Charlton won 1-0 through an Ipswich deflected own goal, the referee gave out three yellow cards to Charlton players and five yellow cards to players from Ipswich, Danny Mills also receiving two yellows which resulted in his sending off. At the final whistle the arguments continued and then spilled over in the tunnel as both teams headed for dressing rooms. Later, in the players' lounge, a tussle between Charlton loanee midfielder Neil Heaney and Argentinean Mauricio Taricco resulted in a broken nose for the volatile Ipswich Town defender.

In the return leg, Shaun Newton scored a spectacular goal in the 36th minute and Ipswich Town's chances of reaching the play-off final had gone. Charlton held out until the final whistle to win the play-off semi-final 2-0 on aggregate and make it through to the First Division play-off final at Wembley.

The board released a press statement informing the Charlton supporters that the West Stand would be completed in readiness for the forthcoming season and a new three-year shirt sponsorship deal had been secured with Mesh Computers worth £1 million. The new Charlton sponsored shirts would be worn at the Wembley final.

PROMOTION PROSPECTS

After Charlton's victory over Ipswich in the play-off semi-final, the streets around The Valley became crowded with supporters in the week leading up to the Wembley final, fans queuing for tickets, the first allocation of 24,000 selling out in one day, and packed into the club shop to buy the officially branded play-off souvenirs and replica match shirts. Unlicensed retailers also did a good trade outside the ground selling flags, scarves, hats, T-shirts and badges.

On the day of the final, which took place on Bank Holiday Monday 25 May 1998, the Charlton Athletic supporters numbered 35,000 in the total attendance of 77,739, a record for a play-off final at Wembley. Charlton supporters living in far-off, distant lands had flown in from all parts of the globe to be there on the day. Other fans, who had already booked early summer holidays before they knew Charlton would be appearing at Wembley, re-arranged flights to either get back early or leave later than planned. Some cancelled their holidays altogether to ensure they were there on the day. Charlton supporters made their way to the final by car, train, coach, bus and even a stretch limousine. Those fans who were unable to attend, either living too far away or unable to obtain a ticket, were able to watch the match broadcast live on Sky, which included Dartford-born sports presenter and Charlton fan, Steve Ryder, who had a monitor set up off camera so he could watch the game while he was broadcasting a live sports programme for the BBC.

The Sunderland supporters in attendance were in a jubilant mood, as their club were regarded as the favourites to win the final and join the elite of the Premier League, taking a share of the riches promotion would bring (estimated to be worth around £10 million). When both teams came out onto the pitch, Charlton wearing their red and white kit, Sunderland in a change of old gold and dark blue, they were met by a great roar coming from both sets of fans, Sunderland supporters seated to the east of the old stadium and Charlton supporters to the west. Twenty-four minutes into the game, however, it was the Charlton fans that were making all the noise, up on their feet and cheering, after Sunderland-born striker Clive Mendonca scored the first goal.

Charlton held onto the slender lead going into the second half before Niall Quinn scored the equaliser. Sunderland then went 2-1 up 8 minutes later, through a goal from on-form striker Kevin Phillips that broke Brian Clough's post-war goalscoring record. Mendonca then scored his second of the day to make it all level at 2-2. In an enthralling encounter which went from one end of the pitch to the other, Niall Quinn scored his second goal of the final to put Sunderland back into the lead with 17 minutes remaining. In the 85th minute, defender Richard Rufus came up for a Charlton corner and, rising up high above the Sunderland defence as the ball was crossed into the area, headed past the out-rushing 'keeper, Perez, and into the empty net, to score his first ever senior goal for the club, to make it 3-3 and take the final into extra time.

In the first period of play, a through ball knocked in towards the Charlton area was taken on by Nicky Summerbee, who shot low, past Saca Ilic, to make it 4-3 to Sunderland. Three minutes before the break, Sunderland lost possession in their own half through a crunching Steve Brown challenge, the ball falling to the feet of midfielder Mark Kinsella who passed it out to Steve Jones on the wing. Taking the ball up and into the Sunderland penalty area, Jones crossed the ball in towards the waiting Mendonca and, with his back towards goal, the striker flicked the ball up with his right foot, turned, and as the ball dropped, volleyed it past the Sunderland 'keeper and into the back of the net, sending 35,000 Charlton supporters into wild celebrations. Mendonca's third goal, the first ever hat-trick scored in a play-off final, made it 4-4 with 17 minutes of extra time remaining. With no more goals scored before the referee blew his whistle to end the game, the play-off final drama continued into a penalty shoot-out to decide which club would be promoted to the Premier League.

The penalties were taken in the goal at the Sunderland end of the stadium, which could well have put more pressure on the Charlton penalty takers. First-up Clive

Mendonca showed no fear and he confidently put the ball away. From then on, both sides scored their five allocated penalties to take it forward into a sudden death shoot-out. With Charlton leading 7-6, it was down to full-back Michael Gray to score his penalty to draw level.

As Gray took a long run up, Charlton manager Alan Curbishley was sat on the bench, with his head in his hands, unable to look. Striking the ball low, to the right of the Charlton goal, 'keeper Sasa Ilic dived to his left to stop the ball dead. Then, picking the ball up, he ran towards the middle of the pitch where his teammates fell upon him as he sank down onto the Wembley turf, the substitutes and members of the squad running over from the touchline to dive on top, making a pyramid of bodies with the 'keeper underneath. Charlton Athletic football club had won promotion to the Premier League in the most dramatic game ever played at Wembley Stadium.

The players taking part on the day were all worthy of a place in the history of Charlton Athletic, the starting line included Sasa Ilic, Danny Mills, Richard Rufus, Eddie Youds, Mark Bowen, Keith Jones, Mark Kinsella, Shaun Newton, Neal Heaney, Mark Bright and Clive Mendonca. All three substitutes, Steve Jones, John Robinson and Steve Brown, came on to play their part in the final. The order of Charlton penalty takers were, Clive Mendonca, Steve Brown, Keith Jones, Mark Kinsella, Mark Bowen, John Robinson and Shaun Newton, Charlton heroes all.

After the Sunderland team collected their runners-up medals, Charlton captain Mark Kinsella led his squad of players up the thirty-nine steps to the Royal Box, where they were presented with winners' medals and the 1998 First Division play-off winners' trophy. The following evening, the players, management team and club staff travelled aboard an open-top bus from The Valley to the town hall at Woolwich for a celebratory civic reception. It was estimated that almost as many Charlton supporters lined the route as there were at the Wembley final. As the bus passed through the streets of Charlton and Woolwich, the players on the top deck waved to the fans below, and took it in turns to hold up the Cup in triumph while the euphoric fans below, many dressed in red and white and waving Charlton flags and scarves, cheered them on their way. The 1998 First Division play-off final between Charlton Athletic and Sunderland was later voted as one of the greatest Wembley matches ever played, recording the highest number of goals ever scored during a single match including penalties, which totalled twenty-one in all.

The challenge of winning promotion came at great financial cost to the club, even though attendances at The Valley had increased in Charlton's promotion-winning season, to an average of 13,275, the club made a record trading loss for the year of just over £2 million. Before the play-off final, Alan Curbishley's right hand man, Les Reed, made the decision to return to the FA and manage the development of Premier League and Football League club academies, the announcement of his departure held back until after the final was played.

12

A PREMIER EXCURSION

For the new season in the Premier League, Alan Curbishley brought in Mervin Day, who the Charlton manager knew well from their days together at West Ham, to take over as team coach, with Keith Peacock moving up from first-team coach to assistant manager.

Although the club had made a substantial financial loss during the previous season, the expected income from promotion into the Premier League would be allocated for use on player purchases and investment in the ongoing development of The Valley, with a reserve fund deposited in the club's bank account for use in emergencies.

Managers of clubs promoted through the play-offs had less time to deal in the transfer market than those promoted automatically, who had at least two weeks head start. After a well-deserved short break, Curbishley's first job was to find some new players to strengthen the squad to be ready to compete in the Premier League. Curbishley signed three experienced players ready for pre-season training. Defender Chris Powell came from Derby for £825,000, midfielder Neil Redfearn from relegated Barnsley for just over £1 million and forward Andy Hunt from West Bromwich Albion on a free contract.

With their club favourites for relegation, Charlton supporters had no preconceptions that competing in the top division would be anything less than extremely challenging. At the very least, they were expecting an eventful and highly entertaining campaign in the Premier League with the top clubs in the English game coming to The Valley. The supporters were also offered the opportunity of attending all of Charlton's away matches in the Premier League by purchasing an away season ticket. Many took the offer up, believing that this may well be Charlton's only season playing in the top division.

The Supporters' Club were also busy during the close season organising the away travel service to transport fans by train and coach to all of Charlton's away fixtures during the 1998/99 Premier League season, many supporters travelling up to the St James' Park for the opening match against Newcastle United on 15 August 1998. Going down to ten men against Newcastle after Richard Rufus was sent off, which the club later unsuccessfully appealed, Charlton came away with a credible 0-0 draw. In Charlton's first Premier League match at The Valley, visitors Southampton attracted a near maximum-capacity attendance of 16,488, which would have been more if the top tier of the new West Stand was not awaiting completion, and the away end had been completely full.

A goal each from John Robinson and Neil Redfearn gave Charlton a 2-0 lead, before Saints 'keeper Paul Jones brought down Clive Mendonca in the penalty area, resulting in the Southampton players being sent off. Mendonca scored from the penalty spot and then went on to score two more to record his first hat-trick in the Premier League, the 5-0 win taking Charlton to the top of the table.

For the third match in a row, there was another sending off when Charlton went to Highbury to play Arsenal, Emmanuel Petit getting his marching orders an hour into the game after receiving a second yellow card. Charlton kept another clean sheet in the 0-0 draw. Although brought back down to earth after losing 4-1 away to eventual Premier League champions Manchester United, Charlton continued to perform well up until the away match against Chelsea at Stanford Bridge on 17 October 1998. Going 1-0 down after Sasa Ilic conceded a penalty in the 18th minute, Charlton then lost their 'keeper after he was knocked unconscious in a nasty collision, and was carried from the pitch just before the end of the first half.

While Saca Ilic received treatment in the dressing room, before being taken by ambulance to Chelsea Hospital for a precautionary brain scan, his teammates battled away in an attempt to get a deserved equaliser, which came in the second half through a goal from defender Eddie Youds. With the match coming to a close, Charlton were looking comfortable in coming away with a point before midfielder Gus Poyet scored with just 2 minutes of the match remaining, the game finishing 2-1 to Chelsea. Dropping down into a more realistic mid-table position, Charlton's performances proved the team were capable of holding their own against the elite of the Premier League. However, although Charlton's first-choice 'keeper Ilic only missed one game, a 4-2 win over West Ham United at the Valley, on his return, Charlton failed to win a single game in the following twelve, until a 2-0 win over Wimbledon at The Valley on 8 February 1999 ended the run. By then, the Wembley penalty-saving hero Sasa Ilic had lost his place in the side to Simon Royce, the big 'keeper losing form and apparently some confidence after the injury sustained at Chelsea.

During the January transfer window, Curbishley signed former Liverpool player and England international John Barnes, on loan until the end of the season. Barnes not only brought some Premier League experience into the team, he also added a touch of class. Results began to improve towards the end of the season, but by then Charlton were third from bottom in the division. Although down in the relegation zone, Charlton had earned the respect of the football population during the club's first excursion into what many believed was the best and most competitive Football League in the global game of football.

In the penultimate match of the season, Charlton travelled to Aston Villa on 8 May 1999 and required a win to ensure any chance of staying up. The Charlton supporters packed into the away end at Villa Park were celebrating within just 3 minutes, when defender Gareth Barry scored an own goal that gave Charlton a 1-0 lead. The fans' celebrations were to last only 4 minutes when the future England international Barry then went up the opposite end to equalise, the first half finishing 1-1. Clive Mendonca scored for Charlton just before the hour, and then, Julian Joachim made it 2-2

10 minutes later. Charlton's lively midfielder John Robinson scored Charlton's third, within 2 minutes, to make it 3-2. Charlton conceded again through another goal from Joachim to make it 3-3. A minute later, Charlton 'keeper Andy Petterson was sent off after pulling down the Aston Villa goalscorer just outside the penalty area, and with no substitute 'keeper on the bench, Robinson went off to be replaced by Steve Brown who pulled on the 'keeper's shirt to take up position in goal. Brown set a club record by making seven appearances in goal at all levels for an outfield player. Steve Brown's first action came when making a dramatic diving save to keep the ball out from the Villa free-kick. It was then all-out attack from Charlton to secure the win. With a minute to go, Charlton's Martin Pringle was brought down by Steve Watson, which resulted in a red card for the Aston Villa defender and a free-kick for Charlton. Taken by right-back Danny Mills, the ball took a slight deflection from his driving shot, before it flew past the Villa 'keeper and into the goal. At the final whistle, Charlton won 4-3 to gain three precious points to save the club from relegation, for another week at least.

On the last day of the season, Charlton's only chance of survival was by beating Valley visitors Sheffield Wednesday, and then hoping Southampton lost at home against Everton, to move up into seventeenth place and stay safe from relegation on goal difference. It was not to be however, as Southampton won 2-0 and Charlton lost 1-0 and the dream of competing in the Premier League for another season was over.

Although it had been a disappointing end to the club's first Premier League campaign, everyone associated with Charlton Athletic could be proud of what had been achieved throughout the season. The club's financial turnover increased to just over £16 million and the club made a profit of £1,249,105. With the West Stand now fully open, attendances at The Valley averaged 19,823, the highest since the 1957/58 season. After dropping back into the First Division, the board now needed to ensure the club continued to maintain that support for the forthcoming season.

The board need not have been too concerned however, as season ticket sales were soon reaching the same levels as those of the previous season. Although it was inevitable there would be some player losses during the close season, they were expected to be fringe players who were out of contract or reaching the end of their careers at the top level of football. Two players moving on were John Barnes and Mark Bright, with both Gary Poole and Matt Holmes forced to retire through injury. Charlton also lost the service of full-back Danny Mills, after Leeds came in with a bid too good to turn down and with Mills making it clear he wanted to play Premier League football, he was sold for a club record fee of £4,375,000.

The board gave Alan Curbishley money to spend in the transfer market and he brought in 'keeper Dean Kiely for £1 million, right-back Greg Shields from Dunfermline for £400,000 and midfielder John Salako on loan from Fulham, who later signed on for a fee of £250,000. With attendances expected to reach the same numbers as the previous season and the club now financially sound, Charlton were in a good position to make a realistic attempt to win promotion back to the Premier League at the first attempt.

The increase in Valley attendances had not only been due to Charlton competing in the Premier League, the Charlton Athletic Supporters' Club had also been working hard to fill any spare seats at The Valley. This was first through Target 10,000, and then, as the ground developments were completed to increase capacity, through the successful ticketing initiatives.

The Supporters' Club had also been busy in widening the club's fan base through the formation of new satellite branches, now running in Anglia, Brighton, West Sussex, Hastings and Bexhill, Lewisham, Northwest Kent, West Kent and the West Country. Also coming under the Supporters' Club wing was an organisation known as the Charlton Bobbies, a group of retired police officers and civilian support staff who were dedicated Charlton supporters. The group had been formed prior to the play-off final and had a membership of around sixty across a broad base of ages, background and gender. Leading up towards the new season, Supporters' Club chairman Mick Gebbett, a local businessman and tradesman, came to the end of his two-year term serving as VIP director and Supporters' Club co-ordinator Wendy Perfect was then elected in his place, making Charlton history by become the club's first woman director.

DISABILITY MOBILISATION

Another addition to the Supporters' Club group was the Charlton Athletic Disabled Supporters Association, their formation coinciding with a recently-published report by the Football Task Force which focused on improving facilities for supporters with disabilities. Now with a directive to provide better ground facilities, a majority of football clubs throughout the divisions were required to actively promote inclusion for supporters with disabilities, and Charlton were one of the very first to have had a dedicated area installed at the ground for use by disabled supporters, long before all other clubs were required to do so. Officially opened on 25 November 1978 for a televised home match against Fulham with the highlights shown on ITV the next day, the facility had been financed by club director Fredrick Boswell. Although open to the elements, as much of the ground was back in the '70s, the area gave supporters with disabilities a safe, accessible enclosure from where to watch the match. Since the club's return to The Valley, which resulted in the redevelopment of the whole ground, the club had put into place a number of initiatives in consultation with disabled supporters to ensure they were able to have the best matchday experience possible.

13

INTO A NEW CENTURY AS CHAMPIONS

The 1999/2000 season began with two home matches. Charlton won both of these, the first a 3-1 win over Barnsley, which saw Clive Mendonca score a hat-trick, and the second, Richard Rufus scoring the only goal in a 1-0 win against Norwich City. Although Charlton lost the first away fixture 2-1 to Fulham, the team then went on a six-match unbeaten run to go top of the table. Over the following eleven fixtures, Charlton won five, drew two and lost four, and were third from top, behind Manchester City and Huddersfield Town. After two consecutive away draws, Charlton then went on a magnificent run of twelve consecutive wins, followed by two further away draws.

In January, with the team back at the top of the table, the board announced a further share issue to raise £3.5 million for the manager to use in the transfer market to help strengthen the squad.

In a match broadcast live on Sky, Charlton's sixteen-match unbeaten run came to an end when they lost to Huddersfield Town at The Valley on 14 April 2000. The 1-0 defeat did not alter Charlton's position in the division, ten points clear of second-placed Manchester City and eleven points ahead of third-placed Ipswich Town. During Charlton's magnificent run of results, the world celebrated the turn of a new century. Greenwich was the centre of the Millennium festivities, having the historic meridian line, from where all time is measured, running through the middle of the town and dividing the world's east and west hemispheres.

Once the celebrations were over, there was ongoing speculation on what the future would hold for the Millennium Dome, a huge, circular, white exhibition centre to the north of the Greenwich Peninsula. Although a majority of the Peninsula would be allocated for housing projects prior to the centenary celebrations, bids had been invited from interested parties in developing large vacant areas of the Marsh, with the prospects of building a sports and leisure complex, and perhaps even a new football arena, close to the dome. This speculative development resulted in hearsay and rumours that West Ham United or even Tottenham Hotspur were interested in moving to the site. Other interest parties included the British Olympic Association, the New Millennium Experience Company and Sky, intending to redevelop the site by demolishing the dome to make way for apartments and offices.

To ensure that no other football club lodged an interest in the proposed sports dome bid, Charlton chief executive Peter Varney had plans drawn up for a new 45,000 all-seater stadium to be constructed next to the Dome as part of the development project, which initially caused an uproar among supporters who believed the Charlton board had intended to move the club from The Valley. The Charlton board eventually withdrew their interest in the bid, which left supporters questioning whether the club had any serious intentions of building a new football stadium on the Peninsular, with the plans potentially only submitted to block any other professional football club showing an interest in moving to the site. A large indoor football arena was eventually built close to the Dome in 2005, managed by the David Beckham Football Academy.

After the loss to Huddersfield Town, the Sky cameras returned to The Valley a week later for the Friday evening match against Portsmouth, Charlton needing a win to secure promotion to the Premier League. With The Valley packed to a capacity of 20,430, a fantastic attendance for a match shown live on television, Portsmouth took the lead 5 minutes before half-time. In the second half, Graham Stuart scored Charlton's equaliser and the game finished 1-1. Dependent on rivals Manchester City's and Ipswich Town's results, players and supporters were left waiting until the following day to find out if they had been promoted. Although Manchester City won, the Ipswich Town result ensured Charlton's promotion. In the next game, away to Blackburn Rovers on 24 April 2000, Charlton were still two points off becoming First Division Champions.

Charlton forward Matt Svensson put his team 1-0 up after 23 minutes and the Charlton supporters were ready to celebrate taking the First Division title. With just over an hour of the match played, Svensson then gave away a penalty, and Blackburn Rovers' Lee Carsley scored from the spot to make it 1-1. It was now most likely the Charlton players and the supporters, who had travelled up to Ewood Park, would have to wait at least another week to get the point required to take the title. Then, news began to filter through from the Charlton crowd that Manchester City were drawing 2-2 away at Portsmouth. If both games finished as draws, Charlton could not be caught.

When the referee blew the whistle to end the match and it was confirmed that Manchester City had drawn, Charlton Athletic became First Division Champions of the new millennium. The Charlton players were joined by their supporters in celebrating together on the pitch, congratulated by thousands of Blackburn Rovers supporters who had waited behind to applaud the triumphant Charlton team and their ecstatic fans. Charlton lost the last two matches of the season, but finished two points clear at the top of the table.

In the modern world of football, promotion into the Premier League had become more important to clubs than winning domestic cup competitions with the lucrative financial benefits available in the game's richest domestic-League competition. Even relegation would bring a small fortune through parachute payments, finances which helped the club survive for a season at least. Building a team to compete in the top division would be expensive. Inflated transfer fees and high wages could be crippling to any club dropping straight back down after just a season in the Premier League. Once promoted, the main objective was staying up, as it was highly unlikely a club the size of Charlton Athletic would ever make a serious challenge for the title or win a place in the Champions League. The very best clubs could expect would be to win a place in the UEFA Cup, where qualification would mean more matches to play and travelling long distances throughout Europe, which clubs with small squads operating on low budgets could well do without.

Charlton supporters were not expecting the club to make any serious attempt to win a place in Europe; staying in the Premier League or perhaps winning some domestic silverware would have been reward enough. Towards the end of the season, the Charlton board expanded their football interests overseas by forming a partnership with Italian Serie A giants Internazionale Milano, where young players from each club would be exchanged on loan deals. The club would also form similar partnerships with several other clubs and football academies around the globe, which included the New Zealand Knights; Spanish club Valencia; Finnish side Myllykosken Pallo-47 and Asec Mimosas in South Africa. These partnerships were the beginnings of the club's pioneering overseas football development programme, especially in working within the disadvantaged communities in Africa, and were projects which would later bring the club a series of well-earned national community awards.

At the end of Charlton's promotion-winning season, manager Alan Curbishley was also rewarded by the League Managers' Association, with the First Division Manager of the Year award, for his accomplishments in guiding his team back into the Premier League at the first attempt. Much to his surprise, Curbishley also won the overall Manager of the Year Award, beating recently-knighted Sir Alex Ferguson, who had won the Premier League title with Manchester United. The Charlton players had also broken several club records during the season, achieving a record points total of ninety-one, winning six consecutive away matches, scoring the most number of away goals and equalling records for most wins, most clean sheets and most doubles.

Andy Hunt finished the season as top scorer with twenty-five League and Cup goals, with John Robinson becoming the club's most capped player after winning his twentieth international cap for Wales. Clive Mendonca finished with eight goals, his season blighted by a series of injuries, which kept him out of half of Charlton's fixtures, and the prolific goalscorer was eventually forced to retire.

As the club prepared for another season in the Premier League, with Alan Curbishley signing a new contract and plans progressing on the building of the new upper tier on the North Stand, at a cost of £9 million, the board's attention turned towards the women's team.

THE NEW AGE OF WOMEN'S FOOTBALL

Although the football club and the Charlton community scheme had been carrying out some excellent work within the community, through projects to engage boys and girls and people with disabilities in football, women's football at the top level had been to some extent neglected. As young girls progressed up through the age groups in the Charlton School of Excellence, which had its own team in each group, there was no official women's team for players to progress onto. The most talented of the players, therefore, moving on to play for other women's football teams.

With the club now back in the Premier League and the women's game receiving much more attention in the media and on television since the Women's League had been taken over by the FA, Charlton was presented with an opportunity to take the women's game forward to a higher level. Although there was an existing Charlton Ladies football team, formed and run independently from the club, the officials at Charlton Athletic did not feel it was appropriate to bring them into the development plans at the top level. Instead, Charlton made the decision to take over the Croydon Women's football team, after several of the players had approached Charlton to discuss a possible link up.

At the time, the Charlton Ladies team had been playing in a local League, while the Croydon Women's team had just won the Women's FA Premiership and FA Cup, and although successful at the top level of the game, they did not have a structured development plan to bring young players through into the first-team squad. When it was first announced that Charlton was intending to take over the Croydon team and rename them Charlton Women's Football Club, while there was little interest shown among the majority of Charlton supporters who followed the men's team, the proposed arrangement was not well received by members of Charlton Ladies team and their dedicated band of followers.

At Croydon Women's Football Club AGM, which took place in June 2000, the players controversially voted in favour of the takeover, a decision which shocked the Croydon chairman Ken Jarvie and team manager Debbie Bampton, leaving her questioning a future role in women's football. The Croydon committee declared an affiliation with Charlton Athletic to be against the rules and chairman Jarvie attempted to block the move. The FA looked closely at the decision made by the Croydon players and how the whole matter had been handled, ruling that the correct procedures had been followed when voting for a change of name and in the proposed takeover of the team by Charlton Athletic. This left the Croydon chairman and committee feeling the players had shown no consideration for other people's feelings, their decision being made for personal gain rather than for the right reasons.

Richard Redden, who had written and published a comprehensive history of Charlton Athletic, wrote a damning article condemning the Charlton Athletic takeover of Croydon women's team, which appeared in the local media. He wrote that, in his opinion, Charlton Athletic had been ruthless in bringing Women's FA Premiership League football to the club, with disregard to the players of the existing Charlton Ladies team and those of Croydon WFC.

The players of the existing Charlton Ladies team were given an opportunity to trial to play for the new women's team. However, the players from Croydon, now the official Charlton Women's team, had all played at the highest level of women's football with a majority playing internationally, and it was highly unlikely any of the Charlton Ladies players would have made it into the newly formed team. After Croydon became part of Charlton Athletic football club, competing as Charlton Athletic in the FA Women's Premiership for the 2000/01 season onwards, the team won its first piece of silverware under the new name before to the start of season. Charlton were League title winners under the name of Croydon, sharing the Community Shield with League Cup winners Arsenal after the match ended in a 1-1 draw.

While the Charlton board carried out the controversial negotiations over the formation of the Charlton Athletic Women's team, manager Alan Curbishley had been carrying out negotiations of his own by bringing in four new signings for

£10-million. Midfielder Claus Jensen, defenders Radostin Kishishev and Karim Bagheri and forward Jonathan Johansson were all international players and the transfer fees were offset against the revenue the club would receive through winning promotion.

Even though Charlton were now bringing in more experienced players, better suited to competing in the Premier League, the club would continue to promote from within, bringing talented young academy players into the squad. One of those promising players, Pierre Bolangi, had been chosen to accompany the first team on a pre-season tour to the West Country, where he made a great impression on the management team and the players. Then, tragically, while the first team were away in Denmark playing in a pre-season friendly, he lost his life at the age of seventeen while taking part in a club pre-season training exercise with the Army at Aldershot, drowning during one of the assault course activities.

When the Charlton players ran out onto The Valley pitch to face Manchester City for their first match of the 2000/01 Premier League season, the players from both teams gathered in the centre circle before kick-off to hold a minute's silence in memory of the young, talented Charlton academy player.

Charlton won the first game back in the Premier League with some ease, beating Manchester City 4-0, the win taking Charlton to the top of the table for a week at least, before dropping down to fourteenth after two straight defeats. Charlton only won three away matches all season with victories over Chelsea, Newcastle United and Manchester City. However, it was the club's excellent home form that ensured mid-table stability, including wins over London rivals Arsenal, Chelsea and Tottenham Hotspur.

One of the most dramatic matches to take place at The Valley during the season came against reigning Premier League champions Manchester United. In front of another capacity crowd of 20,034, Charlton took the lead within 10 minutes through a goal from South African international loan player Shaun Bartlett. Holding on to the lead, Charlton were just 3 minutes away from the end of the first half when Ryan Giggs scored to draw level. Then, only a minute later, Ole Gunnar Solskjaer made it 2-1 to the visitors. After the break, Manchester United came out expecting an easy second half and three points at the final whistle, especially after Roy Keane scored United's third with just over 20 minutes of the game remaining. When Charlton midfielder John Robinson replaced John Salako, he made an immediate impact in Charlton's fight back from 3-1 down. The enthusiastic Robinson, booked for dissent soon after coming on, rallied his teammates onwards to score another goal, forward Bartlett obliged by getting his, and Charlton's, second.

With only 10 minutes of the match remaining, Charlton's equaliser came through none other than the lively Robinson, the ball finding the back of the Manchester United net from a strike across the area, sending the Welsh International on a sprint around the pitch, supporters cheering him on his way as he celebrated his goal. The match, which finished 3-3, was hailed by the sporting media as one of the greatest played during the season.

Charlton's first season back in the Premier League had been an unquestionable success. They finished ninth and went through to the fourth round of the FA Cup, losing 4-2 to Tottenham Hotspur at The Valley. The Cup tie brought in a record gate receipt of £331,711. The club's turnover had risen to £28,317,000, and after spending £12 million in the transfer market, Charlton made a small profit at the end of the season. Charlton also had an England International playing in the squad when left-back Chris Powell was picked by manager Sven-Goran Eriksson to play against Spain in February 2001.

Towards the end of the season, the roof of the North Stand had been removed in readiness to begin work on its redevelopment. The new two-tier stand would wrap around and link up with the East and West Stands to increase The Valley capacity to just over 26,000. For the nineteen Premier League games played at The Valley through the season, all but three had been sell-outs. The progress of the club during the previous eight years, on and off the pitch, since the club returned to The Valley had been remarkable. Success, unsurprisingly, had brought with it new levels of expectation from Charlton supporters, players, board and management.

With Alan Curbishley proving his worth as a Premier League manager, there had been rumours linking Curbishley with the managerial position at West Ham that had been vacated by Harry Redknapp. West Ham had been Curbishley's club since he joined them as a schoolboy, but never having the opportunity to make it onto the pitch once in the first-team squad, he had moved on to play for Birmingham City. To get away from the constant press enquiries on whether he was about to leave Charlton and join West Ham, Curbishley took up an opportunity to take a break and join the Charlton Athletic Veteran's team on their short tour to Spain at the beginning of the close season break.

14

A TEAM OF VETERANS, FORMER PLAYERS AND ARCHIVISTS

The Charlton Veterans' team was first formed during the late 1980s, and began playing matches in South East London and Kent while Charlton Athletic were playing matches at Selhurst Park. The Charlton Veterans' team was made up from ex-professional players and staff who had played or worked for the football club.

Former player Keith Peacock kept close associations with many of his former teammates, one of whom, Brian Kinsey, while still playing local football, was working in sports development for Sevenoaks Borough Council. When the two Charlton legends met up one day they came up with the idea to get together with a few other former players and put on some exhibition matches to raise money for local charities.

While awaiting the day when the former Charlton players could turn out at The Valley once more, the Charlton Vets team, as they became known, played matches at Welling United and at venues around Kent. When Steve Gritt's young daughter was diagnosed as suffering from a brain tumour, he began raising funds for the British Brain & Spine Foundation, a charity which Peter Varney had been associated with before joining Charlton Athletic. Charlton Vets organised a charity football match at The Valley soon after the club returned, playing against a Millwall former players' team at the end of the 1992/93 season. In a line-up that included the joint club manager Steve Gritt, Vets founders Keith Peacock, Brian Kinsey and Charlton Athletic all-time record goalscorer Derek Hales, who came home to The Valley to score a hat-trick in the 4-1 win over Millwall. Keith Peacock scored the first goal which he recalled came from an 18-yard shot, but the other members of the team continue to remind him was more like eight yards. The match raised around £20,000 overall, with local Turf Accountant and Charlton fan John Humphrey assisting with the raising of funds. After the club had moved back to The Valley, the Charlton Vets team had more opportunities to play in more charitable fundraising matches.

It was around the same time the Charlton Athletic Former Players Association was formed and players from the Charlton Vets team were invited to attend matches at The Valley. A group of dedicated Charlton supporters, who had been supporting the club since well before it had moved across London to South Norwood, set up the association to link up former players with their club after its return to The Valley.

Both the Charlton Vets team and Former Players' Association joined forces to pool their resources with support from the football club and sponsorship from local businesses. John Rooke, known as 'Rookie' by everyone at the club, who had been working for Charlton Athletic since before the club moved from The Valley, became the main link between both groups, having been involved with the Charlton Vets since the team began playing matches and as one of the founder members of the Charlton Athletic Heritage Committee.

The Heritage Committee had been formed shortly after the club returned to The Valley, and was set up to ensure that the club's historical material was saved and archived for future posterity. The committee included John Rooke; club statistician Colin Cameron; Richard Redden, author of the historical publication *The Story of Charlton Athletic, 1905–1990*; football club development officer Mick Everett; Supporters' Club members Wendy Perfect and Rick Everitt, and selected Charlton fans who had an interest in keeping the club's long history alive. They all set about the task of searching for and listing all that remained of the club's historical memorabilia, records and trophies, much of which had been boxed up and stored during the club's exile from The Valley between 1985 and 1992.

On the club's return to The Valley, two large shipment containers situated behind the portable cabins in the club's main car park held a large amount of what still remained of the club's artefacts and historical material. Even after the main stand at The Valley had been rebuilt, there was little, if any, sufficient space within the West Stand to store Charlton's historical memorabilia. On completion of the stand, various trophies and artefacts were put out on display in exhibition cabinets situated in the boardroom and several function suits, while the remainder was locked away in any available space, including a broom cupboard and a building contractor's storeroom.

Some years before Charlton had moved out of The Valley to groundshare, shirts that the players had worn for the 1947 FA Cup final, which were found in an old laundry basket in poor condition and covered in mildew, had been promptly thrown onto a pile of rubbish and burned. The members of the Heritage Committee were determined to ensure any other items of historical significance that were discovered would not suffer a similar fate.

One of the Heritage Committee members drew up plans for a purpose-built museum to be incorporated within the construction of the new West Stand. However, with the club needing to utilise every space for its commercial activities, the museum concept would go no further. Later, when the supporters' bar Floyds, located on the lower level of the West Stand, was undergoing redevelopment, the Heritage Committee put forward a proposal to turn the space into a club museum, which transformed into a bar on matchdays. Again, the idea went no further than the production of a series of drawings and floor plans.

Once a majority of the club's historical material had been listed and stored in whatever space could be found, the Heritage Committee turned their attention towards the club's centenary in 2005, making proposals to the club to produce an historical video and commissioning a bronze statue of the late great Sam Bartram, two projects which were later taken on by the Charlton Athletic Centenary Committee when the Heritage Committee disbanded.

Over the next few years, the museum debate continued, leading to further discussions on the feasibility of housing a small museum in the top tier of the newly constructed North Stand, an area allocated as a possible educational study centre. Many years on, the football club has finally decided to proceed with the development of a museum.

Although several Premier League and Football League clubs had former player associations, the Charlton Athletic Former Players' Association had been one of the most active since its formation. Football clubs' player associations operate under various areas of activity, some run as an independent group while others are part of the main football club structure.

The Charlton Athletic Former Players' Association had been formed independently but had strong links with the main football club. Concentrating mainly on reuniting players after the club's return to The Valley, the association encouraged former players to meet up at group events, attend matches, make appearances at special events, and become involved in functions and fundraising activities in partnership with the football club, the Charlton Athletic Supporters' Club and the Charlton Vets team.

The first Former Players' Association committee was made up from passionate long-time Charlton fans who had been involved in organising golf days and Vets matches for the former players. The Former Players' Association was supported by Charlton chief executive Peter Varney, who had also been involved in the Charlton Vets team activities. Varney secured some operating funding from the football club before the association became financially self-sufficient. Several former players joined the committee and Derek Ufton was elected as the association's president.

John Rooke, who had kept in contact with many of the Charlton former players, was enrolled onto the committee from the outset. For a former player to become a member of the association, they were required to have made at least one appearance for the club in the first team playing in League, or Cup, during their time on the books of Charlton Athletic. Once the news was spread about the formation of the Charlton Former Players' Association, the membership grew to over 250.

Although Peter Varney had acted as the focal point for the association when first formed, the Charlton Former Players' Association chairman's role was later taken on by Charlton supporter and contributor to the North Stand Patron's Scheme, Bernard Wickham. The retired insurance broker not only spent a lot of his spare time supporting Charlton, he was also heavily involved with the Charlton Vets team before joining up with the Former Players' Association. Well known and well liked by the players and Charlton staff, Wickham was the ideal personality to take on the role of chairman.

Former players from many eras of the club's illustrious history still fit enough to play travelled extensively overseas on annual Charlton Vets tours, playing in Greece, Spain, Italy and in two trips to the Far East to take part in the Hong Kong Football Masters Sevens, facing teams from Germany, Japan and Australia. In the first tour to Hong Kong, the Charlton Vets found themselves up against some very strong opposition, and to give themselves a more competitive edge for the next tour out to the former British colony, a few more younger players were drafted into a squad which included Steve Gritt, Garry Nelson, Paul Williams, Paul Walsh, Paul Mortimer,

Mike Salmon, Phil Chapple, Mark Penfold, John Bumstead and Colin Walsh. The Charlton Vets finished third on goal difference. Although not losing a match in the group stages, they were beaten by eventual winners Happy Valley in the plate competition, with the tournament highlights broadcast on Sky in June 2006. The sponsor of Charlton Athletic football club at that time, Llanera, part funded the trip for the team and hosted a party for players, officials and local dignitaries.

As well as playing in darts and snooker fundraising events, the former players also competed in regular charity cricket matches up against local based clubs and the All Stars of Lashings.

Unsurprisingly, golf tournaments became an important sporting activity among Charlton's former players, and each summer the Former Players' Association held a society golf day played at courses around Kent.

In the association's early days, the ever-evolving committee members would meet up at The Valley on a monthly basis to plan former player events and organise charity fundraising days. With the redevelopment of the Upper North Stand, the Charlton Former Players' Association had the opportunity to invite former players to matches in an area reserved in the Crossbars lounge, situated next to the aptly named Legends Restaurant. Former players were able to meet up with their old teammates that they had not seen since their playing days.

The former-player matchday events not only became extremely popular with the attending former players, but also with the Charlton supporters who used the Crossbars lounge as an opportunity to meet and talk to many of Charlton's past legends. The Former Players' Association held a very successful exhibition of Charlton memorabilia situated in the Millennium Lounge, lasting over two days and organised by committee member John Rooke. Here, Charlton supporters were able to view a vast array of club memorabilia, programmes and match photographs collected by the association.

Although entry was free, attendees were asked to make a donation to help fund the association's activities. Meeting up at former player events had always been an extremely entertaining experience, when playing colLeagues came together to reminisce about their playing days at Charlton. Former player Bobby Ayre always had a good story to tell during his visits to The Valley, one in particular involving fellow striker Jimmy Gauld. The Scottish-born forward had a quick turn of pace and powerful shot, however, although his individualism made Gauld an entertaining player to watch, it also meant he would often keep the ball to himself, which frustrated the rest of his teammates. This resulted in his strike partner, Ayre, going to see Jimmy Trotter to complain that Gauld would not pass to him. The manager replied that if he wanted to get the ball from Gauld he should go and tackle him!

The player who Gauld had replaced in the team after a move to Italy, Eddie Firmani, went on to have an extremely successful career after retiring from playing, travelling the globe in the role of coach and manager. Unable to attend as many former player functions as he would have liked, then living in America and busy working in football well into his late sixties, he was one of the most well-respected and well-liked members of the association, always ready and willing to talk about his time playing for and managing Charlton, playing in Italy, coaching in America or the time he was caught up in the first Gulf War. After almost a decade of managing clubs in the Middle East, Firmani was living and coaching in the Gulf when Iraq invaded Kuwait in August 1990 and Firmani and his wife were trapped in the country as the troops moved in. Held hostage for three months in a Bagdad hotel by the forces of Saddam Hussein, Firmani eventually made contact with football friends in Iraq who were able to use their influence to negotiate a release, and then safe passage, out of the country.

A great camaraderie had grown between the former players of all eras since the formation of the association and football club's return to The Valley, which was especially evident when they were travelling to tournaments together overseas.

A few days away with the Vets team had given Alan Curbishley some time to enjoy a break in the sun, away from his managerial responsibilities. He played football not only with some of his former teammates, but also a few players he once managed too.

On the return of the Charlton Vets team from the successful tour to Spain, Curbishley was then off on a family holiday to Italy, having decided while he had been away with the Vets team to sign a new contract with Charlton on his return from the family holiday. However, Curbishley continued to be linked with the manager's position at West Ham while he was away. Although it seemed that the manager's role at the East End club was his if he chose to take it, on his return, although tempted by the prospects of taking over the club he hadsupported as a boy and later joined as a youth player, Curbishley signed a new four year contract to continue with Charlton.

The close season brought more action in the transfer market, with Shaun Bartlett signing on a permanent deal after impressing the manager during a loan spell the previous season where he won the Premier League goal of the season for a superb volley, in a 2-0 win over Leicester City at The Valley. The South African forward gave Curbishley a further option up front, after striker Andy Hunt was forced to retire due to post-viral fatigue syndrome. Jason Euell was signed from Wimbledon and defender Luke Young came in from Tottenham Hotspur, all three signings coming to £10,750,000.

Midfielder Gavin Peacock, son of Charlton's assistant manager Keith Peacock, joined up with his father when moving from Queens Park Rangers to Charlton on loan. Even with those new signings, Charlton's start to the 2001/02 season would prove to be problematic, with ten regular first-team players out through either suspension or injury. In the first fixture of the season, Charlton were beaten by Everton 2-1 at The Valley. In the following match Richard Rufus came back into defence after suspension and Charlton were back to their winning ways, beating Ipswich Town 1-0 away.

The team performed reasonably well from then onwards. The upper tier of the North Stand was partially open for the home match against Liverpool on 27 October 2001, which Charlton lost 2-0, the attendance of 22,658 a record at The Valley since the club's return. Charlton supporters travelling to North London for the match against Arsenal the following weekend would witness one of the club's best performances in the Premier League. The Sunday afternoon fixture at Highbury was shown live on pay-per-view, where the television viewers and an almost capacity crowd of 38,025 were in for an exciting and unexpected football display.

With striker Thierry Henry, who would finish the season as the club's top scorer with twenty-four League goals, odds on to score the first, Arsenal were the favourites to take all three points. With only 6 minutes of the match gone, Henry knocked the ball past Charlton 'keeper Dean Kiely to put Arsenal a goal up, and for the next 10 minutes it was all-out attack by the home team. Steadily, Charlton began to get back into the game and, just after the half hour mark, Steve Brown scored Charlton's equaliser from a header, which seemed to put the Arsenal players into shock. 3 minutes before the break, Arsenal 'keeper Richard Wright gifted Charlton a second goal from a free-kick, taken by defender Paul Konchesky, Wright pushing the ball up and back into his own net. Within 5 minutes of the second half kicking off and the Charlton players matching up well against their opponents, the classy midfielder Claus Jensen chipped the ball from a tight angle up, over 'keeper Wright, and in off the post to make it 3-1 to the away team. Charlton were now playing some exceptionally good football against the team, which would go on to be crowned Premier League Champions at the end of the season.

Forward Jason Euell then scored Charlton's fourth before the referee awarded a dubious penalty to Arsenal, after defender Mark Fish was adjudged to have tripped Thierry Henry in the box. A television replay later proved that the defender had got the ball, and not the diving Henry. Although the Arsenal striker scored from the spot, Charlton held out for the last 30 minutes to win the match 4-2. This was the first time that Charlton had beaten Arsenal at Highbury since 1956.

For another season Charlton recorded an impressive series of results in London derbies against Arsenal, Chelsea, Tottenham Hotspur, West Ham United and recently promoted Fulham. The team took twenty points from a possible thirty, losing just two, at home to Arsenal and away to West Ham United. The points gained in the derby fixtures went a long way towards maintaining Charlton's mid-table position.

During the season, Charlton had lost several experienced defenders through injury, resulting in Alan Curbishley drafting in a player who would become a cult hero to the Charlton fans during his short stay. The Portuguese international defender Jorge Costa signed for Charlton on loan from FC Porto in December, and played in every League match up to the end of the season, Costa bowing out at Old Trafford in Charlton's 0-0 draw against Manchester United on the last day of the season. The week before, Charlton had secured the point required to guarantee retaining a place in the Premier League with a 2-2 draw against Sunderland at The Valley. Before the match, Clive Mendonca, after retiring from football through injury, came back out onto The Valley pitch for one more time to receive a presentation from Charlton PLC chairman Richard Murray and Charlton Athletic Club chairman Martin Simons, a very emotional occasion for the player, his former teammates, Charlton staff and the fans.

Although only finishing the season in fourteenth place on forty-four points, it had been another very successful year for the football club. After the new Upper North Stand had been fully opened mid-way through the season, Charlton's average home attendance had risen to 24,135, the highest since Charlton played in the top division of the Football League in the 1956/57 season.

With young midfielder Scott Parker now playing regularly alongside Claus Jensen in the heart of midfield, Mark Kinsella was featuring less often in the Charlton starting line-up. When the opportunity came, he reluctantly decided it was time to move on, joining Aston Villa in the close season. Several new players were signed to strengthen the playing squad including defender Garry Rowett, bought from Leicester City for £2.7 million, and Paul Rachubaka, joining from Manchester United for £200,000. Rachubaka was bought as cover for first-choice 'keeper Dean Kiely, after Sasa Ilic had moved onto Portsmouth. Two free signings also joined in the summer, midfielders Jesper Blomqvist from Everton, and Robbie Mustoe from Middlesbrough.

Charlton season ticket sales had risen to a record 21,000 leading up towards the commencement of the 2002/03 season. The supporters were in for a disappointing start to the season with the team losing the first five home matches. By the beginning of October, Charlton had dropped to second from bottom of the Premier League, becoming one of the favourites for relegation. Charlton's fans never faltered in their support and attendances at The Valley regularly reached in excess of 26,000.

In a Premier League national fan survey, published in 2002, Charlton were placed fifth for the highest percentage of fans attending home matches who lived within a ten mile radius. Manchester United and Chelsea were placed nineteenth and twentieth. For value for money, Charlton came out on top, with 64 per cent of the fan base believing Charlton offered good value for money for ticket prices, facilities and team performances.

Unfortunately, only 28 per cent of Charlton's fan base liked the club mascots Floyd the dog and Harvey the cat, which put them down into thirteenth place, but much better positioned than Newcastle's Monty Magpie, who came bottom with just a 12 per cent approval. Charlton were also placed as one of the lowest clubs for fans witnessing any form of racism aimed towards players at matches. The reliability of such surveys, however, are dependent on many factors such as the size of the club, the club's location, the proportion of fans in the survey and how the data collected is interpreted. Despite all this, it did seem that a majority of Charlton fans taking part in the survey were positive about the club and its future prospects. Even though Charlton were down in a relegation position, attendances at The Valley were regularly reaching close to full capacity. Any fans becoming concerned about the club's position in the division would not be concerned for too long, as results soon began to improve and Charlton moved away from the bottom of the table.

SUPPORTING A CAUSE

The Charlton Supporters' Club, continuing to build upon the success of the football club, now had one of the highest membership levels in the country. Bringing new and lapsed fans to The Valley was made easy by the team's accomplishments on the pitch. With less to do in order to attract support at The Valley with almost all home seats now occupied by season ticket holders, the Supporters' Club increased their workload in organising travel to home and away matches, overseeing the ongoing development of the regional branches, and working in partnership with the football club in varied and various community projects throughout the borough, South East London and large areas of Kent.

The days of campaigning when all was not well with the club were now in the past. The Supporters' Club continued acting on behalf of the members, and all Charlton supporters in general, by working with the football club to set up a fans' forum, gave supporters the opportunity to put forward any matters relating to the club to Charlton's board.

In December 2002, the Supporters' Club organised an extremely successful tenth anniversary, 'Back to The Valley' dinner, to celebrate the club's return and achievements since. Returning as a Second Division club to a ground which held just over 8,000, to then playing in the Premier League at a stadium with a capacity of 26,500 within just a decade, was a remarkable accomplishment for everyone who had made it possible – the Charlton Athletic board, club staff, coaches, players, managers and without doubt, the supporters themselves.

The month before the anniversary took place, a 1-0 win at Main Road ended Manchester City's run of three wins and was the beginning of Charlton's eight match unbeaten run, which came to an end at Stanford Bridge on a pitch which resembled a beach.

After the turf had been removed due to problems with the playing surface, sand had been laid down in readiness for the laying a new pitch. After losing the game 4-1, Charlton made a formal request to have the game replayed on grass to comply with Premier League rules, but after an investigation by the League authorities, the request was denied. Over the remaining sixteen games of the season Charlton won six, drew two and lost eight, to finish in thirteenth place with forty-nine points.

Long-serving, Welsh international midfielder and supporters' favourite John Robinson was granted a free transfer in recognition of his long service with the club, and joined Cardiff City at the end of the season. Although one international player had left the club, Charlton had two players receive their first caps, midfielder Scott Parker and defender Paul Konchesky, who were called up to play for England.

When West Ham United were relegated from the Premier League at the end of the season, the East London club's star player, Paolo Di Canio, made it known that he wanted a move from Upton Park andAlan Curbishley immediately moved in to sign him up. Curbishley had already signed Icelandic international Hermann Hreidarsson, from Ipswich Town towards the end of the season and he was joined by Republic of Ireland international, and previous Ipswich teammate, Matt Holland, signed during the summer. Defender Chris Perry came in from Tottenham Hotspur. Paul Konchesky moved in the opposite direction on loan, with former Charlton 'keeper Simon Royce returning after going out on loan to several clubs while on the books of Leicester City. England Under-20 striker Carlton Cole also came in on loan from Chelsea. In Charlton's 2003/04 first-team squad of twenty-six players, eighteen had been capped by their country at Under-21 and senior level, Charlton becoming a club full of international football stars.

Losing the first match of the season 3-0 against Manchester City at The Valley, Alan Curbishley's six-hundredth match as Charlton manager, which included his joint managerial partnership with Steve Gritt, Charlton came back with a 4-0 win away to newly promoted Wolverhampton Wanderers. Although drawing two and losing two of the next four fixtures, Charlton were back into their winning ways with three victories in a row, and everything seemed to be going well at the club.

After beating Chelsea 4-2 at The Valley on Boxing Day, a game where Scott Parker put on a fantastic performance, Chelsea made an offer for the midfielder during the

January transfer window. This was the second time Chelsea had shown interest in the Charlton midfielder, after making an initial approach the season before, for a derisory offer of £5 million. Curbishley made it clear to his board he did not want to let Parker go, however, as far as the player was concerned, he wanted the move to Chelsea. This resulted in several meetings taking place between player and manager with Parker demanding to leave and Curbishley refusing to let him go. Eventually, Parker got the move he wanted and Charlton received a fee of £10 million, a very nice sum for the club to deposit in the bank, however, the loss of Parker and the disruption the transfer caused affected the club throughout the second half of the season.

Charlton were fourth in the table before the sale of Parker, a position which Curbishley believed may have been maintained if the influential player had not left. After his move to Chelsea, the team's form took a dip and Charlton finished the season in seventh place. The club's turnover of £42,660,000 for the season was the largest in the club's history, with wages taking up a massive 70 per cent of the total. Attendances at The Valley were up again to an average of 26,293, with the largest gate of the season, 26,768, coming against Chelsea.

Alan Curbishley had brought in midfielder Jerome Thomas towards the end of the season for £100,000, but found it impossible to replace Scott Parker during the close season. Then, to add to his problems, Paulo Di Canio decided to accept an offer to join home town club Lazio of Rome, instead of extending his contract with Charlton. Claus Jensen then put in a transfer request to join Fulham and two central defenders, Gary Rowett and Richard Rufus, retired through injury.

With Carlton Cole returning to the West London club after his loan ended and Matt Svensson having already moved on to join Norwich City in December, Charlton were now short of attacking options up front. Even though Curbishley brought in a few new players to strengthen the squad at the beginning of the close season, Stephan Andersen, Brian Hughes, Dennis Rommedahl and defender Talal El Karkouri, the Charlton manager failed to secure the services of three quality players he attempted to sign, Tim Cahill, James Beattie and Mathieu Flamini. Danny Murphy and Francis Jeffers were both persuaded to sign just before the start of the new season for a total of £5.1 million.

After almost finishing in a European qualification place the previous season, Charlton struggled to find any consistency throughout the 2004/05 season and, once accumulating the points required to ensure Premier League safety, suffered an end of season slump, only taking three points from the remaining nine games to finish thirteenth in the division.

15

100 YEARS OF HISTORY

The 2004/05 season had been chosen to officially celebrate the centenary of Charlton Athletic Football Club, which had been founded in June 1905. During the centenary year, the Former Players' Association organised a former players' dinner which took place on 26 September 2004, attended by over ninety players, several travelling from overseas to be at the prestigious event. These included Allan Simonsen, Hans Jeppson, Eddie Firmani, Peter Reeves and Graham Tutt.

To start off proceedings, the Charlton Former Players' Association President, Derek Ufton, made a speech to welcome his fellow Charlton Athletic professionals back to the club and then the centenary dinner was underway. During the evening's celebrations, the Former Players' Association organised several activities to raise funds to go towards the bronze statue of Sam Bartram that the club's Centenary Committee had commissioned. Apart from the traditional selling of raffle tickets, an innovative computer-generated centenary cup competition was devised, where teams from different eras throughout Charlton's 100-year-long history played in a knock out series of cup ties, shown on a television monitor positioned in the lounge while the guests dined.

The computer-generated teams included the 1947 FA Cup final winning side, the 2000 Division One Champions, the Wembley play-off winners of 1998 and Charlton's first ever team from 1905, plus many more teams from different periods throughout the history of the club. Each team played in a series of knock-out matches, with the two finalists competing for the Charlton Centenary Cup. Every Charlton team in the knock-out competition had been purchased by a table of former players and guests but Charlton Athletic football club chairman Martin Simons, unhappy with the team his table had drawn, decided to swap his team with another table. Subsequently, the 1935 team that he traded went through to reach the final, but were then beaten by the team from 1985, the eventual Charlton centenary cup winners.

Throughout the evening, videos were played showing Charlton matches from the past and each player attending had their photograph and playing statistics displayed in succession on the overhead monitors. Sky Sports were also in attendance, filming the event that would be shown prior to Charlton's live match against Blackburn Rovers, broadcast the following day. The official festivities concluded with a speech from sports writer and long-time Charlton fan, Patrick Collins. Afterwards, each of the former players were presented with original colour player caricatures depicting them during their playing days, drawn in the style of the famous artist Syd Jordon, who produced humorous illustrations of players and match action for newspaper publications during the 1930s–50s.

Afterwards, the former players, guests and association members spent the remainder of the evening talking about times past and the glory years of Charlton Athletic. The following day, many of the Charlton former players stayed over to attend the match against Blackburn Rovers at The Valley as guests of the club, Charlton winning the match 1-0.

The finale of the football club's centenary celebration came on 9 June 2005, the same day the club had been formed 100 years before, and the bronze statue of the late great Charlton Athletic 'keeper Sam Bartram was unveiled.

The statue, produced by local artist Andrew Hawken from Blackheath, was erected outside of the football club's main entrance of the West Stand. When an appeal was made to raise the £50,000 required to fund the project, most of the money came from generous donations made by supporters, raised within eleven months of the commission being undertaken. Sam Bartram's daughter, Moira, who was then living in Canada, travelled over for the unveiling and was joined by a host of former Charlton Athletic 'keepers for what became a very emotional day. Along with the club producing a special limited edition centenary club shirt, available for supporters to purchase as a unique centenary souvenir, a lavish three-hour centenary video and DVD had been produced, introduced by Charlton fan Michael Grade and presented by Jim Rosenthal. The production included archive footage of the club's very earliest matches from the early 1900s up to the present day, along with interviews of many of the club's former and current players, managers, directors and fans.

The club also launched the Charlton Athletic centenary awards. Generations of supporters from all eras voted to select a player for ten categories. Sam Bartram won Charlton's greatest ever 'keeper award; Richard Rufus, greatest defender; Mark Kinsella, greatest midfielder; Derek Hales, greatest striker; Alan Curbishley, greatest manager and Eddie Firmani, the greatest overseas player. The Wembley play-off final against Sunderland was voted as the greatest ever match and the greatest season as 1999/2000, with Charlton wining promotion to the Premier League as First Division champions. The cult hero award went to Derek Hales and the lifetime achievement award to Keith Peacock. Each award winner received a miniature copy of the Sam Bartram bronze statue. Chris Powell and Steve Brown accepted the award on behalf of the players for the greatest season and Clive Mendonca on behalf of the players for the greatest game. The awards were presented at the football club's official centenary dinner, held on 11 December 2005 at the Royal Lancaster Hotel in central London.

A HIGH PRICE FOR PREMIER LEAGUE SUCCESS

Despite finishing the centenary season in a respectable eleventh place, the position could well have been improved if Charlton's firepower had been better. Shaun Bartlett finished top scorer with just six goals. During the season, Charlton's most capped England player, Chris Powell, went out on loan to West Ham United and then joined the East London club on a free transfer in December. Also moving on during mid-season were Graham Stuart, Michael Turner, Paul Rachubka and Jamal Campbell-Ryce.

In January 2005, Charlton began running The Valley express, a return coach service from thirty towns across Kent, which aimed to bring in as many people as possible to fill up The Valley. This was an initiative which was not well received by Kent club Gillingham, who believed Charlton were attempting to steal their fans away by tempting them with Premier League football at The Valley. In reality, the majority of fans using the service were Charlton supporters who had moved from London, out into Kent.

To take Charlton forward into a fifth consecutive season playing in the Premier League, Alan Curbishley had a budget of approximately £6 million to spend in the transfer market, a sum of money which he would need to use wisely as is it would not go very far in signing top-quality players to compete in the top division. The first name on the list of players Curbishley wanted to bring in during the close season was Darren Bent. The striker was still playing in the First Division play-offs for Ipswich Town, and it was doubtful his club would have welcomed any enquiries while the matches were ongoing.

Happily for Charlton, but not Ipswich Town, when Bent's team lost in the semi-finals, Charlton put in an offer for the prolific goalscorer of £2.5 million. Alan Curbishley made five other signings before the start to the 2005/06 season, bringing in Darren Ambrose from Newcastle United for £1.5 million and three players on loan, Gonzalo Sorondo from Internazionale, Jonathan Spector from Manchester United and Alexei Smertin from Chelsea. Chris Powell was also back at the club on a year-long deal after failing to agree terms to stay on with West Ham United. With Charlton's spending budget one of the lowest in the division, there was no doubt a huge gap was opening up financially between clubs at the top of the Premier League, and clubs finishing mid-table and below.

Income earned in the Premier League from positional prize money and television rights differed considerably depending where clubs finished at the end of each season. For the 2005/06 season the winners would expect to receive just over £52 million. In comparison, the club finishing at the bottom who received a little over £16 million. For a club such as Charlton, who finished around mid-table and brought in approximately £23 million, it was almost impossible to keep up and compete with those regularly finishing towards the top of the division, especially when a majority of those clubs also had higher stadium capacity, which brought in more in gate receipts. With the income the top clubs received from finishing higher up the table, they were able to spend more money in the transfer market to offer higher wages and bring in top-class players. This left clubs like Charlton continuously attempting to play catch-up.

Some football clubs, in an attempt to chase the dream of winning promotion to the Premier League and gain a European qualification place, would deliberately get into serious financial debt, in expectation of recouping the money from the riches on offer in the Premier League and Champions League. In many cases, this resulted in financial ruin. Even the most astute and successful businessmen appeared to lose all sense of reason, spending without regard to the consequences if it all went wrong. This had been the case with Leeds United, Manchester City and Derby County.

Charlton Athletic, however, had always been regarded by the people in the game, and the football media, as being a model example of how a football club should be run.

Four straight wins at the start of the season took Charlton up into second place, three points behind leaders Chelsea with a game in hand, both clubs making their best ever start to a Premier League season. The West London side were the next opponents at The Valley, and with Charlton having a good record in the Premier League against Chelsea, the home supporters were full of expectation that their team were capable of getting a winning result. The first half was an evenly matched game. Then, in the second half, Chelsea pushed higher up the field and, under pressure, Charlton conceded two well-taken goals to lose the match 2-0. Charlton's new striker, Darren Bent, had scored in every match prior to the loss against Chelsea. With the World Cup final in Germany coming up during the summer, he would soon add to his tally of five League goals and be in contention for a call up into the senior England squad, after impressing in the under-21s.

Going into the second half of the season, Charlton dropped down to mid-table after a terrible run of results. Although supporters continued to come out in force, and home attendances were regularly in excess of 26,000, there were a minority of fans beginning to show impatience with recent performances. In the modern game of football, supporters now had the opportunity to express their views about the clubs they supported, the performances of their team, players and the manager, almost immediately after the referee had blown the final whistle, through call-in radio shows and internet forums, or blogs as they became known. Some Charlton supporters were becoming openly critical of not only team performances, but also the direction in which the club was heading. Fans suggested that Alan Curbishley had taken the club as far as he could, and that perhaps it may be time for him to move on, and for a new man to take Charlton further up the Premier League table to finish in an automatic European qualifying position.

When European Champions Liverpool visited The Valley on 8 February 2006, Charlton recorded their fourth sell-out of the season, with an attendance of 27,111. On this occasion the home fans were far from discontent with the performance of the team, Charlton outplaying their opponents by putting on a fantastic display of football to win the match 2-0, Darren Bent scoring from a penalty and full-back Luke Young getting the second on the stroke of half-time. Unfortunately, shortly after that win over Liverpool, influential midfielder Danny Murphy decided he wanted a move and joined Tottenham Hotspur on the last day of the mid-season transfer window.

ENGLAND CALLING?

Although there may have been some discontent shown by a minority of Charlton supporters with Alan Curbishley and the team's performances during the season, the Charlton manager was still considered good enough by the FA to be included on a shortlist of candidates to take on the England managerial position when the current manager, Sven-Goren Eriksson, announced he would leave the post after the forthcoming World Cup finals. Rumours circulated that Curbishley was a prospective contender for the role, confirmed when photographs appeared in a national newspaper of the Charlton manager meeting up with FA chief executive Brian Barwick.

In March, eight weeks before the end of the season, Alan Curbishley, in agreement with Charlton chairman Richard Murray, had a meeting at his brother Bill's house in West London with Brian Barwick, for informal and discreet discussions regarding the England managerial position. However, unbeknown to Barwick, a photographer following the FA chief executive around had taken photographs of the men standing at the doorway of the house before their meeting. The photograph then appeared in the *Sunday Mirror* with a headline suggesting that Curbishley was in contention for the England manager's position.

With the season coming towards an end, and having gained the points required to secure the club's place in the Premier League for another season, Alan Curbishley met with Charlton chairman Richard Murray to discuss an extension to his contract. Even though Murray had wanted Charlton's long-serving manager to continue, Curbishley did not commit to extending his contract, wanting to consider his options at the end of the season. However, his options did not include an opportunity to become the England manger, as Curbishley later admitted he never really believed he had been in contention for the role.

It was decided at the meeting between the Charlton manager, his chairman and club chief executive Peter Varney, that as Curbishley was reluctant to commit his future to the club, it would be best for all concerned if he left at the end of that current campaign to give the club an opportunity to bring in a new manager to prepare to take the club forward into the following season.

At the last home match of the season on 29 April 2006 against Blackburn Rovers, Richard Murray made an announcement on the pitch prior to the start of the game that Alan Curbishley's time with Charlton Athletic had come to an end, thanking him for his service to the club as a player and a manager. The somewhat embarrassed Curbishley then made his own short speech to the supporters, a majority shocked to hear the news of his departure and a minority believing it was time for him to go. After losing the last home game of the season 2-0, Charlton travelled up to Old Trafford a week later to take on Manchester United for Curbishley's last match as manager. On the day, the Charlton travelling supporters in the record Premier League attendance of 73,006, the fans gave Alan Curbishley a great round of applause, with the appreciative Manchester United fans joining in, as he made his final farewell. Unfortunately for Curbishley and the club's supporters, Charlton lost the match 4-0.

Finishing the season in thirteenth place of the Premier League, Charlton received positional prize money of £21 million, over half of which would later be spent in the transfer market by the new incoming Charlton Athletic manager. Charlton striker Darren Bent had scored twenty-two League and Cup goals in his first full Premier League season with Charlton. However, with the club's supporters expecting their striker to be automatically included into the England squad for the World Cup finals in Germany, after winning his first senior cap in March, the highest scoring Englishman in the League was left behind and Arsenal's Theo Walcott, an unproven young striker at international level was unexpectedly chosen ahead of him.

As the England international squad prepared to travel off to Germany in an attempt to win the World Cup, the Charlton board of directors were on their own quest to find the right man to take over the Charlton managerial role. There was plenty of speculation surrounding the appointment of a new man to take over from the successful Curbishley, which included the names of Hull City manager Peter Taylor, Preston North End's Billy Davies, Colchester United's Phil Parkinson and Bolton coach and former Liverpool player Sammy Lee.

The Charlton board, however, made no indication whether any prospective managers had been approached, or even considered, once the decision was made for Curbishley and the club to part. When the announcement was then made that the board had appointed Ian Dowie as the new manager, chairman Richard Murray informing the media that twenty candidates had been interviewed with Dowie the most impressive, it came as a disappointing surprise for a majority of Charlton supporters.

Ian Dowie was never going to be a popular choice among Charlton fans. He had recently been in charge of bitter rivals Crystal Palace, when relegated from the Premier League after drawing 2-2 against Charlton at Selhurst Park a year before. The Palace manager then missed out on promotion through the play-off final at the end of the 2005/06 season, leaving Palace by mutual agreement in May, where it had been reported that Dowie had wanted a move to be close to his family living in Bolton.

Despite this, eight days later Dowie was appointed as the new Charlton manager. This resulted in Crystal Palace owner Simon Jordan taking his former manager to court over claims that Dowie had misled him about his reasons for quitting Selhurst Park. Ian Dowie stated that his was never the case and was publicly backed by both Charlton chief executive Peter Varney and chairman Richard Murray. For a club which had once been considered a model example of how a football club should be run, the managerial mishap was just the beginning of a series of disastrous episodes which would beset the club over the coming months.

When Ian Dowie took over the managerial role, he was given £12 million to spend in the transfer market before the start of the season, more money than any previous Charlton manager had received. Dowie used the transfer fund to sign Djimi Traoré from Liverpool, Amdy Faye from Newcastle United, Andy Reid from Tottenham Hotspur and Souleymane Diawara from French club Sochaux-Monbéliard. Scott Carson joined from Liverpool on loan and Jimmy Floyd Hasslebank came in from Middlesbrough on a free transfer, but on high wages.

Losing seven of the first ten matches of the 2006/07 season, Charlton were down at the bottom of the Premier League, not the position the Charlton supporters had expected the club to be in, under a manager who was supposedly appointed to take the club forward.

Despite suffering a disastrous start in the League, Charlton did reach the quarter-finals of the League Cup for the first time in the club's history. First beating Carlisle at home in the second round, then Bolton at home and Chesterfield away in a difficult and hard-fought match, Charlton managed to scrape through into the next round after extra time. At the end of the match, the Charlton supporters began booing Dowie as he came onto the pitch, resulting in the under-pressure manager throwing his Charlton manager's jacket towards the disgruntled fans. By the time Charlton were knocked out in the quarter-final by Second Division Wycombe Wanderers, Ian Dowie had been sacked and his number two, Les Reed, was signed up as manager on a permanent deal, Reed having returned to the club as head coach on Dowie's appointment.

Ian Dowie later claimed in a television interview he would have kept Charlton safe from the drop if he had not been dismissed. As far as the Charlton supporters were concerned, however, Dowie had been appointed to improve upon his predecessor's outstanding work, rather than save the club from dropping out of the Premier League.

The appointment of Les Reed appeared to be a panic move by the board, unable to decide the best way forward after paying off Dowie's contract compensation which left the club with very little money to bring in an experienced manager.

Undoubtedly an excellent first-team coach, Les Reed's only previous managerial experience had been when assisting Alan Curbishley a decade before. Winning just one League match in seven, before losing 2-0 away to Middlesbrough, Reed's short managerial reign came to an end when he left the club by mutual consent, his removal resulting in another compensation payout for the club.

On Christmas Eve, Charlton supporters' favourite for the job, Alan Pardew, became the club's third manager in seven months. Sacked as manager from struggling West Ham United just three weeks before, the Charlton fans had been calling for Pardew's appointment ever since. The board obliged by signing the former Charlton midfielder on a reported £3.5-million, three-and-a-half-year deal.

Alan Curbishley was then appointed as manager of his boyhood club, West Ham. This resulted in both Pardew and Curbishley competing against each other to keep their new clubs safe from relegation, Charlton in nineteenth place with twelve points and West Ham United one place above on eighteen points.

In Charlton's first game under Pardew, the team drew 2-2 against Fulham on 27 December 2006, which was followed by a 2-1 win over Aston Villa three days later, both games played at The Valley. Then came two losses, 4-0 away at Arsenal and 3-1 at home against Middlesbrough. Charlton supporters knew, if they didn't already, that even with their preferred choice of manager in charge, he would have an extremely difficult job on his hands to keep Charlton up. In the remaining fifteen fixtures of the season, Charlton won four, drew six and lost five. Although not a bad run of results, the final points total of thirty-four was not enough to save the club from relegation. West Ham United, on the other hand, finished with a total of forty-one points, which kept Curbishley's new club up.

With relegation came an almost immediate mass exodus of players from the club, with Darren Bent, who had finished the season as top scorer with thirteen League goals, sold for a record club fee of £16.5 million. Alan Curbishley had made an offer to take Darren Bent to West Ham United, but the Charlton striker rejected the deal and chose to go to Tottenham Hotspur instead.

Other players leaving with Bent were Dennis Rommedahl, Luke Young and Souleymane Diawara, sold to offset the expected losses the club faced, and to reduce the club's wage bill. Hermann Hreidarsson, Radostin Kishishev, Bryan Hughes, Talal El Karkouri, Thomas Myhre and Kevin Lisbie left on free transfers, and the never fully fit Jimmy Floyd Hasselbaink, released after the club decided not to extend his contract.

Relegation not only saw a reduction in the playing squad, it also saw the club make cuts in staffing through redundancies. The board also took the decision to disband the Charlton Athletic Women's team as a cost-saving measure, almost all of the first-team players moving on to play for other women's teams. After causing so much controversy just six years before when taking over the Croydon Women's team, women's football at Charlton Athletic was now in complete disarray. Charlton chief executive Varney explained that the decision to disband the team was down to a lack of exposure in the media, along with under investment financially in women's football by the Football Association.

Charlton's relegation had caused financial turmoil throughout the club, with significant losses expected from the drop in television revenue, gate receipts, sponsorship and positional prize money. Although the club would receive a parachute payment from the Premier League, spread out over two years to help ease Charlton's transition back down to the Championship, the club was operating on an infrastructure that was reliant on income secured through playing in the top division, something that could never be maintained playing in the Championship.

Promotion back to the Premier League was crucial if Charlton wanted to avoid their debts spiralling out of control. When it became clear towards the end of the season that Charlton were heading for relegation, in an attempt to maintain support for the next season and bring in much needed revenue for the season ahead, the club ran a season ticket promotion scheme for all supporters renewing before the end of April 2007. This offered a free season ticket for the 2008/09 season, provided Charlton were promoted back into the Premier League at the first attempt.

In August, the club announced that sponsorship had been secured through the Charlton Athletic Community Trust to reform the Charlton Athletic Women's team, and that former Charlton Athletic player Paul Mortimer would take on the role of team coach after Keith Boanas, the previous women's team manager, had been made redundant.

Charlton's successful community scheme had become a charitable trust in 2003, independent of the running of the football club. This meant, whatever happened to the football club financially, the Charlton Athletic Community Trust would not be affected. By the time funding had been secured to continue with the Charlton Athletic Women's team, only two of the original players were still available to play. A new team was then formed and entered into the FA Women's Premier League National Division. Although a few of the previous players did return during the 2007/08 season, the team, no longer strong enough to compete in the top tier of the women's game, were relegated at the end of the season and dropped into the Women's Southern Division.

Even with the club's financial circumstances in a precarious state of affairs, Alan Pardew was given a substantial amount of money to spend on players who he believed would bring Charlton success by winning promotion back to the Premier League.

In came Luke Varney, Paddy McCarthy, Yassin Moutaouakil, Dean Sinclair, Izale McLeod, Zheng Zhi and Therry Racon, all signed for just under £6 million. Pardew also added to the squad by bringing in players on free transfers, including Chris Iwelumo and former player Chris Powell, who would pair up with his old full-back partner from the Premier League days, Danny Mills, who joined Charlton on loan. Going into the 2007/08 season, Charlton were one of the favourites to win promotion straight back up into the Premier League, and after ten games with only one loss, they were second in the Championship table with nineteen points. There was a confidence among the supporters that Pardew's squad of players were more than capable of making an immediate return.

Things then started to go wrong for Pardew during the second part of the season. Charlton dropped outside of the play-off places when he began making changes to the first-team line-up, which resulted in a succession of frustrating performances. The final ten games of the season secured two wins, Charlton drawing two and losing six to finish in eleventh place, seven points off a play-off place. With attendances at The Valley dropping to an average of 20,894, failure to secure promotion cost the club financially, resulting in a net loss of £11.5 million.

Against all expectations and despite it seeming likely that Charlton would offload some of the higher earners after the substantial losses the club incurred after failing to win promotion, Alan Pardew managed to keep hold of a majority of his first-team squad of players. One influential member of the club unexpectedly moving on at the end of the campaign was chief executive Peter Varney, who decided to leave Charlton after eleven years due to personal reasons. His position was taken on by Charlton Community Trust chief executive Steve Waggott.

To add to Charlton's financial hardship, the club lost a second shirt sponsor in succession through bankruptcy. After previous sponsors Allsports went into administration in September 2005, Spanish property developer Llanera followed, going bust halfway through a sponsorship deal worth £6.6 million.

Although Charlton had been tipped to make another strong challenge for promotion, the team dropped down towards the relegation places with just four wins from sixteen matches at the beginning of the 2008/09 season, and a humiliating 5-2 home defeat to Sheffield United on 22 November 2008 cost Alan Pardew his job. Leaving by mutual consent, Pardew received a profitable pay-off, and his assistant, Phil Parkinson, was appointed as caretaker manager. The former Colchester United and Hull City manager had been one of the reported candidates for the Charlton job after Curbishley had left, however, after leaving Hull by mutual consent, Parkinson joined up with Pardew at Charlton, both having previously worked together at Reading. The Charlton board then appointed Parkinson on a permanent basis, despite him not having won any of his eight matches while in the caretaker role. Charlton dropped to the bottom of the table with nineteen points and were in grave danger of a second relegation.

The constant changes made in team selection through the inclusion of loan signings throughout the season produced a series of inconsistent performances. Out went Luke Varney to Derby County, Izale McCloud left for Millwall and Amdy Faye joined Stoke City. In came Deon Burton from Sheffield Wednesday, Hameur Bouazza from Fulham and former Charlton defender Linvoy Primus arrived from Portsmouth. The player rotations did give some of the young squad members a chance to impress when selected for the first team and full-backs Chris Solly and Grant Basey, midfielder Jonjo Shelvey and forward Chris Dickson all had opportunities to prove themselves during the season.

With Charlton now in financial disarray, the cash-strapped board of directors had no other option than to consider looking for new investors to assist servicing the club's increasing debt. Several high profile names were speculatively linked to a possible takeover, including Tony Fernandes, who later bought Queens Park Rangers, David Sullivan, who went on to buy into West Ham United and even former

Leeds United chairman Peter Ridsdale was believed to have offered £11-million in a takeover bid, which thankfully for the Charlton supporters was apparently no more than hearsay.

A bid from Swiss-based fund manager Sebastien Sainsbury was reportedly rejected before Dubai-based Zabeel Investments put forward an offer of around £50 million, which was later withdrawn due to a slump in the global economy. While Phil Parkinson was in the Charlton managerial hot seat, the team created an unwelcome record of eighteen matches without a win, which began under former manager Pardew and came to an end in Parkinson's first win as manger when Charlton beat Crystal Palace 2-1 at The Valley on 27 January 2009. With only three further wins coming after the victory over Palace, Charlton were cast adrift at the bottom of the table by twelve points, relegated before the season had ended with a debt of some £24 million.

During the close season, Phil Parkinson began putting together a team in an attempt to get Charlton straight back up into the Championship. Out went the club's higher earners, including midfielder Zheng Zhi and 'keeper Nicky Weaver, and in came new signings and loanees, midfielder Leon McKenzie, forwards Nicky Forster and David Mooney and defenders Christian Dailly and Miguel Lliera. Along with the new players coming in, the Charlton squad would be wearing a new kit for the 2009/10 season, sponsored by Kent Reliance Building Society, in a three-year undisclosed six-figure deal. Even with the extensive changes in playing staff, Charlton were considered as one of the favourites for automatic promotion. The season started off better than anyone could have hoped or expected, Charlton only losing one match in the first fourteen. Parkinson's new look team went into second place of the First Division.

Results throughout the season kept Charlton up in the top six places, eventually finishing the season in fourth, only three points off automatic promotion to go into a play-off semi-final against fifth-placed Swindon Town. Charlton lost the first leg away 2-1 and then drew level in the return leg by winning 2-1 after extra time. The outcome was decided by a penalty shoot-out, which Charlton lost 5-4, a disappointing end to a season that had so much promise.

Attendances at The Valley fell to an average of 17,407 and advanced season ticket sales had also dropped to just 6,528, the total number including 400 already allocated to supporters who had purchased a discounted five-year season ticket package after the club had been relegated from the Premier League. The club's debt had mounted to an estimated £34 million and during the summer the club wound up its existing companies after an extraordinary general meeting, leaving club chairman Richard Murray in control of a new holding company Baton 2010 Ltd. This replaced Charlton Athletic plc and Charlton Athletic Football Company Ltd, resulting in the directors depositing a further £5 million into the club to avoid any possibility of administration.

The continuing survival of Charlton Athletic had become ever more dependent on the finances generated by the board of directors. The funding included £5.5 million that had been raised in 2005 through a share issue, a £5-million loan made in 2007 and the £14.6 million convertible corporate bond issue in 2008, allowing the club to repay short-term bank loans and to provide the club with working capital. Afterwards the directors provided a further £7 million in loans, with Richard Murray making available an additional £3 million in August 2010.

Since the club had reached its peak in the Premier League in 2006, the income the club had once received had fallen by more than £30 million. With players' wages also falling in line with the loss of annual income, the club was no longer able to afford to bring in the type of player capable of winning automatic promotion, or, as it had proved at the end of the season, players capable of winning promotion through the play-offs. The emergence of young Jonjo Shelvey in the first team had been one of the highpoints of the season. Shelvey joined Charlton as a youth player from West Ham United in 2004 and the talented midfielder made forty-two League appearances before he was sold to Liverpool after Charlton lost out in the play-offs for an initial fee of £1.7 million.

16

A CHANGE IN FORTUNES AND CLUB OWNERSHIP

Despite the lack of proven quality players at the club, Charlton were once again named among the promotion favourites going into 2010/11 season. Remarkably, it seemed as if those predicting promotion might well be correct, as after nine wins and four draws out of seventeen matches played, Charlton were up into second place by November.

Four months after Richard Murray made the financial contribution to keep the club afloat, a consortium, represented by former Charlton chief executive Peter Varney, offered to buy a controlling interest in Baton 2010 Ltd through an acquisition company incorporated in the offshore tax haven of the British Virgin Islands. The new potential owners, lawyer Michael Slater and an international property developer and former vice president of Newcastle United Tony Jimenez, operating as Charlton Athletic Football Club Holdings Ltd, would take over controlling interest as major share holders, leaving Richard Murray with a 10 per cent stake in the club.

While these negotiations were taking place, the team's promising start to the season had fallen away by the time the takeover was officially announced on 31 December 2010. Charlton manager Phil Parkinson had never been a favourite with the club supporters but, on a limited budget and a reliance on loan signings, team performances under his leadership at the start of the season had been impressive. The new owners also showed no intention of making any managerial changes, intending to give Parkinson every support. However, after Charlton were beaten by Swindon Town 4-2 at The Valley in the week after the takeover, manager Phil Parkinson, assistant Mark Kinsella and first-team coach Phil Breaker left the club and Keith Peacock took over as caretaker until a new manager could be found.

Charlton chairman Michael Slater explained that the dismissal of Parkinson was because performances had not been good enough. Less than two weeks later, former player Chris Powell became the twentieth full-time Charlton Athletic manager. Although inexperienced in the role of manager, only acting in a caretaker capacity for one match while coaching at Leicester City, Powell had carried on his coaching role after the appointment of Sven-Goran Eriksson until he moved back to The Valley as manager.

The forty-one-year-old Powell, who had played over 250 League and Cup games during three periods at the club, signed a three-and-a-half-year deal to keep him at

Charlton until the summer of 2014. Winning his first game in charge 2–0, at The Valley against Plymouth Argyle, this was Charlton's first victory since November and Powell's excellent start to his first managerial post continued with a further three victories. There then followed a dreadful series of results, Charlton going eleven matches without a win. With the recent high turnaround in managers, supporters were doubtful whether Powell would make it through to the end of the season, let alone to the end of his contract. The Charlton supporters' respect for Chris Powell brought very little criticism from the terraces and although things were not going well on the pitch, he was backed wholeheartedly by the Charlton fans, who sang out his name and made sure the new men in charge of the club were aware that the fans were fully behind the club's manager.

Results began to improve towards the end of the season, but by then it was much too late to make a challenge for a play-off place. Charlton ended the season in thirteenth place with fifty-nine points. Despite finishing in a mid-table position after dropping out of a prospective automatic promotion place, the average attendance at The Valley was the third best in the First Division, and higher than fourteen Championship clubs, including local rivals Millwall and Crystal Palace. Chris Powell had little time after his appointment to do any significant business in the transfer market, but he did bring in striker Bradley Wright-Phillips from Plymouth Argyle for an undisclosed fee. The majority of the players used during the second half of the season while under his charge were signed by the previous Charlton managers, so he had no opportunity to make the team his own. This situation, however, would change the following season.

During the summer break, Chris Powell began a complete squad restructure. Out went almost all of the previous signings, including Therry Racon, Jose Semedo, Miguel Llera and Christian Dailly. Those who could not be moved on would go out on loan, including Paul Benson, Simon Francis, Leon Clarke and Gary Doherty. Two players who had come through the Charlton academy would also be sold on, keeper Rob Elliott, who did not want to extend his contract, and prospective young full-back Carl Jenkinson, sold to Arsenal for around £1 million.

With a limited amount of funding made available by the new owners to sign players who had the potential to bring the club promotion, the manager nevertheless made eighteen signings between May and early September, players who would prove crucial to Chris Powell's aim of winning promotion at the end of his first full season in charge. Those new signings included 'keepers Ben Hamer and Nick Pope; defenders Cedric Evina, Matt Taylor, Rhoys Wiggins, Michael Morrison and Andy Hughes; midfielders Danny Hollands, Bradley Pritchard, Mikel Alonso, Danny Green, Dale Stephens and Ruben Izquierdo and forwards Paul Hayes, Michael Smith, Yann Kermorgant and former Charlton striker Jason Euell. Although moving a majority of the previous season's squad out of the club, the players Chris Powell kept, Johnnie Jackson, Chris Solly and Bradley Wright-Phillips, would play significant roles in Charlton's push for promotion.

Charlton went unbeaten in twelve games at the beginning of the 2011/12 season. Then, after losing 1–0 away to Stevenage, they went on a six-match winning run to keep them at the top of the table after nineteen games, on forty-six points.

Charlton became uncatchable throughout the remainder of the season and won promotion back into the Championship with four matches to spare, after a 1-0 victory away at Carlisle United on 14 April 2012. They were confirmed as First Division Champions a week later, after a 2-1 home win over Wycombe Wanderers. Charlton received the First Division Champions trophy on 5 May 2012 after a 3-2 win over Hartlepool at The Valley, with an attendance 26,749.

Having been on top of the table since September, Charlton ended the campaign with the club's highest ever League point's total of 101, more than any professional European League that year. Over half of Charlton's total of eighty-two League goals had been scored by three players, Bradley Wright-Phillips with twenty-two, Captain Johnnie Jackson with twelve and Yann Kermorgant also with twelve. The supporters' belief in Powell had proved correct, despite some media pundits making the presumption that he would become another Charlton Athletic managerial casualty after the first few difficult months of his managerial reign.

With virtually a whole new squad of players, Chris Powell had carried out what many believed was an impossible task of winning promotion in his first full season as Charlton manager. Charlton's average home attendance had risen to 17,485, the third highest in the division with only the two Sheffield clubs finishing higher. The increase in matchday attendances at The Valley had not only been due to the team's marvellous performances during the season, they were also boosted by the club's discounted ticket promotions, such as the offer of 'football for a fiver' where tickets to selected home games had been priced at just £5.

The owners' initial intentions when taking over the club had been to make Charlton Athletic financially sustainable, after the club had been surviving on investments from directors and player sales since relegation from the Premier League. While the owners' objective would be promotion back up into the Premier League, which could only be achieved without risking the financial stability of the club.

The financial investment the owners made in the playing squad, which had brought the club success on the football field, was expected to secure an increase in revenue through winning promotion and securing extra income from television rights. However, the television money for the coming season would be far less than expected when none of the broadcasting companies, apart from Sky, had shown any interest in screening live League football. This lack of interest resulted in a £23-million reduction in the rights money available for League clubs each season, when Sky secured the broadcasting package with a much smaller bid.

Charlton's operating finances would also be affected by the negotiations of players wages after promotion through the Football League's scheme to lower clubs' spending on wages. This had been modelled on UEFA's Financial Fair Play regulations and Championship League clubs would no longer be allowed to spend out more than they earned each financial year.

The owners of Charlton stressed the importance of bringing talented young players into the first team through the football club's successful youth academy, as this provided long-term financial benefits for the club. Even though Charlton would not be able to compete with the wages that young players could expect to earn at clubs in the Premier League, Charlton had an impressive record of developing young players and bringing them through to play first-team football. To ensure that Charlton Athletic offered the very best player development opportunities available, and to oversee the development of academy at New Eltham to meet the required category-one standards, Paul Hart was appointed as the club's Academy Director, bringing a wealth of knowledge and experience to the role.

With very few transfer dealings carried out during the close season, Chris Powell retained a majority of the squad which had won the club promotion and brought in four players on free transfers, defender Dorian Dervite, forwards Jordan Cook and Ricardo Fuller and midfielder Salim Kerkar, along with 'keeper David Button and defender Lawrie Wilson joining for undisclosed fees.

Charlton season ticket sales topped 11,000 before the start of the club's first season back in the Championship, an increase of 27 per cent compared to the previous year. The 2012/13 season, however, did not start off well, and after drawing the first game away, Charlton then won the first home match against Leicester City 2-1 but failed to record another League victory at The Valley until the thrilling 5-4 win over Cardiff City at the beginning of November. Down in nineteenth place after fifteen matches played, Charlton supporters continued to have faith that Powell would turn the poor run of results around, optimistic that the new ownership duo of Michael Slater and Tony Jimenez shared their views. The last thing that the club needed now was another change in management. Charlton's inconsistent performances, however, continued and although going seven matches undefeated, Powell's team lost three in a row and were unable to move away from the bottom half of the table.

Rumours began to circulate that the club was once again in financial difficulties, even though promotion the previous year should have brought an increase in operating revenue. The club announced an operating loss of £7.5 million on a turnover of £8.5 million, which indicated the club had been falling into debt at an alarming rate. In January 2013, supporters who had paid for five-year season tickets in the restyled Valley Investment plan had a chance to quiz the chairman over the club's ongoing financial predicament. Michael Slater explained to the VIPs in attendance that he had been transferring £1 million a month over to the club to cover the operating shortfall. This was money that he maintained was his alone, although the chairman was non-committal over his own financial situation regarding the transfer of such large funds. While both Slater and Jimenez were the club's major shareholders, there had been some speculation among the Charlton supporters regarding the actual ownership of the club. There was a belief that there may have been silent partners with financial interests in Charlton Athletic Football Club Holdings Ltd, which operated its financial dealings from an offshore bank account. With loans outstanding to previous club directors, repayable once the club attained Premier League status, it was questionable how the football club would continue to survive without the riches that promotion to the top division would bring.

17

TRUSTING IN THE LOYAL SUPPORTERS

A group of supporters who were concerned about the ongoing welfare of the club decided to come together and form a Supporters' Trust, officially launched in Bartram's bar at The Valley on the eve of the 'Back to The Valley' twentieth-anniversary dinner. The formation of the trust began as a steering group, when supporters who had been involved with the Valley Party and a few younger fans, who barely remembered the dark days of playing at Selhurst Park, met up in the Beehive public house in New Eltham in the summer of 2012 to vote on forming a trust and to elect a chairman and vice chairman. There had been previous attempts to form such a trust, but at the time, even with Charlton dropping down the divisions, fans were still backing the board of directors, who shared the same passions and dedication as the supporters.

Supporters' trusts had evolved as formal, democratic and not-for-profit organisations run by the fans of the clubs they supported, initially formed in times of financial crisis which threatened the existence of the club. Trusts would raise funds and purchase shares in the club to place a member on the board or, in some instances, gain control of the football club altogether.

The first supporters' trust was formed by fans of Northampton Town FC in 1992, when their club faced closure due to mounting financial arrears. Raising funds to assist in taking control of the club, the former directors were voted out, and a new board, which included two members of the Northampton Town Trust, were elected in their place after administrators were called in to rid the club of debt.

The Charlton Athletic Supporters' Trust was formed primarily to give a network of fans an independent democratic voice in how the club was run, act as a positive force to unite the Charlton Athletic fans, contribute to the ongoing success of the club and, in the worst case scenario, to be there to safeguard the club's existence.

At first, owners of football clubs were suspicious of the motives behind the formation of supporters' trusts, which had much more power behind them than a supporters' club, groups that were usually under the directive of the football club. However, supporters' trusts became commonplace among football clubs throughout all four football divisions, and were regarded as a positive link between the club and the fans.

For a small subscription, anyone with an interest in the football club could become a member of the Charlton Athletic Supporters' Trust, and former football club chairman Martin Simons was one of the first to sign up. Subscribers then had the opportunity to vote on selecting the committee, or stand for election themselves. The trust's interim committee included chairman Barnie Razzle, vice chairman Craig Soloman, secretary Richard Wiseman, treasurer Kevin Messerre, press officer Math Morrison, liaison Ken Sinyard, membership Richard Hicks and commercial liaison Richard Hunt, the man behind the successful Valley Party advertising campaign.

One of the Supporters' Trust's first actions was to carry out a fans' survey on a range of club related subjects, the results used to influence the trust's priorities, which included the debate on safe standing areas at football stadia, ticket pricing, catering and fans' matchday experiences. Later, however, the trust would become involved in a debate over the possible relocation of the club.

18

BOARDROOM TRANSITION

During the latter part of the season, results began to improve, the team moving up from fifteenth place at the beginning of March to ninth position at the end of the season, just six points off a play-off position. Losing only two matches in the final twelve, drawing four and winning six, which included an impressive 6-0 away win at Barnsley, the run had given supporters a reason to celebrate a successful end to Charlton's first campaign back in the Championship. While everything was progressing well on the pitch, things were not going well at boardroom level, with several members of the backroom staff moving on during the Slater and Jimenez era. First, Peter Varney, acting as vice chairman, left soon after the takeover, and then director Alex Newell resigned after a restructuring of the Charlton board. Newell was later followed by chief executive Steve Kavanagh, first resigning from the board of directors and then from the club, which resulted in both Varney and Kavanagh pursuing legal redress.

At one stage, the Charlton Athletic board only had three acting members, Michael Slater, Tony Jimenez and Richard Murray. Then, head of club development Rick Everitt was sacked after a disciplinary hearing process, which resulted in another claim for unfair dismissal. This was followed by communication manager Matt Wright tendering his resignation before head of conference and banqueting Paul Ellison was suspended, pending further investigations. Dave Archer, head of commercial sales, handed in his resignation and left the club the following season, to join non-League Ebbsfleet Town. Ebbsfleet Town were managed by former Charlton player Steve Brown and assisted by former Charlton player and manager, Steve Gritt, with Peter Varney now acting as the Kent club's vice chairman.

A majority of those leaving the club, either through dismissal or resignation, were not only long-term members of the senior management team; they were supporters of the club too. Rick Everitt, not afraid to criticise the running of the club when criticism was necessary, brought back the Charlton fanzine *Voice of The Valley*. The ongoing concerns surrounding the club in regard to finances, sale of the club and a possible move from The Valley featured in the first revived publication, and would be expanded upon in future editions. The fanzine also featured articles contributed by former club staff members and executives, including Matt Wright, Steve Dixon and Peter Varney.

The club had once again finished the season with a financial deficit. With operating costs rising to just over £19 million, the club's losses were estimated at £6,588,000. Although attendances at The Valley had increased to an average of 18,499, this figure included a higher number of away fans who attended Championship fixtures. The slight increase in season tickets sales had not been matched by tickets sold on a matchday, with large numbers of complimentary tickets given away to schools and groups associated with the Charlton Community Trust in order to help fill the ground out.

A new shirt sponsorship deal with local firm Andrews Air Conditioning, worth around £220,000 for one season, was secured on the club's return to the Championship. The income received from television rights also brought in further additional income. The club's overall commercial activities, however, had reduced compared to the previous season, putting Charlton twelfth in the Championship by commercial income. For a club with the fourth highest attendance in the division, this was unexpectedly poor. The financial problems facing Charlton were indicated by Chris Powell's dealings in the transfer market. His four major signings for the 2012/13 season came in through free transfers. Forward Simon Church, defender Richard Wood, 'keeper Ben Alnwick and midfielder Mark Gower joining after a period on loan. Ten players left on free transfers, and 'keeper David Button was sold to Brentford for an undisclosed fee.

A CHANGE IN CLUB FORTUNES

The lack of any significant summer signings gave the Charlton supporters an indication that the owners were not prepared to invest further on improving the squad, and with more than half of Charlton's players, along with manager Chris Powell, in the final year of their contracts, the board were showing no urgency to enter into contract negotiations. This all lead to further speculation the board were intending to sell the club.

The uncertainties surrounding the future of the club, and the future of the players and manager, appeared to have an effect on team performances on the pitch. Charlton lost the first two games of the season, drew the next and then went 3-0 down within 23 minutes in the fourth match at a rain-drenched Valley against Doncaster Rovers on 24 August 2013. The game was suspended because of the poor weather conditions and when play finally resumed, forward Simon Church pulled a goal back for Charlton to make it 3-1 before Doncaster had a player sent off. At the half-time break, the conditions became much worse as the rain continued to fall, neither side coming back out onto the waterlogged pitch. After the referee made an inspection he called a halt to the game and abandoned the match.

The once excellent Valley pitch was now in an exceptionally poor condition. This had also been a cause for concern the previous season, and the current severe wet weather conditions had not helped the club groundstaff resolve the problems of the waterlogged playing surface. Later, it become apparent that the drainage system, hastily installed for the club's return to The Valley in 1992, had collapsed and totally failed. As Charlton's poor run of form continued, the supporters were faced with unsubstantiated reports in the media and social networking sites that several interested parties were making enquiries with the owners into purchasing the club.

In the August 2013 edition of *Voice of The Valley*, Charlton fan and Sky News City editor Mark Kleinman wrote an article which gave an account of details of a leaked club document of proposals to sell the club, even though the owners had previously made a public statement claiming the club was not for sale. There was also speculation that one of those interested parties had an option to relocate the club to a purpose-built ground on the Greenwich Peninsular close to the O2 Arena, the exhibition centre formerly known as the Dome.

Any interested prospective owners, however, would find relocating the club from The Valley to a new stadium problematic, as the Charlton Athletic Supporters' Trust had, by then, begun making an official application with Greenwich Council to list The Valley as an asset of community value. If successful, anyone who owned the club would be required to inform the council and the Supporters' Trust of any intention to sell part, or all, of the ground, before proceeding with any such sale. The conjecture surrounding the relocation to the Greenwich Peninsula, as part of this new buyout deal, was not the first time the club had been associated with such a move. The club had first proposed building a new stadium in the area prior to the return to The Valley in 1992, and again later when stadium plans were submitted by Charlton as part of a bid on the millennium site after the centenary celebrations.

The rumours of such a move raised debate among Charlton supporters. Some were in favour of building a new ground on the Peninsula, while others, who had fought long and hard to bring the club back to The Valley, were totally opposed to any such move. The Valley had the potential to become a 40,000 all-seated stadium, capacity enough for Charlton if promotion was ever won back to the Premier League. However, staying at The Valley, a ground situated in the centre of a residential area with limited public access, could well restrict the commercial development opportunities necessary to ensure long-term viability of the club in the modern, corporate business world of football.

A purpose-built stadium on the Peninsula, however, in an area full of commercial potential, might improve the financial opportunities necessary to enable Charlton to successfully compete with clubs in the top division. Greenwich Council had already published a plan to develop the west side of the peninsula that would include waterfront and light-industrial development, education facilities and a 40,000 seated outdoor multi functional open air arena. The plans included new road and pedestrian access, as well as an extension to the Docklands Light Railway, the council conceding that such a large-scale, long-term project would have significant logistical obstacles to overcome if the proposed development were ever to proceed.

As further names emerged in media circles regarding prospective buyers, from American billionaires to corporations situated in the Far East, the Charlton board of directors continued on a policy of silence over any prospective buyout transactions. With the board unwilling to enter into any discussions with the fans over the sale of the club, the Charlton Supporters' Trust were more successful in engaging the club owners in discussions regarding the listing The Valley as an asset of community value, the board seemingly very positive over the proposals.

The Supporters' Trust, working with the Charlton Athletic Fans' Forum, also attempted to encourage the board to be more open with the fans concerning any subsequent sale of the club and the future prospects of the manager and players, whose contracts would be coming to an end during the close season. Supporters were obviously concerned that if, at the end of the season, a majority of the squad left as free agents during the transfer window, Chris Powell, even if he continued as Charlton manager, would be fielding a team of academy players. Now with half the season gone and Charlton down in nineteenth place, Powell's job was by no means safe. Not only was his contract up at the end of the season, the poor form of the team could well give the existing owners, or any new prospective owners coming in during the current campaign, a reason to relieve him of his managerial duties.

During the winter months, staging matches at The Valley was becoming a serious cause for concern as any heavy fall of rain left the pitch covered in surface water, completely waterlogged and unplayable. In the modern game of football it was now expected that clubs competing in the League's top divisions should have the very best pitch surfaces to play upon and to ensure the safety of the players, and there was no doubt The Valley pitch was falling short.

After the match against Doncaster was postponed, more heavy rain caused a delay to the start of the Leeds United match in November and over the Christmas holiday period; supporters were constantly monitoring the club news feeds to see if Charlton's home matches had been postponed.

At the end of December, after months of speculation surrounding the sale of the club, chairman Michael Slater released a short press statement on the club website informing supporters of negotiations taking place with Belgian businessman Roland Duchâtelet for the sale of Charlton Athletic. With plenty of rumour and gossip among Charlton supporters already posted on social network sites relating to a Belgian multimillionaire interested in buying the club, the official statement now confirmed that the proposed takeover of the club was true.

At the beginning of the new year, halfway through the 2013/14 season, Charlton Athletic Football Club came under the ownership of Belgium businessman and political activist Roland Duchâtelet. His company Staprix NV acquired 100 per cent of the club's shares for a reported £15 million. The electronics entrepreneur was estimated to be worth in the region of £400 million, and although one of the richest men in his home country, he was not one of the wealthiest of foreign owners who were buying into the English game of football.

The Charlton supporters now had high expectations that with the financial support of the Belgian, Chris Powell would now have the funds available to bring players in before the end of the January transfer window to give Charlton a realistic chance of winning enough points to pull clear of the relegation places.

On stepping down from the board, along with Tony Jimenez and chief executive Martin Prothero, Michael Slater's parting remarks were that they had left the club in a far better state than when they had taken it over three years before. Charlton Athletic had been in a precarious financial predicament until Slater and Jimenez took over ownership of the club, and by appointing Powell and then making the funds available for him to invest in the transfer market, they had undoubtedly been influential in the club's success in winning promotion. Nonetheless, the lack of further financial investment in player acquisitions had made Powell's job of Championship consolidation an extremely difficult task to achieve.

Michael Slater also reported that prior to the sale of the club to Staprix NV, the board had been approached by at least twenty-five interested parties since Charlton had won the First Division title, either directly or indirectly through their agents making enquiries into the purchase of the club, but that only two had made any serious offer. One bid made by a consortium failed the Football Leagues full legal and financial due diligence procedures because investors were expecting anonymity and the buyout was blocked. The second offer, made by Belgium businessman Roland Duchâtelet, was cleared by the Football League and accepted by Slater and Jimenez.

On leaving the club, the usually uncommunatative silent partner in the club's previous joint ownership team, Tony Jimenez, released a long parting statement that gave the reasons why the club had been sold. Jimenez praised both his and Slater's achievements while owners of the club, paying tribute to Chris Powell, his staff and players for the significant role they had played during the promotion-winning season. Jimenez explained that the decision to step aside was not taken lightly, and that, as custodians of the club, they had only relinquished control once they found a buyer who would make a positive difference to the club. Whatever views the Charlton supporters held regarding the motives behind Slater's and Jimenez's purchase of the club and sale just three years later, part of his statement, whether written by Tony Jimenez, or his press officer, was certainly true.

> Owners, managers, coaching and playing staff. Eventually, they will all come and go. But the fans – the heartbeat of the club – remain. Let us not forget that Charlton Athletic was founded all the way back in 1905 as a community football club. It is important that those traditions, ethos and heritage are preserved.

UNDER A NEW REGIME IN A EUROPEAN PARTNERSHIP

As soon as the transfer of ownership from Michael Slater and Tony Jimenez to Staprix NV had been completed, Richard Murray, who had continued to serve on the board of directors since selling the club, was appointed as non-executive chairman and, within a week, Duchâtelet had placed lawyer and business associate Katrien Meire onto the board as a director to oversee the running of the club and report back to her boss based in Belgium.

The Belgian businessman was no newcomer to the world of football, having long-term business interests in several other football clubs located throughout Europe, which included Belgian club Standard Liège, Spanish Second Division side AD Alcorcon, German Fourth Division side Carl-Zeiss Jena and Hungarian champions Ujpest. After taking over control of Standard Liège, Duchâtelet infuriated the club's supporters by selling off the club's best players to stabilise the club financially. He also made several managerial changes in succession while the club's restructuring took place. The unrest caused among the club's fans resulted in protesting in the streets outside the club's stadium. However, through the owner's imposed changes, Standard Liège, already one of the top clubs in Belgian football, was now run much more economically than before, continuing to be a major force in the Belgian League.

The Belgian football entrepreneur had a reputation of loaning out players between the clubs he had interests in, either as an owner or chairman. Soon after taking over the ownership of Charlton Athletic, three Standard Liège players were making their way over to join up with Charlton on loan to the end of the season – midfielder Astrit Ajdarevic, 'keeper Yohann Thuram-Ulien and winger Anil Koc. Perhaps to dispel the initial fears that the new club owner may be swift in making changes in the managerial role, Duchâtelet made it clear in a club statement that he was having regular discussions with Chris Powell about the manager's plans for the rest of the season, and for the football club overall.

The fact remained, however, that with Charlton hovering just above the relegation places, there would be no firm guarantee that Roland Duchâtelet would allow Powell time to put those plans into action. When the first match under Roland Duchâtelet's ownership was postponed, Charlton's FA Cup, third-round tie against Oxford United, due to the poor condition of the pitch, it became apparent that not only would he be overseeing the rebuilding of the team, but also the refurbishment of the pitch, which was evident when the League fixture against Barnsley was also called off at short notice a week later when the referee declared the pitch to be unsafe, even though the groundstaff had had the pitch covered with a plastic dome for over a week.

The FA Cup tie eventually took place during the following week. Charlton went 2-0 down to visitors Oxford United in the first half on a pitch which was still in an extremely poor condition. In the second half Charlton defender Michael Morrison scored to make it 2-1, followed by star striker Yann Kermorgant scoring an acrobatic equaliser, 10 minutes before time. In the replay at the Kassam Stadium, French striker Kermorgant scored twice, and his fellow forward Simon Church, once, in an emphatic 3-0 win that eased Charlton through to the next round, away to Huddersfield Town. Charlton's top scorer Yann Kermorgant would play once more for Charlton before the new owner decided to sell him to Bournemouth for £400,000, after it was reported negotiations over an extension to his contract broke down.

Midfielder Dale Stephens had also left Charlton the day before to join Brighton for an undisclosed fee, and the Charlton supporters were understandably angry over the sale of two influential players. The diplomatic Charlton manager, Powell, explained through the media that the sale of both players was very disappointing, but the decision had been made in the interests of the club. Kermorgant made it clear through an interview in the South London press that he had never wanted to move from Charlton but had become worried where the club was heading, and whether Powell would still have total control of the team with the new owner seemingly bringing in his choice of players. When negotiations then broke down over wages and the length of an extended contract, the Frenchman said he felt he had been pushed out of the club, moving to Bournemouth when Charlton accepted the first offer that came in for him.

On deadline day of the mid-season transfer window, 'keeper Ben Alnwick, who had taken over from the injured Hamer, and then made himself Charlton's first choice after a series of excellent displays in goal, was sold to Leyton Orient for an undisclosed fee. Powell admitted this was something he was not happy about, and explained that although the supporters had every right to think this was a little bit confusing, and that he had wanted to keep Alnwick, the club could not guarantee an extension to his contract. Subsequently, after just one appearance for Orient, Alnwick had his contract cancelled by mutual consent after signing off work for personal reasons.

Other players coming into the club were Iranian forward Reza Ghoochannejhad, from Standard Liège, and Loic Negro from Ujpest, a club also owned by Roland Duchâtelet, both signed for an undisclosed fee. The new owner had begun on his player restructuring programme almost as soon as he had taken control of the club, and supporters were now becoming increasingly concerned over the fate of the manager. In a press conference, Duchâtelet, who had admitted previously that he had not communicated well with Standard Liège supporters over the actions he had taken in streamlining the club, gave a brief breakdown on his plans for his new football club.

Initially, Duchâtelet had expected the club to quickly break even through the sale of players going towards paying the bills. This was nothing new for Charlton supporters, with the club often selling the most talented players to balance the financial books. Impressed with the club's youth academy, Duchâtelet was also expecting to develop young players to bring into the Charlton squad to send out on loan, or sell to other clubs in the Belgian businessman's network, with players coming to Charlton in the opposite direction.

After beating Huddersfield 1-0 in the fourth round of the FA Cup in January, Charlton's League performances failed to improve. They lost three and won one of the four fixtures leading up to the fifth round of the Cup, away against Sheffield Wednesday. The supporters of both clubs were aware of which team the winners of this match would play in the next round, as the Cup tie at Hillsborough had been postponed previously due to a waterlogged pitch, and the quarter-final draw made before the rescheduled match was played. The winners of the game between Sheffield Wednesday and Charlton Athletic would be up against the Steel City's other club, First Division Sheffield United.

The football media were understandably expecting, and even hoping, that Sheffield Wednesday would beat Charlton and go into the next round to set up a local FA Cup quarter-final derby. However, it was the South London club that went through winning 2-1, preventing an all-Sheffield quarter-final Cup tie. Before the Cup tie against First Division Sheffield United, managed by Nigel Clough, Charlton lost their League match against top of the table Leicester City 3-0 away, and were now third from bottom of the table. However, with three games in hand over the five clubs above them, Powell was confident his team would be safe from relegation by the season's end. In spite of Powell's positivity, rumours were now circulating that the Charlton manager's job may well be on the line.

On the day of the quarter-final, the supporters were in a jubilant mood, anticipating Charlton going through to a semi-final FA Cup appearance at Wembley. While Charlton fans were gathering at the away end concourse at Bramall Lane and taking some refreshments before kick-off, there were rumours spreading throughout the crowd that manager Chris Powell was expected to play the Belgian 'keeper Yohann Thuram-Ulien, instead of Charlton's first choice, Ben Hamer. When both teams came out onto the pitch, none of Duchâtelet's players featured in the Charlton starting line-up, including 'keeper Yohann Thuram-Ulien. The only player in the team who joined Charlton after the takeover was Marcus Tudgay, brought in on loan from Nottingham Forest.

In a disappointing display during the first half of the match by the players Powell had put his faith in to win their place in a Wembley semi-final, the First Division opposition were the better team from the start. Although neither side came close to finding the target with Charlton playing a holding game, the home side did have a goal disallowed for offside before the half-time break. It would be much the same going into the second half, until Charlton's Callum Harriott had a chance to score from a knock down by Marcus Tudgay. The young midfielder, however, shot wide of the open goal. Five minutes later, Sheffield United scored from a deflection and within 2 minutes were winning 2-0, ending Charlton's dream of making it to Wembley. Chris Powell made three substitutions during the second half and two of the three players that came on, Ajdarevic and Ghoochannejhad, were Duchâtelet players.

Two days after going out of the FA Cup, supporters were faced with the news that Charlton manager Chris Powell had lost his job. A week after he had agreed financial terms for a new contract, awaiting assurance from the new owner over the club's football strategies before agreeing to sign. A statement made by Duchâtelet explained that both men could not reach an agreement over the football strategies for the club going forward, resulting in a decision for Powell to leave. No sooner had the popular Powell left the club, than Belgian football coach José Riga came in to replace him, apparently already at the training ground while Powell was packing his bags. A former Standard Liège head coach and already well associated with Charlton's new owner, Riga took charge of the team for the match against Huddersfield at The Valley on 2 March 2014. A majority of the supporters, disgusted by the way Powell had been dismissed, gave a great round of applause 3 minutes into the game to show a mark of respect and appreciation for the former Charlton manager, the time of 3 minutes chosen as the former full-back had worn the number three on his shirt during his playing days at the club.

Although Charlton fans had nothing against the club's new head coach, supporting him from the outset, many supporters had concerns about how Duchâtelet was beginning to impose his authority over the club, not only off the pitch but on it, with little information coming forth over the long-term plans and intentions for his new acquisition. José Riga secured a point in the 0-0 draw with Huddersfield, followed three days later, with another point from a 0-0 draw away to rivals Millwall, only one place above Charlton in the table.

The Supporters' Trust, after successfully having The Valley designated as an Asset of Community Value, now turned their attentions to supporters' concerns regarding the position of Charlton Athletic in Roland Duchâtelet's European football club network. The trust made a request for the owner to address the fans in person, rather than through a press release on the club website or in a recorded interview, to make clear his own intentions on the short and long term strategies for Charlton Athletic.

FOOTBALL FRANCHISING DIVIDING OPINION

Opinion was divided among supporters whether Charlton would lose self determination, independence and identity if all the clubs in Roland Duchâtelet's football franchise were run as similar business models for the benefit of the whole group, or possibly the club at the top of the pyramid. At the time, this was Standard

Liège, a club more likely to qualify and compete regularly in the financially lucrative European cup competitions than any of his other clubs, including Charlton.

UEFA and its national associations had different rules regarding multiple club ownership. This caused a conflict of interests if multi-owned clubs ever competed against each other in European competition, and resulted in only one of those clubs being eligible to participate at one time. Although unlikely to affect Charlton in the short term, if at all, it was a rule that could have affected Charlton in the future.

The supporters justifiably expected an explanation as to the future role and position that Charlton would now play in Roland Duchâtelet's growing European football empire. The Supporters' Trust, in co-operation with the fans' forum and members of the Supporters' Club, requested a meeting with the Charlton board and, more specifically, the owner, to discuss the concerns Charlton supporters had over the direction the football club was heading, the club's future domestic football policy after the sacking of Chris Powell, and whether there would be a different type of managerial structure put in place for player recruitment and team selection. In response, director Katrien Meire, acting as Duchâtelet's spokesperson, assured the trust representatives that as soon as the season had come to a conclusion, these issues would be addressed, recognising that a good dialogue with the fans was essential.

Meanwhile, with the club's long-term future now under debate, the team were battling it out on the pitch in an attempt to ensure that by the season's end, Charlton would still be a Championship club. José Riga put together a team from a squad of players he was unfamiliar with, and although his assistant coach, Karel Fraeye, had been appointed alongside him after the departure of Powell, Duchâtelet retained the services of the former manager's backroom staff. The owner had kept assistant manager Alex Dyer, first-team coach Damian Matthew, football advisor Keith Peacock and goalkeeping coach Ben Roberts, all on hand to offer Riga advice on the attributes of the players in the first-team squad and the demands of playing English League football.

Surprisingly, over the next series of matches, hardly any of the new signings brought in since the takeover, apart from midfielder Ajdarevic, would find a regular place in the first-team line-up, resulting in 'keeper Thuram-Ulien refusing to travel to an away game against Leeds United. There was also an ever-widening division growing among Charlton supporters, some in favour of the new ownership and managerial changes and others against, with divided views over the merits of selling forward Kermorgant at a time when other players in the team were struggling to score goals.

During March, Charlton submitted plans to Greenwich Borough Council for the construction of a new training ground complex at Sparrows Lane in New Eltham. The plans had been formulated before the club was sold to Duchâtelet but the new owner was fully in support of the development, which would fit neatly within his own youth development policies. Players could then be brought through the academy system to go on to play for Charlton, other clubs in the owner's football network, or sold to provide working capital.

The new development was a joint venture between the football club, the independently-run Charlton Community Trust and several other local partners to provide a top class sports and education facility for the first team, academy, Community Trust activities and local community football projects, the building of the complex was financed through the Premier League and FA Facilities Fund. On approval, it was expected that the facility would take up to two years to complete, enabling the club to move from category-two up to category-one status under the Elite Player Performance Plan academy guidelines. The development of the club's training facility would not be affected by the club's failure to stay in the Championship, which had now become a real possibility. The team continued to find it difficult to win the points needed, even with games in hand, to push on up the table and away from the relegation area.

By the time bottom of the table Barnsley visited The Valley on 15 April 2014, playing in one of the games in hand, Charlton had won four, drawn two and lost four under Riga's command, and were one place and one point above the bottom three relegation places. Charlton needed a win and three points from the Barnsley game to move up three places into eighteenth. The supporters, however, were once again left disappointed. Taking a two-goal lead over the home side, Barnsley won the game 2-1, Charlton's goal coming from midfielder Ajdarevic who bundled the ball over the line in the 90th minute. Since the sale of Kermorgant, Charlton's strike force had scored just three League goals between them. With games running out fast, Charlton drew with Bolton at home and, in an away fixture against Sheffield Wednesday, came back from 2-0 down to win 3-2, with Charlton forward Marvin Sordell scoring the first hat-trick of his career.

Before the season came to a close, prices for the 2014/15 season were announced and application forms were sent out to existing and lapsed season-ticket holders, the club making changes to the seating price structure throughout all home stands, with reductions in some blocks and rises in others.

With the club's fate still undecided, supporters were offered the opportunity to renew their season tickets before a cut-off deadline date of 9 April 2014, when it was expected there would be a price rise across all areas. Controversially, season ticket holders in the first rows of the upper North Stand faced a price rise of over 50 per cent, as their season ticket included automatic membership to the Crossbars lounge. The football club commercial department then had to send letters out to existing season ticket holders in the Upper North to clarify the purchase conditions not made clear in the application form, explaining it was not compulsory to pay the increase for membership to Crossbars, and if existing season ticket holders decided not to take up this option, the price of the season tickets would remain the same as the current season. Although Charlton season ticket prices were one of the most competitive in the division, sales were down in comparison to the same period the previous year, which was unsurprising as team performances at The Valley had been poor all season. It was more than likely that supporters were awaiting the club's fate before filling out their new season ticket application form.

Down in nineteenth place, with only two fixtures remaining and three points from safety, Charlton supporters arrived at The Valley for the last home match of the season against Watford. Nervous but optimistic, they would not have to wait until the final game away to Blackpool for the team to secure Championship survival. In the finest performance at home all season, and at this stage of the campaign the most significant, Charlton won the match 3-1 to secure the club's place in the championship. Young midfielder Callum Harriott scored two goals, his second, a volley, worthy of winning goal of the season, while the captain, Jonny Jackson, scored one to put Charlton 2-1 up after Watford had equalised in the first half. The Charlton starting line-up on the day did not include a single player brought in after the club had been purchased by Duchâtelet, five players coming through the Charlton youth academy and six players signed by former manager Chris Powell.

In the final match of the season, away to Blackpool, young Callum Harriott went one better than in the previous match by scoring a hat-trick in Charlton's emphatic 3-0 win. With the team now playing much better than during the first half of the season, fans continued to be divided over whether the club would have survived if Powell had not been sacked and Riga appointed.

Along with celebrating survival, the football club could also celebrate the achievements of its youth academy, the Under-18s squad winning the Professional Development League Two – South title, beating rival contenders Queens Park Rangers 4-3 away in their final fixture of the season. The Charlton Women's team also won the London Capital Cup, after coming back from a goal down to beat Queens Park Rangers 2-1 in the final.

Before the season had concluded, the football club applied to the local council for planning permission to lay a new pitch at The Valley with under-soil heating, a new drainage system and artificial turf laid around the perimeter. While work was underway to make the new pitch ready for the start of the 2014/15 season, work was now required to build a new Charlton Athletic football team to play upon it. Once the club's Championship future had been secured, Charlton Athletic owner Roland Duchâtelet began restructuring the club to fit in with his football business model.

Less than three weeks after the final game of the season, Paul Hart left his position of Academy Director and was replaced by Steve Avory, under a new title of academy manager. Head coach José Riga, brought in to manage the team on a short-term contract, left on the same day. Although interested in continuing in his role, he failed to agree with Duchâtelet over Charlton's future plans and decided it was time to move on.

The man appointed to replace him, Bob Peeters, moving from his position of manager of Belgium club Waasland-Beveren, took up the managerial role at Charlton Athletic in May 2014, in readiness to prepare the team for what the Charlton supporters expect to be an extremely eventful and unpredictable Championship season.

The collective groups which have grown and developed alongside Charlton Athletic Football Club for over 100 years all had significant and specific roles to play in creating the history and heritage of the club. Over time owners, directors, managers and players of the football club come and go, and as domestic cup competitions and Leagues transform and evolve, with European club football becoming ever more important in the game, the constant that will ensure the future success of Charlton Athletic Football Club will be the steadfast support, loyalty and devotion of its fans.

BIBLIOGRAPHY

Bartram, Sam, *Sam Bartram: The Autobiography* (1956).
Bristowe, Anthony, *Charlton Athletic* (1951).
Cameron, Colin, *The Valiant 500* (1991).
Cameron, Colin, *Home and Away with Charlton Athletic, 1920–2004* (2003).
Curbishley, Alan, *Valley of Dreams* (2006).
Everitt, Rick, *Battle for The Valley* (1991).
Firmani, Eddie, *Football with the Millionaires* (1960)
Inglis, Simon, *The Football Grounds of England and Wales* (1983).
Redden, Richard, *The History of Charlton Athletic: Valley of Tears, Valley of Joy* (1993).
Seed, Jimmy, *The Jimmy Seed Story* (1958).

If for any reason I have not accredited any material used in this publication to people or organisations where necessary, or failed to trace copyright holders as required, then I should like to apologise for any oversight.

ACKNOWLEDGEMENTS

The assorted images produced within this publication come from my own collection and those supplied by The Former Players' Association and The Charlton Athletic Disabled Supporters Association. Some material, information and photographs were also given by family, friends, supporters, players past and present and organisations associated with the football club.

My thanks go to:
Colin Cameron, John Rooke (former CAFC staff member – CA Former Players Association Committee), Committee members of CA Former Players Association – Mark Baines, Sue Copus, Sarah Ellis, John Hutley, Keith Peacock, Luciano Masiello and Graham Sadler, Tony Farrell and Tony Garrett (CA Disabled Supporters Association), Tom Morris and Steve Bridge (Club Photographers), Tony Mitchell (Photographer), Jim Jelf, Arthur Jensen, Mick Berry, Percy Castle, John Chadwick, Peter Croker, Keith Ferris, Harry Field, Eddie Goatman, Andy Grierson, Paddy Hawkins, Ernie Hurford, Harold Lugs, Eric Keep, Ken Little, Bob Nokes, Charlie Revell, John Roth, Ken Starkey, Archie Star, Peter Barrett, Bill Swingler, Harry Trew, Dennis Butcher, Frank Beech, Don Freeman, George Daily, Christine Lawrie, Peter Dutton, Gladys Dutton, Jean Tindell, Dot Blackwell, Eddie Marsh, BN Poulter, Dorothy Barrom, Betty Read, Dot Blackwell, Andrew Hawkins, Ron Weston, Lester Trask, Iris Hemmings, John Wimbury, Jim Walker, Lee Poynter (Bugle Horn-Charlton), Geoff Billingsley, Andrew Billingsley, Norman Billingsley, Dave Headley, Steve McHattie, Alan Armstrong, Gerry McCarthy, Stuart Jeffries, Colin Barker, Fred Clarkson, Graham Clark, Alan Russell, The Greenwich Heritage Centre and Charlton Athletic FC (past and present): Peter Varney, Roy King, Rick Everitt, Mick Everett, Bobby Ayre, Harry Gregory, Justin Fletcher, and the CA Supporters Trust.